"Finally, a book about the 'New Atheism' that is not only hard-hitting, but also accessible and engaging for the average reader. Sean McDowell and Jonathan Morrow have assembled some of the finest thinkers in the Christian world and have turned them loose to provide clear and articulate answers to the questions 'backyard skeptics' in our lives ask. You get only a few pages into this book before you see the shallowness and blindness of the popular New Atheism and, by stark contrast, the rationality of belief in the God of the Bible. This is a book to buy for all of your skeptical coworkers, neighbors, or family members. Then challenge them to meet with you weekly as you work through the chapters. They (and you) will never be the same."

—Craig J. Hazen, PhD
Founder and director of the MA program in
Christian Apologetics, Biola University,
and author of *Five Sacred Crossings*

"Fashion trends come and go. Music trends come and go. New ways of challenging historical Christian faith come and go. Truth lasts. But sadly, many miss the difference between truth and trends. In another time period of challenges to faith, this book provides well-thought-out, intelligent, and very practical responses. These are *the* questions that we cannot ignore today. Sean McDowell and Jonathan Morrow guide us to see unshakeable truth in the midst of what can feel like unnerving and scary questions."

—Dan Kimball
Author of *They Like Jesus but Not the Church*

"Sean McDowell and Jonathan Morrow ask questions that deserve to be discussed between believers and their atheist friends. I hope this book will be a springboard for that dialogue. I, for one, want to debate it with them!"

—David Fitzgerald
Atheist author/activist and director of the
Atheist Film Festival and Evolutionpalooza!

Is GOD Just a Human Invention?

And Seventeen Other Questions Raised by the New Atheists

Sean McDowell | Jonathan Morrow

Kregel
Publications

To our professors at Talbot School of Theology.
You taught us not only how to love God with our hearts and
souls, but also with our minds.

Contents

A Tale of Two Oxford Atheists

I therefore put to my former fellow-atheists the simple central question: "What would have to occur or to have occurred to constitute a reason for you to at least consider the existence of a superior Mind?"

—Antony Flew

On March 26, 1941, little Clinton made his grand entrance into the world in Nairobi. The expansive Kenyan skies would be his first laboratory and would launch his investigation of a very big world. By the age of six, Clinton was already boring his sister with facts about the planets and how they worked.[1] Eight years later, his family moved back to England (his father joined the Allied Forces in Britain during World War II). It was the big questions of life—Why are we here? Where did we come from? What is our destiny?—that led Clinton to science. But around the age of sixteen, after encountering Darwinism for the first time, he lost his "harmless Anglican faith" and went off to Balliol College at Oxford University. Upon graduation in 1962, he decided to continue his studies at Oxford by pursuing a doctorate in zoology, specializing in ethology, under Niko Tinbergen. Then, following a brief stint lecturing at the University of California at Berkeley, Clinton returned to Oxford as a professor in 1970.

In 1953, young Alister made his grand entrance in the capital city of Belfast in picturesque Northern Ireland.[2] Like Clinton, Alister was fascinated by how the world worked. At the age of ten, he built a small reflecting telescope so that he could "study the wonders of the heavens."[3] As he would later put it, "By the age of thirteen, I was hooked. There was no question what I would do with the rest of my life. I would study the marvels of nature."[4] This passion for discovery fueled his study of chemistry and physics at the Methodist College in Belfast. But along the way and coming of age in war-torn Northern Ireland, it had become evident to him that "the sciences had displaced God, making religious belief a rather pointless relic of a bygone age."[5] So, in 1971, Alister was off to Oxford University to pursue a doctorate in chemistry, specializing in molecular biophysics. And after a season of teaching at Cambridge University and other professional opportunities, he joined the faculty at Oxford in the early 1990s.

Both Clinton and Alister cut their intellectual teeth on atheism. One of these boys would grow up to doubt his atheism; the other would fully embrace it. One would come to be known by such colorful titles as the "Devil's Chaplain" and "Darwin's Rottweiler"; the other would doubt the intellectual foundations of atheism and go on to earn a second doctorate—this time in theology. Both of them joined the faculty of Oxford, the oldest university in the English-speaking world.[6]

As you may have guessed, Clinton is the atheist and author of *The God Delusion*, the prominent evolutionary biologist Clinton Richard Dawkins. Alister is the Christian theist and author of *A Fine-Tuned Universe: The Quest for God in Science and Theology*, theologian Alister McGrath.

How can two intelligent, inquisitive, Oxford-trained scientists arrive at such different conclusions about God? We will return to that fascinating question later in the book.

THE NEW ATHEISM: COMING TO A BOOKSTORE OR BUS STATION NEAR YOU

Atheism is making a comeback. From bookstores to bus campaigns, the question of God's existence is up for public debate.[7] Perhaps you've seen some of these books topping the best-seller lists: *The God Delusion* (Dawkins), *God Is Not Great: How Religion Poisons Everything* (Christopher Hitchens), *The End of Faith: Religion, Terror and the Future of Reason* (Sam Harris), and *Breaking the Spell: Religion as a Natural Phenomenon* (Daniel C. Dennett). Yes, atheism of a certain flavor is making a comeback and Clinton Richard Dawkins is leading the charge with *The God Delusion* (which has now sold over 2 million copies). With evangelistic zeal he writes, "If this book works as I intend, religious readers who open it will be atheists when they put it down."[8] And these atheists are taking their newfound commitment seriously—some are even getting "debaptized" with a hair-dryer ceremony.[9]

If you peruse the books mentioned above, you will encounter some bold claims:

- "Religion has run out of justifications. Thanks to the telescope and the microscope, it no longer offers an explanation of anything important."[10]
- "When one person suffers from a delusion, it is called insanity. When many people suffer from a delusion it is called Religion."[11]
- "The God of the Old Testament is arguably the most unpleasant character in all fiction: jealous and proud of it; a petty, unjust, unforgiving control-freak; a vindictive, bloodthirsty ethnic cleanser; a misogynistic, homophobic, racist, infanticidal, genocidal, filicidal, pestilential, megalomaniacal, sadomasochistic, capriciously malevolent bully."[12]
- "I would be the first to admit that the prospects for eradicating religion in our time do not seem good. Still, the same could have been said about efforts to abolish slavery at the end of the eighteenth century.... The truth is, some of your [Christians'] most cherished beliefs are as embarrassing as those that sent the last slave ship sailing to America.... Clearly, it is time we learned to meet

our needs without embracing the preposterous.... Only then will the practice of raising our children to believe that they are Christian, Muslim, or Jewish be widely recognized as the ludicrous obscenity that it is."[13]

One thing is crystal clear from reading these books: these authors—who are leaders of a group the media has dubbed the New Atheists—are on a crusade against religion. And while they are against religion in general, they aim most of their criticisms and complaints at the fastest growing religion in the world and the almost two billion people who embrace it—Christianity. If you were to use their writings to create a New Atheist mission statement, it would read, "Christianity isn't just false; it's dangerous and must be eliminated." The aim of this book is to respond to such claims.

Now to be fair, not all atheists are cut from the same cloth and many do not employ or endorse the New Atheists' shrill rhetoric. In fact, some of the strongest criticisms of the aforementioned books have come from professionally trained, atheistic philosophers. For example, New York University Professor of Philosophy Thomas Nagel found Dawkins's attempts at philosophical argument "particularly weak" and the work of an "amateur."* Unfortunately for Dawkins, the vast majority of *The God Delusion* is not the popularized scientific writing for which he has become famous, but philosophical arguments against God, religion, and Christianity. Nagel is not the first to point out that Dawkins is

---

* See Thomas Nagel, "The Fear of Religion," review of *The God Delusion*, by Richard Dawkins, *The New Republic* (October 23, 2006). One of the leading theistic philosophers in the world, Alvin Plantinga, called Dawkins's philosophical arguments sophomoric: "You might say that some of his forays into philosophy are at best sophomoric, but that would be unfair to sophomores; the fact is (grade inflation aside), many of his arguments would receive a failing grade in a sophomore philosophy class. This, combined with the arrogant, smarter-than-thou tone of the book, can be annoying. I shall put irritation aside, however and do my best to take Dawkins' main argument seriously." "The Dawkins Confusion," review of *The God Delusion* by Richard Dawkins, *Books and Culture*, March/April 2007, http://www.booksandculture.com/articles/2007/marapr/1.21.html (accessed April 17, 2009).

clearly out of his element. Prominent Darwinist philosopher Michael Ruse went as far as to say that "*The God Delusion* makes me embarrassed to be an atheist."[14]

WHY ALL THE HOSTILITY AGAINST RELIGION?

It wasn't too long ago that the idea of books like these becoming *New York Times* best-sellers would have been hard to imagine. So what happened? Why are people reading books bashing God and ridiculing the faithful? Well, that's a complex question, but we think two reasons must be included in any answer.

First, we live in a post–9/11 world. The events of that terrible day, when three thousand people lost their lives, are seared in the collective memory of our nation, and Americans had front-row seats to see where religious fanaticism can lead. Until that point, such fanaticism had always been going on "somewhere else." It is hard to overstate how drastically this event changed our world.

In the days that followed, the cultural conversation turned to the role and value of religion in the public square and in our global society. Such conversations are certainly legitimate and appropriate and can be healthy if done in the right way. But events like 9/11 helped create the cultural context in which the hyperaggressive claims of the New Atheists could actually be entertained by a nation founded on Judeo-Christian principles.

Second, there is a growing undercurrent of unbelief in America. A *Newsweek* cover story, "The End of Christian America," reported that "the number of Americans who claim no religious affiliation has nearly doubled since 1990, rising from 8 to 15 percent."[15] Why is this? While sociologists of religion have more than enough polling data to analyze, we think Timothy Keller offers a plausible explanation in his excellent book *The Reason for God: Belief in an Age of Skepticism*:

> Three generations ago, most people inherited rather than chose their religious faith. The great majority of people belonged to one of the historic mainline Protestant churches

or the Roman Catholic Church. Today, however, the now dubbed "old-line" Protestant churches of cultural, inherited faith are aging and losing members rapidly. People are opting instead for a non-religious life, for non-institutional personally constructed spirituality, or for orthodox, high-commitment religious groups that expect members to have a conversion experience. Therefore the population is paradoxically growing both more religious and less religious at once.[16]

Behold the fruit of pluralism and secularization. It seems a growing number of people—on both sides of the God question—are no longer content to "play church." Either what people believe is true and they are going to attempt to live out their faith *in all areas* of life, or it's false and people shouldn't waste their time going through the motions of their childhood faith if it really doesn't make any difference.

So these two factors have generated a cultural conversation about faith and God in the twenty-first century. This is both an opportunity and a challenge for people of faith. But these phenomena also created space for a small yet well-publicized and increasingly vocal New Atheism, whose advocates tell anyone who will listen that if we simply get rid of religion, we can free ourselves from childish nonsense and be about the business of living. Or as the atheist bus campaign ad says, "There's probably no God. Now stop worrying and enjoy your life."

IS ATHEISM NEW?

Is atheism new? No, it isn't. Atheism has been around for quite a while.[17] It had its heyday in America during the "God is dead" movement of the 1960s.* What *is* new is the biting and

---

* See the April 8, 1966, cover of *Time*. The "God is dead" movement so popular in philosophy departments during the 1960s is being reversed by the resurgence of contemporary philosophers who are theists. See the cutting-edge arguments for God's existence in William Lane Craig and J. P. Moreland, *The Blackwell Companion to Natural Theology* (Malden, MA: Wiley-Blackwell, 2009). An interme-

powerful rhetoric, as well as the cultural visibility of the New Atheists due to the explosion of the Internet, blogs, and 24/7 coverage of anything and everything—the more controversial and polarizing the better.

Why engage the New Atheists? As we have already seen from the critiques of the New Atheists by fellow atheists, serious doubts have been raised as to whether their arguments are sound. But we must also remember that ours is a society driven by images and slogans, not carefully reasoned discourse or critical analysis. We like our updates in 140 characters or less. We don't have time for the whole story—the sound bite will have to do. Let's be honest: our attention span can handle Twitter, Facebook, and *American Idol*, but long, detailed explanations are, well ... *too* long.

So in a world of sound bites and unexamined slogans, the New Atheists' forceful rhetoric can seem emotionally compelling and disturbing to those who are unfamiliar with the solid evidence for God in general and Christianity in particular. This is especially true of the emerging generation, which is skeptical of authority and has not been given a compelling, whole-life vision of Christianity, including the hows and whys to faith's honest questions.[18]

We have talked to enough people under the age of thirty to know that these books are causing some to walk away from their faith. We felt it was important to speak to the issues raised by the New Atheists in an accessible yet rigorous manner and from a distinctively Christian perspective so that people can make up their own mind after considering the evidence.

ENGAGING THE CLAIMS OF NEW ATHEISTS

Our task will be responding to the major arguments and complaints raised against Christianity. The New Atheists support

---

diate work is Paul Copan and Paul K. Moser, *The Rationality of Theism* (London: Routledge, 2003). To begin exploring these questions, see Francis Beckwith, William Lane Craig, and J. P. Moreland, *To Everyone an Answer: A Case for the Christian Worldview* (Downers Grove, IL: InterVarsity Press, 2004).

their central thesis that "Christianity isn't just false; it's dangerous" by appealing to two main lines of evidence—*scientific/philosophical* and *moral/biblical*. Accordingly, we have divided our book into two parts addressing each of these in turn. By the end of the book, we will have explored eighteen important questions raised by the New Atheists.

Before we outline where we are headed in this book, a quick word is needed regarding the New Atheists' tactical approach in their writings and public debates (which thousands are watching on YouTube). Hoping that *something* hits the mark, the New Atheists tend to throw everything and the kitchen sink at people. They provide examples and anecdotes designed to appeal primarily to the emotions, and they skillfully use sarcasm and humor—this is especially true of Christopher Hitchens. But humor is not an argument; neither is ridicule (and neither is having a British accent). As with any issue, keep an eye out for whether the claims are actually supported by the evidence or if they are just eloquently communicated. In questions as important as these, you want to base your decisions on a firm foundation.

In part 1 we will deal more specifically with scientific and philosophical challenges to belief in God. Part 1 will include topics such as the nature of faith and its relationship to reason, the possibility of miracles, the origin of the universe, the existence of the soul, and whether Darwinian evolution is really the only game in town.

Part 2 will deal more specifically with moral and biblical challenges to belief in God. Some of the topics discussed will include whether religion is inherently dangerous, the nature of hell, whether the Bible endorses slavery and genocide, the problem of evil, and whether there is any relevant difference between believing in the flying spaghetti monster and believing in Jesus of Nazareth.

We will round out the book by sharing from our spiritual journeys before returning to our "tale of two Oxford atheists" to see how it is that they could end up at such different places on the question of God. At that point, it will be up to you to decide if the New Atheists have made their case or if the uncaricatured view of Christianity expressed in this book emerges as the most compelling worldview.

The vast amount of literature on these topics can be overwhelming. To help navigate through the literature, we have listed two books at the end of each chapter for further engagement. Also, be sure to check out the appendixes at the end of the book that cover a few other relevant issues (such as, how faith and doubt can coexist, and whether the Bible has been corrupted through the centuries).

CHANGING THE TONE OF THIS CULTURAL CONVERSATION

The truth about God is too important *not* to be seriously investigated and honestly discussed. Unfortunately, it doesn't take very long for friendly conversations to devolve into shouting matches—and this helps no one. The fact of the matter is that belief and unbelief are here to stay: neither one will be disappearing anytime soon. So it does no good to vilify the other side. If any real progress is to be made, we must change the tone of this conversation.

In his thought-provoking book *No One Sees God: The Dark Night of Atheists and Believers*, Michael Novak contends that "unbelievers and believers need to learn a new habit of reasoned and mutually respectful conversation."[19] We agree. And that is the spirit we hope found its way into the pages of this book.[20]

FOR FURTHER ENGAGEMENT

Berlinski, David. *The Devil's Delusion: Atheism and Its Scientific Pretensions*. New York: Basic Books, 2009.

Flew, Antony, and Roy Abraham Varghese. *There Is a God: How the World's Most Notorious Atheist Changed His Mind*. New York: HarperOne, 2007.

PART 1

Responding to Scientific and Philosophical Challenges

CHAPTER 1

Is Faith Irrational?

Faith, which is belief without supportive evidence, should not be given the respect, even deference, it obtains in modern society. Faith is always foolish and leads to many of the evils of society.

—Victor Stenger

A distinct mark of the New Atheists is their belief that religion is blind, irrational, and stupid. This is evident in the title Richard Dawkins gave to one of his recent books—*The God Delusion*. The take-home message is clear: those who believe in God are fools who have been hoodwinked into believing something absurd. Dawkins thinks religious people are deluded.

What could possibly cause Dawkins—and the rest of the New Atheists—to be so staunchly opposed to religion? Why resort to attacking those whose lives are enriched by belief in God? One reason for Dawkins's hostility seems to be his view that religious belief is not evidentially based: "In all areas except religion, we believe what we believe as a result of evidence."[1] In other words, religious faith is blind but in other disciplines—and especially science—we demand evidence for what we believe. Thus, Dawkins concludes that religion is a "nonsensical enterprise" that "poisons everything."[2]

The idea that faith is opposed to reason permeates the writings of the New Atheists. Dawkins calls faith a "delusion," which he describes as "persistent false belief held in the face of strong contradictory evidence."[3] Daniel Dennett claims that Christians are addicted to blind faith.[4] According to Sam Harris, "Faith is generally nothing more than the permission religious people give one another to believe things strongly without evidence."[5] In *The End of Faith*, Harris writes,

> Tell a devout Christian that his wife is cheating on him, or that frozen yogurt can make a man invisible, and he is likely to require as much evidence as anyone else, and to be persuaded only to the extent that you give it. Tell him that the book he keeps by his bed was written by an invisible deity who will punish him with fire for eternity if he fails to accept every incredible claim about the universe, and he seems to require no evidence whatsoever.[6]

If this were true, then we would happily abandon our religious faith and join the ranks of the New Atheism. And we would suggest that you do too. But on what basis can we conclude that religious faith is blind? Since the New Atheists claim to value beliefs that are evidentially supported, *where is the evidence to support their belief that religious faith is blind?* They cite no one who holds to the beliefs they reject.* The New Atheists regularly proclaim the irrationality of religious faith, and yet they offer no evidence to back it up.

WHAT ABOUT DOUBTING THOMAS?

"Not so fast," you might be thinking. "What about doubting Thomas? Didn't Jesus scold Thomas for demanding proof while praising those with simple faith?" The story of doubting Thomas is frequently cited as proof that Christianity requires

---

* Perhaps they've met some people claiming to be Christians who fit this profile. As David Kinnaman, president of the Barna Research Group, has pointed out in his provocative book *UnChristian*, "outsiders" have a pretty low view of Christians: "Our research shows that many of those outside of Christianity, especially younger adults, have little trust in the Christian faith, and esteem for the lifestyle of Christ followers is quickly fading among outsiders." David Kinnaman and Gabe Lyons, *UnChristian* (Grand Rapids: Baker, 2007), 11.

blind faith. When the other disciples reported that they had seen the risen Jesus, Thomas refused to believe until he could see the nail marks and put his hands where the nails had been and into Jesus' side where he had been speared. A week later, Jesus showed up and gave him the very evidence he demanded. Then Jesus spoke these words to Thomas, "Because you have seen me, you have believed; blessed are those who have not seen and yet have believed."[7]

Dawkins cites this text in *The Selfish Gene* as proof that Christianity opposes reason. He writes, "Thomas demanded evidence.... The other apostles, whose faith was so strong that they did not need evidence, are held up to us as worthy of imitation."[8] If we isolate Thomas's story from its context, then it could plausibly be interpreted as a repudiation of evidence-based faith, as Dawkins suggests. But there are several problems with taking this approach.

First, Jesus predicted his resurrection on multiple occasions in the presence of the disciples.[9] Thomas should not have been surprised at the return of Jesus. Second, Thomas heard eyewitness testimony (evidence) from the rest of the disciples and yet still refused to believe. (The vast majority of scientific knowledge we possess depends upon trusting the conclusions of other scientists, which is true for virtually all disciplines.) Third, Jesus did many miracles during his ministry as proof of his identity. In fact, right after the story of Jesus scolding Thomas, John said the miracles of Jesus were recorded "so that you may believe Jesus is the Messiah, the Son of God, and by believing you may have life in His name."[10]

BIBLICAL FAITH

The fact that some Christians may have blind faith is not the same as Christianity itself valuing blind faith and irrationality. Mainstream Christianity has always emphasized that faith and reason go together. Indeed, *biblical faith is trust in God because he has shown himself to be reliable and trustworthy.* Faith is not belief in spite of the evidence, but belief in light of the evidence.

The New Atheists like to lump all religions together and to dismiss them with sweeping generalizations. But Christianity is unique in valuing the role of the mind which includes the proper use of reasoning and argumentation.[11] Jesus said to love God with all your heart, all your soul, and with all your *mind*.[12] The Lord said to the nation of Israel: "Come now, let us reason together."[13] An emphasis on the value of the mind pervades Scripture and church history.

In the Old Testament, God showered Egypt with miracles before inviting Israel to follow him into the wilderness.[14] Rather than asking Israel for blind allegiance, God performed miracles through Moses so they could have reason to trust him. Exodus 14:31 makes this clear: "And when the Israelites saw the great power the LORD displayed against the Egyptians, the people feared the LORD and put their trust in him and in Moses his servant." Miracles preceded the call to belief and laid the foundation for a rational step of faith.

In the New Testament, Jesus specifically did miracles so that people would know who he was and, as a result, confidently place their faith in him. Jesus wanted his followers to exercise an intelligent faith, not a blind one. During a trip to Capernaum, Jesus stopped to preach in a packed house. In a desperate attempt to get their friend healed by Jesus, four men lowered a paralytic down through the roof. After forgiving the man's sins, Jesus said to the crowd, "But that you may know that the Son of Man has authority on earth to forgive sins," and then to the paralytic himself, "I tell you, get up, take your mat and go home."[15] Jesus healed the man so people would *know* he spoke with authority from above. Rather than calling people to exercise blind faith, Jesus provided evidence (miracles) so that people could exercise an intelligent faith in him.

Many religious leaders have asked for people to follow them, but Jesus uniquely showed himself to be a reliable and trustworthy object of faith. As David Clark reminds us, "Faith derives its value not from the intensity of the believer but from the genuineness of the one she believes in. True faith is faith in the right object; faith in an unfaithful person is worthless or worse."[16] In contrast to Jesus, Mohammed refused to perform any miracles in confirmation of his claims to be a prophet from God, and Buddha said, "By this you shall know that a man is *not* my follower—that he tries to work a miracle."*

We will defend the possibility and reality of miracles in chapter 3. For now, we simply want to show that Christians have had evidence of their faith since the inception of the church. And the value placed on both faith and reason has persisted throughout church history. In his article "Faith and Reason," David Marshall traces about thirty great Christian thinkers throughout the history of the church. As Marshall demonstrates, the predominant view of leading historical Christian thinkers has been that faith ought to be supported by evidence.[17] Consider a few examples:

- Justin Martyr: "Reason directs those who are truly pious and philosophical to honour and love only what is true." (*The First Apology*)
- Clement of Alexandria: Philosophy is "a kind of preparatory training to those who attain to faith through demonstration." (*The Stromata*)
- Augustine: "But they are much deceived, who think that we believe in Christ without any proofs concerning Christ." (*Concerning Faith in Things Not Seen*)
- Thomas Aquinas: "Hence it was necessary for the salvation of man that certain truths which exceed human reason should be made known to him by divine revelation." (*Summa Theologica*)

Alister McGrath (the Oxford theist we discussed in the introduction) is one of the world's leading experts on historical theology. In *The Dawkins Delusion* McGrath concludes that the

---

* Part of the purpose of Buddhism is to empty the mind, not to use it to discover truth. Huston Smith, *The World's Religions* (New York: HarperOne, 1991), 91.

characterization of faith as "blind faith" is not the historical Christian understanding but one that Dawkins invented to suit his own agenda.[18] Christianity has always valued the role of evidence and reason for faith.

EVERYONE HAS FAITH

When people hear the word *faith*, they typically think of religious faith. After all, religious people have faith in God, Scripture, and other unseen things such as heaven, angels, and the soul.* But the point that is often overlooked is that Christians are not the only ones who have faith—everyone does. *Everyone* has faith in something, including the New Atheists.

If you didn't have faith, you wouldn't eat, leave your home, or even be reading this book. Take a moment to think about the many things you have faith in:

- You have faith that a pilot is sufficiently trained and won't—intentionally or unintentionally—crash the plane.
- You have faith that other drivers won't swerve into your lane.
- You have faith that your electrical wiring won't spontaneously go haywire and burn down your house.
- You have faith that at a restaurant, the waitress will serve you food that is edible and safe.

Nevertheless, planes do crash, cars occasionally swerve out of their lanes, electrical wiring breaks down, and from time to time restaurants serve unsafe food. These things happen, but they are rare, which is why we move through our daily lives trusting they won't. We have plenty of experience and evidence that cars don't swerve from their lanes and that pilots can be trusted. Thus, our faith in these objects seems to be well grounded.

Therefore, the most important question is not, *Do we have*

---

* "Now faith is being sure of what we hope for and certain of what we do not see" (Heb. 11:1).

faith? but, How well-grounded is our faith? Is our faith rational or irrational? This is true both for routine events, such as driving safely down the road, and for the "big" questions involving God, morality, and the meaning of life.

The New Atheists would like us to believe that only religious people have faith. Thus, Christopher Hitchens asserts of the New Atheists, "Our belief is not a belief. Our principles are not faith."[19] However, take a few minutes to read the New Atheists and it will be quite obvious that they, including Hitchens, have great doses of faith. Some people even argue that it takes more faith to be an atheist than to believe in God.[20] Consider a few examples of "unseen" things that the New Atheists have faith in:

- They have faith that the universe came into existence from nothing.
- They have faith that life spontaneously arose from matter. (Dawkins says he wouldn't be surprised if chemists announce in a few years that they have solved the problem of the origin of life.[21] Why does he believe this? Faith.)
- They have faith that multiple universes exist to help explain why our universe is so exquisitely fine-tuned for life. (Dawkins admits that there is currently no evidence for the "multiverse" theory.[22])
- They have faith that mind can emerge from matter, or that mind is solely matter.[23]
- They have faith that there is nothing beyond the natural (physical) world.[24]
- They have faith that the world would be improved without religion.

It's certainly possible that the New Atheists could turn out to be right. Maybe scientists will detect multiple universes in the future. Maybe they will come up with an explanation for the origin of the universe. Maybe chemists will solve the mystery of the origin of life. Maybe philosophers will explain how mind can emerge from matter. Maybe. Maybe. Maybe. Until such evidence is forthcoming, however, these claims can rightly be considered articles of faith (and arguably *blind* faith).

A DIVINE REVOLUTION

It may have seemed acceptable in the mid-1960s to argue that religious people were irrational and deluded and clung to blind faith. A *Time* magazine cover in 1966 with the headline "Is God Dead?" certainly captured the prevailing attitude of the time. Philosophers and liberal theologians proclaimed the "death of God" movement and believed that Western culture was permanently leaving behind its theistic roots.

Yet as philosopher William Lane Craig pointed out in a recent *Christianity Today* article titled "God Is Not Dead Yet," the news of God's passing was premature.[25] In fact, at the very time theologians were proclaiming the death of God, a new generation of philosophers was beginning a quiet revolution in Christian thought.

The revolution likely began with the release of Notre Dame philosopher Alvin Plantinga's *God and Other Minds* in 1967 (just one year after *Time* magazine's infamous cover story proclaiming God's demise). With the highest degree of philosophical rigor, Plantinga argued that belief in God is rationally justified. Following Plantinga, a new generation of Christian philosophers began writing in scholarly journals, participating in professional conferences, and publishing with the top academic presses in the world. Presently, as a result of the movement, "atheism, though perhaps still the dominant viewpoint at the American university, is a philosophy in retreat."[26] Part of the reason the New Atheists have been so loud and hostile is because atheism has been losing the rational higher ground.

In a recent article bemoaning "the desecularization of academia that evolved in philosophy departments since the late 1960s," atheist philosopher Quentin Smith observes that "in philosophy, it became, almost overnight, 'academically respectable' to argue for theism, making philosophy a favored field of entry for the most intelligent and talented theists entering academia today."[27] Smith complained that atheists simply watched while this revolution swept through the philosophical community. He concludes, "God is not 'dead' in academia; he returned to life in the late 1960s and is now alive and well in his last academic stronghold, philosophy departments."[28]

In recognition of this revolution, *Time* magazine ran a second major story in 1980 titled "Modernizing the Case for God." The article marveled at how modern philosophers were refurbishing the traditional arguments for the existence of God:

> In a quiet revolution in thought and argument that hardly anybody could have foreseen only two decades ago, God is making a comeback. Most intriguingly, this is happening not among theologians or ordinary believers, but in the crisp intellectual circles of academic philosophers, where the consensus had long banished the Almighty from fruitful discourse.[29]

In *The Devil's Delusion*, secular Jew David Berlinski put it this way:

> What is awkward is just that at the moment when the community of scientists had hoped that they had put all that behind them so as to enjoy a universe that was safe, sane, secular, and sanitized, somehow the thing they had been so long avoiding has managed to clamber back into contention as a living possibility of thought. This is *very* awkward.[30]

THE EVIDENCE FOR GOD

The philosophical revolution over the past few decades has lead to the strengthening of the traditional arguments for God's existence with new insights and evidence. In their writings, the New Atheists hardly interact with these arguments, and, until recently, they have refused to engage leading Christian thinkers in public. While we will present these arguments in more depth later, let's take a quick tour of some of the arguments that have brought new vitality to theism. The New Atheists can only ignore these arguments for so long.

The cosmological argument. This argument begins with the observation that the universe had a beginning, which is demonstrable by science and philosophy. Given that something can't begin to exist without a cause, it seems eminently reasonable to believe that a transcendent cause (outside of the universe) is responsible for its existence. Since matter, time, and energy simultaneously came into existence at a finite point in the past, the cause is plausibly timeless, immaterial, intelligent, powerful, and personal. Simply put, the beginning of the universe points to a Beginner.

The design argument from physics. Scientists have learned that the laws of physics that govern the universe are exquisitely fine-tuned for the emergence and sustenance of human life. The universe seems to be uniquely crafted with us in mind. If there were the slightest changes in any number of physical constants, our universe would quickly become inhospitable. The most compelling and reliable explanation for why the universe is so precisely fine-tuned is because an Intelligent Mind made it that way. Simply put, the fine-tuning of the universe points to a Fine-Tuner.

The design argument from DNA. Since the discovery of the structure of DNA in 1953, scientists have learned that cellular organization and the development of living creatures are orchestrated by genetic information. Human DNA, for example, contains the informational equivalent of roughly eight thousand books. Natural forces such as chance and necessity have overwhelmingly failed to explain the origin of biological information. In our everyday experience, we attribute the origin of information to a mind. Simply put, the vast amount of information contained in living organisms points to an Information Giver.

The moral argument. This argument reasons from the reality of objective moral values to the existence of God. If God does not exist, then moral values are ultimately subjective and nonbinding. Yet we know objective moral values are real. We don't need to be persuaded that, for example, torturing babies is wrong. All reasonable people know this. Therefore, since moral values do exist, then God must as well. Simply put, the existence of moral values points to a universal Moral Lawgiver.

While these arguments need to be developed and defended (which we will do in upcoming chapters), this short account should be sufficient to make the key point of this chapter: Christianity is not an irrational religion that glorifies blind faith. In fact, just the opposite is true.

IMPARTING OURSELVES

Faulty views of Christianity (and Christians) are not countered solely by good arguments, but also through relationships. The apostle Paul spoke of imparting not only the truth, but also his very own life.[31] Perhaps Dawkins, Harris, and Dennett simply haven't gotten to know thoughtful and intelligent Christians who value the role of evidence and reason.

If you are a non-Christian, let us close by asking you some questions: How many thoughtful, sincere Christians do you know? Have you taken the time to build relationships with Christians to hear their stories, understand their struggles, and consider why they really believe as they do? And the same question applies to Christians: How many non-Christians do *you* know? Are you imparting not only what you think is true, but your very own life? As we have seen, Christianity is an intelligent faith. This can certainly be learned through reading a book and engaging the arguments, but it's often best understood face-to-face in the context of a relationship.

FOR FURTHER ENGAGEMENT

Craig, William Lane. *On Guard: Defending Your Faith with Reason and Precision.* Colorado Springs, CO: Cook, 2010.

Moreland, J. P. *Love Your God with All Your Mind: The Role of Reason in the Life of the Soul.* Colorado Springs, CO: NavPress, 1997.

WHY I DON'T LIKE THE WORD *FAITH*

I don't like the word *faith.* It's not that faith isn't important. It's just misunderstood by people who should know better. Some believers think that having compelling evidence for Christianity undermines faith. To them, faith and reason are opposites.

Their thinking goes something like this. First, without faith it's impossible to please God (Heb. 11:6). Second, evidence and proof undermine faith since, after all, where's room for faith when you know something is true? Therefore, blind irrational faith pleases God.

Notice the definition of faith lurking in the background? Faith is religious wishful thinking, a desperate lunge in the dark when all evidence is against you. Take the leap of faith and hope for luck.

Curiously, none of the biblical writers understood faith this way. Jesus tells his naysayers, "Though you do not believe Me, *believe the works*, so that you may know and understand that the Father is in Me" (John 10:38 NASB, emphasis added). Peter reminds the crowd on Pentecost that Jesus was "a man attested to you by God with miracles and wonders and signs" (Acts 2:22 NASB).

Paul writes that the evidences from the natural world for God's eternal power and divine nature "have been clearly seen," so much so that those who deny Him "are without excuse" (Rom. 1:20). Later he says that if we believe in a resurrection that didn't really happen, we have hoped in vain and "are of all men most to be pitied" (1 Cor. 15:19 NASB). No religious wishful thinking here.

So let's set the record straight. Faith is not the opposite of reason. The opposite of faith is unbelief. And reason is not the opposite of faith. The opposite of reason is irrationality. Do some Christians have irrational faith? Sure. Do some skeptics have unreasonable unbelief? You bet. It works both ways.

Here's a suggestion that might help you avoid this confusion.

Stop using the word *faith*. Use the word *trust* instead, because biblical faith means active trust. And trust must be earned. Today, just as in Jesus' day, we have "many convincing proofs" (Acts 1:3) that God is real and Jesus is the risen Savior—evidence enough to satisfy your mind and earn your trust.

Is faith irrational? That depends entirely on what you mean by "faith." If you think faith means staking your eternal destiny on a reckless leap of religious wishful thinking, then yes, *that* faith is irrational. But that is not biblical faith.

Biblical faith isn't wishing; it's confidence. It's not denying reality, but discovering reality. It's a sense of certainty grounded in the evidence that Christianity is true—not just "true for me," but actually, fully, and completely true.

God does not want your leap of faith. He wants your step of trust. When you realize you're not just wishing on a star about eternal things, that step becomes a lot easier.

—Gregory Koukl

Gregory Koukl is founder and president of Stand to Reason (www.str.org), and host of Stand to Reason's radio talk show. He is the author of *Tactics: A Game Plan for Discussing Your Christian Convictions*.

CHAPTER 2

Are Science and Christianity at Odds?

The conflict between religion and science is unavoidable. The success of science often comes at the expense of religious dogma; the maintenance of religious dogma always comes at the expense of science.

—Sam Harris

Science is at war with religion. The conflict can be traced back to the Dark Ages, a period in which the Church vigorously asserted its dogma and persecuted anyone who questioned its authority, including scientific pioneers such as Galileo, Copernicus, and Bruno. Fortunately the Enlightenment came along in the eighteenth century and validated methods of acquiring knowledge through evidence and testing. These methods freed scientists to pursue truth without fear of recrimination from the Church. Thus the scientific revolution was born. Yet the war between religion and science continues to this day.

If you believe this rendition of history, there's a good chance you've been reading a public school textbook or the New Atheists. The idea that science and religion are at odds is a popular myth in our culture, perpetuated by news headlines like "God vs. Science" in *Time* magazine. Of the perceived conflict, Christopher Hitchens writes, "All attempts to reconcile faith with science and reason are consigned to failure and ridicule." Richard

Dawkins writes, "I am hostile to fundamentalist religion because it actively debauches the scientific enterprise.... It subverts science and saps the intellect."[1]

Although it is widely believed that science and Christianity are at odds, the *opposite* is actually true. There is no inherent conflict between Christianity and science. We don't mean to suggest that religious antagonism to science has never existed. It has and does. But the history of science shows that such claims of antagonism are often exaggerated or unsubstantiated. "Once upon a time, back in the second half of the nineteenth century," says Alister McGrath, "it was certainly possible to believe that science and religion were permanently at war.... This is now seen as a hopelessly outmoded historical stereotype that scholarship has totally discredited."[2]

The scientific enterprise as a sustained and organized movement emerged in Christian Europe. During the sixteenth century, people from every culture studied the natural world, and yet modern science emerged in Europe, a civilization primarily shaped by the Judeo-Christian worldview. Why? Because Christianity provided the philosophical foundation as well as the spiritual and practical motivation for doing science. The Christian worldview—with its insistence on the orderliness of the universe, its emphasis on human reason, and its teaching that God is glorified as we seek to understand his creation—laid the foundation for the modern scientific revolution.

GOD'S UNIVERSE

Most scientific pioneers were theists, including prominent figures such as Nicolaus Copernicus (1473–1543), Robert Boyle (1627–1691), Isaac Newton (1642–1727), Blaise Pascal (1623–1662), Johannes Kepler (1571–1630), Louis Pasteur (1822–1895), Francis Bacon (1561–1626), and Max Planck (1858–1947). Many of these pioneers intently pursued science because of their belief in the Christian God. Bacon believed the natural world was full of mysteries God meant for us to explore. Kepler wrote, "The chief aim of all investigations of the external world should be to discover the rational order which has been imposed on it by God, and which he revealed to us in the language of mathematics."[3] Newton believed his scientific discoveries offered convincing evidence for the existence and creativity of God. His favorite argument for design related to the solar system: "This most beautiful system of sun, planets, and comets could only proceed from the counsel and dominion of an intelligent and powerful being."[4]

Christopher Hitchens discounts the religious convictions of these scientific pioneers, claiming that belief in God was the only option for a scientist of the time.[5] But this puts Hitchens in a curious dilemma. If religious believers get no credit for their positive contributions to society (e.g., shaping modern science) because "everyone was religious," then why should their mistakes, like atrocities committed in the name of God, discredit them? This is a double standard. One cannot deny religious believers credit on the basis of "everyone was religious" and also assign blame on the same foundation. To make the case that "religion poisons everything," Hitchens has to ignore evidence to the contrary.[6] And he is more than willing to do so.

Dawkins accepts that some early scientific pioneers may have been Christians, but he believes Christian scientists are now a rarity: "Great scientists who profess religion become harder to find through the twentieth century."[7] However, in the same year that Dawkins published *The God Delusion* (2006), three leading scientists released books favorable to theism.[8] Harvard astronomer Owen Gingrich released *God's Universe*, arguing that an individual can be both a scientist and a believer in intelligent design. Internationally renowned physicist Paul Davies published *Goldilock's Enigma*, in which he argued that intelligent life is the reason our universe exists. Francis Collins, former head of the Human Genome Project, published *The Language of God*, in which he presents scientific and philosophical evidence for God. Incidentally, President Barak Obama appointed Francis Collins as the director of the National Institutes for Health, one of the world's foremost medical research centers.

Naming scientists whose Christian worldview motivated

their work doesn't settle the issue of how science and religion relate. Entire books have been written on how science and religion intersect.[9] But we do hope you see that many early scientific pioneers, as well as cutting-edge scientists today, derived their motivation for scientific research from the belief that God created the world for us to investigate and enjoy. These scientists did not view Christianity as incompatible with science.

WHAT ABOUT GALILEO?

The idea that science and Christianity are at odds largely endures because of the reported cases of the Church persecuting scientists such as Copernicus and Galileo. Most people believe that the Catholic Church persecuted Galileo for demonstrating that Earth revolves around the sun, thereby undermining the unique and privileged status of our planet and threatening the intellectual security of the religious dictatorship of his time. The Church's reaction to Galileo is viewed as routine: Sam Harris, for example, claims that the Christian tradition involved "torturing scholars to the point of madness for merely speculating about the nature of the stars."[10]

The problem with this rendition of the story is that it's not entirely true. Scientists before Copernicus and Galileo did not think of the center of the universe as the place of honor and privilege.[11] Aristotle viewed the earth as a "cosmic sump" where air, water, fire, and matter mixed to cause decay and death. In the *Divine Comedy*, Dante placed Satan's throne at the center of Earth. Copernicus, Galileo, Kepler, and other scientists saw the heliocentric model of the universe as exalting the status of Earth rather than denigrating it.[12]

Galileo's problem was not simply that he challenged the authority of the Church. The issue was far more complex. Galileo also upset secular professors whose careers were dedicated to the older cosmology. Prior to the sixteenth century, most educated people (regardless of religious persuasion) accepted the primary cosmological model of the ancient Greeks, who believed Earth sat stationary while the sun revolved around it. When Galileo offered scientific evidence against this model, he "rattled the cages" of both the Church and academia.

Galileo made three costly mistakes in his diplomacy (or lack thereof) that led to his reproof. First, he broke his promise not to teach that Copernicanism was true. Given that the evidence for heliocentrism was inconclusive at the time, Galileo agreed not to teach its truth. But he went back on his word with the release of *Dialogue Concerning the Two Chief World Systems.*

Second, Galileo openly mocked the pope in this same book through a fictitious dialogue between two people—himself and the pope. This was especially odd since Pope Urban VIII was both a friend and supporter. Galileo named the pope *Simplicio,* which means "simpleton" or "buffoon." Galileo's character was articulate and elegant as he responded to the foolish and simplistic remarks of Simplicio. Needless to say, the pope was not amused.

Third, Galileo spoke authoritatively on the meaning of Scripture, which was clearly outside his area of expertise. He spoke with authority on issues that he was simply not qualified to address. Thus, his opponents criticized him not only on scientific grounds, but also because of his theological views and the arrogance with which he presented them.[13]

Galileo was neither executed nor persecuted by the Church for his diplomatic blunders. After his trial before the Inquisition, he was placed under the care of the archbishop of Siena, who housed him in his beautiful palace for five months. Galileo was then released to his home in Florence where he received a Church pension for the rest of his life. He was able to continue his scientific research in areas unrelated to heliocentrism.

What can we conclude about the Galileo incident? The popular claim that the Church persecuted Galileo for advancing science is a caricature. As Dinesh D'Souza points out in *What's So Great About Christianity,* the Galileo episode is a blip on the radar of an otherwise harmonious relationship between scientists and the Church. "Indeed," says D'Souza, "there is no other example in history of the Catholic Church condemning a scientific theory."[14] This myth persists because it's consistently presented as fact in textbooks, history programs, and, most recently, in the writings of the New Atheists. It's time to put it to rest.

NATURALISM VERSUS THEISM

Naturalism is a scientifically oriented worldview that denies the existence of God and the soul. Richard Dawkins put it this way: "An atheist in this sense of philosophical naturalist is somebody who believes there is nothing beyond the natural, physical world, no *super*natural creative intelligence lurking behind the observable universe, no soul that outlasts the body and no miracles—except in the sense of natural phenomena that we don't understand yet."[15]

Theism holds that there is a personal creator and sustainer of the universe who is omnipotent, omniscient, essentially good, omnipresent, and eternal. Christianity believes that the Creator has revealed himself to humankind in the person of Jesus Christ, a member of the Trinity, who was resurrected from the dead in confirmation of his deity.[16] Thus, Christians believe in the supernatural world, including God, the soul, angels, and miracles.

We return now to a point brought up earlier in the chapter: there is no inherent conflict between Christianity and science. Defining these two worldviews shows us the root problem: naturalism and theism are at odds, not science and Christianity. Naturalism is intrinsically atheistic because it sees nothing outside the natural or material world. Here is what's interesting about the foundational beliefs of naturalists: naturalists place enormous trust in nature's order and their powers of reason, but their worldview ultimately undermines any basis for such confidence. Science is only possible if the world is ordered and if we can trust our senses and reason.

Let's consider a basic question: Why does the natural world make any sense to begin with? Albert Einstein once remarked that the most incomprehensible thing about the universe is that it is comprehensible. Why should we be able to grasp the beauty, elegance, and complexity of our universe?

Einstein understood a basic truth about science, namely,

that it relies upon certain philosophical assumptions about the natural world. These assumptions include the existence of an external world that is orderly and rational, and the trustworthiness of our minds to grasp that world. Science cannot proceed apart from these assumptions, even though they cannot be independently proven. Oxford professor John C. Lennox asks a penetrating question, "At the heart of all science lies the conviction that the universe is orderly. Without this deep conviction science would not be possible. So we are entitled to ask: Where does the conviction come from?"[17] Why is the world orderly? And why do our minds comprehend this order?

Toward the end of *The God Delusion*, Dawkins admits that since we are the product of natural selection, our senses cannot be fully trusted.[18] After all, according to Darwinian evolution, our senses have been formed to aid survival, not necessarily to deliver true belief. Since a human being has been cobbled together through the blind process of natural selection acting on random mutation, says Dawkins, it's unlikely that our views of the world are completely true. Outspoken philosopher of neuroscience Patricia Churchland agrees:

> The principle chore of brains is to get the body parts where they should be in order that the organism may survive. Improvements in sensorimotor control confer an evolutionary advantage: a fancier style of representing [the world] is advantageous so long as it... enhances the organism's chances for survival. Truth, whatever that is, takes the hindmost.[19]

Dawkins is on the right track to suggest that naturalism should lead people to be skeptical about trusting their senses. Dawkins just doesn't take his skepticism far enough.

In *Miracles*, C. S. Lewis points out that knowledge depends upon the reliability of our mental faculties.[20] If human reasoning is not trustworthy, then no scientific conclusions can be considered true or false. In fact, we couldn't have *any* knowledge about the world, period. Our senses must be reliable to acquire knowledge of the world, and our reasoning faculties must be reliable to process the acquired knowledge. But this raises a particularly thorny dilemma for atheism. If the mind has developed through the blind, irrational, and material process of Darwinian evolution, then why should we trust it at all? Why should we believe that the human brain—the outcome of an accidental process— actually puts us in touch with reality? Science cannot be used as an answer to this question, because science itself relies upon these very assumptions.

Even Charles Darwin was aware of this problem: "The horrid doubt always arises whether the convictions of man's mind, which has developed from the mind of the lower animals, are of any value or at all trustworthy. Would anyone trust the conviction of a monkey's mind, if there are any convictions in such a mind?"[21] If Darwinian evolution is true, we should distrust the cognitive faculties that make science possible.

I (Sean) was speaking to an atheist student group at a prominent university in northern California. In response to my presentation of this argument, one of the students argued that scientific studies actually demonstrate that the mind cannot be fully trusted.* He claimed science proves that we should distrust our cognitive faculties. While I commended him for a creative challenge, I pointed out that his comment suffered from a fatal flaw: the scientific studies that are meant to disprove the reliability of human reasoning depend on the reliability of human reasoning to come to that conclusion. In other words, the only way these scientists could come to the conclusion that we should doubt the human mind was by using their own minds! To quote C. S. Lewis, "If the value of reasoning is in doubt, you cannot try to establish it by reasoning."[22]

According to Templeton Prize–winning physicist Paul Davies, the intelligibility of the universe points toward a rational grounding:

---

* An evolved mind gives no foundation for trusting reason. Theism gives a foundation for that trust, but also tells us that our reason, like everything else, has been affected by humanity's fall in the garden of Eden.

Science is based on the assumption that the universe is thoroughly rational and logical at all levels. Atheists claim that the laws [of nature] exist reasonlessly and that the universe is ultimately absurd. As a scientist, I find this hard to accept. There must be an unchanging rational ground in which the logical, orderly nature of the universe is rooted.[23]

Atheism provides no such rational ground, but undercuts it. Atheists can certainly do scientific research, but here's the catch: they can do science only if they abandon their naturalistic worldview and borrow from theism because theism provides the necessary foundation for the logical, orderly nature of the universe and the powers of reason.

This point brings us full circle. It's not Christianity that is at odds with science—it's naturalism. Notre Dame philosopher Alvin Plantinga sets the record straight:

People like Dawkins believe there is a conflict between science and religion because they think there is a conflict between evolution and theism; the truth of the matter, however, is that the conflict is between science and *naturalism*, not between science and belief in God.[24]

It's not simply that the order of the universe fits better with theism. The connection goes deeper. An ordered, rational universe is what we would expect from a God who created us in his image. Forming true beliefs about the world is one way we reflect the image of God imprinted in us by our Creator.

Science depends on the assumption that the world is orderly and that our minds can access this reality. Even the most secular scientists presume that nature operates in a lawlike fashion. This conviction is best explained by the pioneers of the scientific revolution, who believed *the cosmos is orderly because it was designed by the rational Creator of the universe who desires for us, as beings made in his image, to understand, enjoy, and explore his creation.*

FOR FURTHER ENGAGEMENT

Collins, C. John. *Science and Faith: Friends or Foes?* Wheaton, IL: Crossway, 2003.

Lennox, John C. *God's Undertaker: Has Science Buried God?* Updated ed. Oxford: Lion, 2009.

[why it matters]

FAITH FOUNDED ON FACT

My studies have been primarily in two areas: apologetics, the discovery and defense of proper religious values; and philosophy of law, with special emphasis on human rights. In both of these areas, I have become convinced that historic, biblical Christianity offers the only meaningful and effective worldview.

Atheists tell us that the universe can rationally be regarded as infinite, or all there is. This is simply not the case.

First, most cosmologists consider the universe to be finite.

Second, the big bang is seen as the beginning of matter, energy, space, and time, and thus requires an explanation. Einstein himself moved from a belief in an infinite universe to an acceptance of big bang cosmology—viewing his own effort to correct his general theory of relativity to support an infinite, nonexpanding universe as his "biggest blunder."

Third, an actual infinite constitutes an irrational notion. Thus, it follows that the universe cannot have this property, whereas God, as a spirit, is not subject to such a restriction. The only rational explanation for the universe's beginning is the existence of a transcendent God not bound by space-time considerations.

Finally, as many physicists and cosmologists have observed, the universe is finely tuned, requiring an intelligent creator. The existence of universes other than our own (the possibility of "multiverses") has zero empirical evidence to support it. But even if a multiplicity of universes exist, we have no grounds for asserting that they would not be finely tuned. And we would need a "multiverse generator" to explain them—which would simply push the need to assert God's existence a step backward, in no sense eliminating it.

My academic work has reinforced one of the most fundamental elements of Christian truth: that the *subjective* must be grounded in the *objective*—that objective fact, not wish fulfillment or political correctness, needs to determine both scholarship and personal religious belief.

"God was in Christ reconciling the world to Himself" (2 Cor. 5:19 NASB): that is an objective fact and my personal religion must be based on it. I must not try to create God (or the world) in my image, but rather accept God and his revelation of himself as the source of my worldview and religious life.

—John Warwick Montgomery

John Warwick Montgomery is professor emeritus of law and humanities at the University of Bedfordshire (UK). He is the author of many books, including *Faith Founded on Fact* and *History, Law, and Christianity*. Visit him at www.jwm .christendom.co.uk.

CHAPTER 3

Are Miracles Possible?

The nineteenth century is the last time when it was possible for an educated person to admit to believing in miracles like the virgin birth without embarrassment.

—Richard Dawkins

"Snow and ice on the equator? That's impossible!" This was the reaction of Europeans in 1849 when German missionary Johann Ludwig Krapf first sighted "two large pillars ... covered with a white substance" towering above a large mountain northeast of Kilimanjaro.[1] Even though Krapf had witnessed the snow on Mount Kenya with his own eyes, his claim was met with disdain and disbelief by the scientific community of his day.

Krapf tried unsuccessfully to persuade his colleagues that snow could exist on mountains near the equator. After all, he argued, it was commonly believed at the time that snow existed near the equator on mountains in South America and Ethiopia. Nevertheless, despite his personal testimony and corroborating evidence, the scientific community ridiculed his claims.

More than thirty years elapsed before Krapf's claims were finally substantiated. In 1883 the Royal Geographic Society commissioned Scottish explorer Joseph Thomson to seek the shortest route from the Indian Ocean to Lake Victoria. As he trekked through the plains of Laikipia (northwest of Mt. Kenya), he spotted the 17,057-feet-tall, snowcapped mountain, confirming

Krapf's original observation. Mount Kenya was later explored in 1887 and finally climbed in 1899.

Scientists' reaction to the discovery of snow on the equator is similar to the way many view the possibility of miracles today. The New Atheists are especially unwilling to consider evidence for a miracle because such an event does not fit their preconceived view of the world. Because of their commitment to naturalism, they discard miracles from the outset, regardless of the strength of the evidence. Richard Dawkins writes, "[There is] nothing beyond the natural, physical world, no *super*natural creative intelligence lurking behind the observable universe, no soul that outlasts the body and no miracles—except in the sense of natural phenomena that we don't understand yet." Christopher Hitchens adds, "The last word on the subject [the possibility of miracles] was written by Scottish philosopher David Hume."[2] We will discuss Hume's view below.

If naturalism is true, as the New Atheists proclaim, then every event and feature of the world requires a natural explanation, making miracles impossible. Rather than actually rising from the dead, Jesus' appearances must have been hallucinations.[3] Jesus could not have fed the five thousand; they must have packed their own lunches. Jesus didn't actually walk on water; maybe conditions on the Sea of Galilee were just right to form a hard-to-see ice patch that he walked on (believe it or not, scientists have recently entertained this possibility).[4]

If naturalism is true, then the New Testament accounts of the life of Jesus must be mistaken. And if miracles are not possible, then Christianity cannot be true. *Christianity crumbles if miracles are impossible.* While other religions report miracles, Christianity is uniquely based upon the occurrence of historical miracles, and in particular, the resurrection of Jesus of Nazareth. If Jesus has not risen, observes the apostle Paul, the Christian faith is "worthless."[5]

Like the New Atheists, can we simply rule out the possibility of miracles before an investigation of relevant facts? Can we settle the issue simply by appealing to the naturalistic world-view? We think such methodology is premature and counter-productive. Here's why: only if atheism were proven to be true could we rationally deny the possibility of miracles. Without such a proof, we ought to be open to the occurrence of a miracle and be willing to follow the evidence wherever it leads. After all, if a transcendent, personal God exists, then it seems eminently possible that he has acted in the universe.

ARE MIRACLES IMPROBABLE?

In *The God Delusion*, Richard Dawkins defines miracles as "events that are extremely improbable."[6] The problem with this definition is that probabilities are always relative to the background information one considers. For instance, suppose Joe is a college student. Imagine, further, that 10 percent of college students surf. Given that background information, it would be quite unlikely that Joe surfs. But what if we found out Joe was a student of a university in Hawaii and 90 percent of those students *do* surf? Obviously, the probability of Joe being a surfer would radically change!

Dawkins claims that miracles are "extremely improbable." But with respect to what? If we begin our investigation assuming naturalism, as Dawkins does, then certainly miracles are improbable. However, if we consider all the evidence for God's existence, including the cosmological argument (chapter 5), the design argument (chapters 6–7), evidence for the soul (chapter 8), the moral argument (chapter 15), and the historical evidence for the resurrection (below), then miracles seem quite probable.

In short, the possibility of miracles depends upon the existence of God. If God exists, miracles are possible. If it's even *possible* that God exists, then we can't rule out his intervention in the natural world before we consider the evidence. Even atheist Michael Goulder, a staunch critic of miracle stories says, "We ought not to rule out 'miracles' as explanations of striking events."[7] In other words, we ought to consider the evidence before determining the verdict.

The New Atheists believe Scottish philosopher David Hume undermined the possibility that we could ever *prove* a miracle occurred. That is, even if a miracle did happen, the wise person would never believe it. Given the New Atheists' appeal to Hume's work, it's worth taking a closer look at his critique of miracles.

DIDN'T HUME DISPROVE THE CASE FOR MIRACLES?

David Hume destroyed any rational basis for believing in a miracle. At least that's what the New Atheists would like you to think. According to Christopher Hitchens, Hume's book *An Enquiry Concerning Human Understanding* (1748) ended debate on the subject and settled the case against miracles more than two and a half centuries ago.[8] Hume challenged the identification of miracles with both "in principle" and "in fact" objections.

Hume's "In Principle" Objection

Hume claimed that belief ought to be justified by probability and that probability is based upon the uniformity or consistency of nature. Nature always behaves in a certain way, Hume said, therefore it is likely that it will always behave that way. Based on this probability, he concluded that exceptions to nature's laws are so infinitely improbable as to be considered impossible. The unchangeable laws of nature outweigh any evidence that could ever be offered for a miracle. Anything that is unique to normal human experience—such as a miracle—should be, according to Hume, eliminated outright.

For example, which is more probable: that the witnesses of Christ's resurrection were mistaken, or that Jesus was raised from the dead? According to Hume's naturalistic methodology, the answer is obvious, even without considering the evidence, because he believes the laws of probability tell us that miracles simply cannot happen.

Despite Hume's continued influence today, philosophers agree that Hume overstated his case.[9] Let's consider two key problems for Hume's position. First, Hume speaks of the "uniform" experience against miracles. But such a way of thinking is guilty of circular reasoning. Here's why: Hume presumes to know the uniformity of human experience *prior* to considering the evidence. To assert that uniform experience counts against miracles is to assume that all miracle claims are false. But how can he make such a claim before examining the facts? Well, he simply assumes it. C. S. Lewis pokes fun at this way of reasoning:

> Now of course we must agree with Hume that if there is absolutely "uniform experience" against miracles, if in other words they have never happened, why then they never have. Unfortunately we know the experience against them to be uniform only if we know that all the reports of them are false. And we can know all the reports to be false only if we know already that miracles have never occurred. In fact, we are arguing in a circle.[10]

Second, Hume's critique of miracles says we should never believe the improbable. While most outcomes do tend to favor the odds, are we in a position to say that we should *never* believe otherwise? Following this train of thought, we should never believe that a person has been dealt a royal flush, since the odds against it are 649,740 to 1 (assuming five cards). Yet occasionally a royal flush shows up in a hand. The odds against winning a state lottery are usually millions to one, yet someone wins. According to Hume, even if you were dealt a royal flush or held a winning lottery ticket, you would not be justified in believing it was true. Similarly, Hume's reasoning would justify denying that a miracle occurred, even if you personally witnessed it! But surely it is perfectly reasonable to believe that an improbable event can at least occasionally occur. Wise people consider the weight of the odds but ultimately base their belief on the facts.

Hume's "In Fact" Objection

Hume gives four "facts" which he believes discount the rationality of believing in a miracle. First, no historical miracle has been sufficiently attested by honest and reliable men who are of such social standing that they would have a great deal to lose by lying. Second, people crave miraculous stories and will gullibly believe absurd stories, which is evidenced by the sheer number of false tales of miraculous events. Third, miracles only occur among barbarous people. And fourth, miracles occur in all religions and thus cancel each other out, since they espouse contradictory doctrines.

As for Hume's first "in fact" argument, it has been shown that the Gospel writers were both interested in and capable of recording accurate history.[11] Eleven of the twelve disciples were put to death because of their convictions that Jesus is the risen Lord. While this does not prove the veracity of their beliefs, it does show the depth of their conviction and the level of their sincerity. Liars make poor martyrs.

We agree with Hume's claim in his second "in fact" argument: some people are willing to believe absurd miracle stories without proper scrutiny. But this only highlights the importance of proceeding carefully and cautiously before accepting a miracle claim as valid. Sure, *some* people are willing to gullibly follow absurd miracle claims, but are we in a position to say this is true for *all* people?

As for Hume's third "in fact" argument, Jesus' miracles did not occur among a barbarous people, but among the Jews who were a highly educated and sophisticated people. Unlike other people groups of the Mediterranean world, the Jews were uniquely committed to studying and following their ancient Scriptures.[12] The literacy rate among Jews in first-century Palestine was likely higher than the Greco-Roman population. This is likely due to the presence of synagogues that functioned as schools for Jewish boys.[13] The Jews valued education, which is why Paul encouraged early Christians to study and show themselves approved to God.[14]

Hume's fourth and final "in fact" argument falls short as well. While it is true that other religions have miracle claims, none of the miracles are as powerfully attested as the miracles of Jesus Christ.[15] Unlike the miracles in the Gospels, these other claims tend to be poorly supported in questionable sources far removed from the events. Miracle stories involving founders of major world religions such as Mohammed, Buddha, or Krishna appear centuries later.* The stories about many religious founders, such as Lao-Tzu and Confucius, contain no miracle claims at all.[16]

We can confidently conclude that Hume's "in principle" and "in fact" arguments fail to undermine the rationality of believing in miracles. While his arguments do serve to make us cautious, the only way we can settle the question of the historicity of a miracle claim is through an investigation of the historical evidence. To this we shall now proceed.

MIRACLE CASE STUDY: THE RESURRECTION OF JESUS CHRIST

So far we have defended the *possibility* of miracles. Now we will consider the *evidence* for the central miracle of the Christian faith—the resurrection of Jesus of Nazareth. While naturalism poses a significant challenge to the possibility of miracles, as we have seen, so too miracles pose a substantial challenge to naturalism. In other words, if naturalism is true, the veracity of the resurrection accounts would be significantly weakened. But

---

* Christopher Hitchens claims that other virgin birth stories, such as of Buddha and Krishna, discount the uniqueness of the Christian claim (*God Is Not Great*, 22–23). Dawkins hints at a similar suggestion for the resurrection (*The God Delusion*, 119–20). While Hitchens and Dawkins cite these supposed similarities between Christianity and earlier pagan mystery religions with bravado, they show surprisingly little knowledge that this theory has been largely abandoned by the scholarly community (T. N. D. Mettinger, *The Riddle of Resurrection: "Dying and Rising Gods" in the Ancient Near East* [Stockholm: Almqvist and Wiksell, 2001]). While we have early eyewitness accounts for the Christian claims (see Luke 1:1–4; 1 John 1:1), other reports, such as those of virgin births, come hundreds of years after the event, and no one has demonstrated that any pagan resurrection claims surfaced before the time of Jesus. For the most part, the pagan deities of the mystery religions were timeless mythical figures who experienced "dying and rising again" annually with the changing seasons. The disciples were very clear about their intentions: "For we did not follow cleverly contrived myths when we made known to you the power and coming of our Lord Jesus Christ; instead, we were eyewitnesses of His majesty" (2 Peter 1:16 HCSB). See also the section in chapter 18 titled, "Did Early Christianity Borrow from Pagan Mythology?"

on the other hand, if the resurrection accounts are shown to be true, naturalism would be defeated. Simply put, *while naturalism challenges resurrection, so too resurrection challenges naturalism.*

Christopher Hitchens is unmistakable in his rejection of the resurrection: "Having no reliable or consistent witness, in anything like the time period needed to certify such an extraordinary claim, we are finally entitled to say that we have a right, if not an obligation, to respect ourselves enough to disbelieve the whole thing."[17] Hitchens asserts this with little justification or interaction with the historical evidence.* Such strong words may have been mainstream in the early part of the twentieth century, but with recent advancements in New Testament studies, few contemporary scholars would agree with Hitchens's assessment of the facts.

Some of the world's greatest intellectuals and people from all walks of life have testified to the strength of the case for Jesus' resurrection, including novelist Anne Rice (who has sold over 100 million books worldwide), lawyer Simon Greenleaf (one of the greatest authorities on legal procedure), professor Thomas Arnold (former chair of modern history at Oxford University), and magician Andre Kole (one of the greatest illusionists of our time). They all examined the evidence closely and came to the same conclusion—*Jesus rose from the grave.* Let's consider why.

In *The Case for the Resurrection of Jesus*, Gary Habermas and Michael Licona cite five historical facts that are well evidenced and granted by nearly every scholar who studies the subject, regardless of his or her theological persuasion.[18] They are agreed-upon facts over which there is little debate. The question is not whether these facts are true, but which theory best explains them. Let's consider three of the known facts.†

---

* Hitchens would need to interact with arguments made by New Testament historians Gary Habermas and Michael Licona, *The Case for the Resurrection* (Grand Rapids, MI: Kregel, 2004).

† The two facts not under consideration in this chapter are that two men's opinions suddenly changed: Paul the church persecutor and James the skeptic and brother of Jesus.

Fact 1: Jesus Died on the Cross

The evidence for Jesus' death by crucifixion at the hands of the Romans is considerable. First, all four Gospels report Jesus' death.[19] Historical events that are attested in multiple sources are considered to be on firm ground.

Second, the nature of crucifixion virtually guaranteed death. Crucifixion was scientifically honed by the Romans to cause maximal pain over the longest possible time. The great historian Will Durant wrote that "even the Romans... pitied the victims."[20] Crucifixion was so brutal that a new word had to be created to describe the anguish victims felt—*excruciating*. Given the custom of whipping, the crown of thorns, the crossbar burden, and his crucifixion with nails, it is virtually certain that Jesus was dead.

Third, the spear in the side reported by John that caused water and blood to flow is medical evidence that Jesus died. Many medical doctors have agreed that the release of blood and water from such a spear wound is a sure sign of death.[21]

Fourth, extrabiblical writers record the death of Jesus. These include Cornelius Tacitus (A.D. 55–120), who is considered by many to be the greatest ancient Roman historian; the Jewish scholar Josephus (A.D. 37–97); and the Jewish Talmud (A.D. 70–200). The death of Jesus is on such solid historical ground that John Dominic Crossan, the liberal Jesus Seminar scholar says, "Jesus' death by execution under Pontius Pilate is as sure as anything historical can ever be."[22]

Fact 2: Jesus' Tomb Was Empty

On Sunday after the crucifixion, Mary and the other women went to anoint the body of Jesus. To their surprise, the tomb was open and the body was gone. There is good reason to believe the tomb was actually empty as the women reported. Let's consider two lines of evidence.

First, the disciples of Jesus did not go off to Egypt or China to preach the resurrection of Christ; they went right back to the very city of Jerusalem where Jesus was crucified. Had the tomb of Jesus been occupied, they could not have maintained the resurrection for a moment. Why not? Philosopher Stephen Davis explains:

> Early Christian proclamation of the resurrection of Jesus in Jerusalem would have been psychologically and apologetically impossible without safe evidence of an empty tomb.... In other words, without safe and agreed-upon evidence of an empty tomb, the apostles' claims would have been subject to massive falsification by the simple presentation of the body.[23]

Second, one of the most compelling evidences supporting the empty tomb story is that women first discovered it. In first-century Palestine, women had low status as citizens or legal witnesses. Except in rare circumstances, Jewish law precluded women from giving testimony in a court of law. So why would the disciples, if they were contriving the story, have used women as the first witnesses to the empty tomb? Typically when people concoct a story to deceive others, they don't invent information that discredits their story. The fact that the disciples include the women as the first witnesses to the empty tomb tells us one thing—*they were reporting the truth.*

Fact 3: Jesus' Disciples Sincerely Believed He Appeared to Them

Scholars agree that the early disciples sincerely believed that Jesus rose from the dead and personally appeared to them. A convincing line of evidence can be found in 1 Corinthians 15:3–8, which is a short creed that records the death, burial, resurrection, and appearances of Jesus to Peter, James, the twelve disciples, a group of five hundred, and finally to Paul. Even though the book of 1 Corinthians was written around A.D. 55, scholars believe the short creed in chapter 15 predates the writing of the book itself. One reason is because at the beginning of the creed Paul says, "For I delivered to you as of first importance what I also received" (NASB). In other words, Paul is passing on to the Corinthian church what had previously been given to him. When did Paul receive the creed? Since Paul first visited Peter and James in Jerusalem three years after his conversion (Gal. 1:18-20), many critical scholars believe that Paul received the creed from them on this initial encounter. This would date the creed to within five years after the death of Jesus. Historically speaking, this is remarkably early evidence for belief in the death, burial, and appearances of Jesus.

FOLLOWING THE EVIDENCE WHERE IT LEADS

Many naturalistic theories have been suggested for the resurrection, but none of them can account for all the facts.[24] Only one conclusion takes into account all the accepted historical facts and does not adjust them to preconceived notions. It is the conclusion that Jesus rose from the dead—a miraculous event in history.

The New Atheists boldly claim that miracles are impossible. Yet, as we have seen, this denial is not based on any scientific or historical evidence, but rather comes out of a philosophical commitment to naturalism. If naturalism is true, then the New Atheists are right—miracles are impossible. But if naturalism is false, then miracles are possible (arguably even *likely*). Rather than ruling out the possibility of miracles from the outset, shouldn't we be open to the historical and scientific evidence? We think so. And we will do our best to lay out this evidence in the rest of the book.

FOR FURTHER ENGAGEMENT

Geisler, Norman L. *Miracles and the Modern Mind: A Defense of Biblical Miracles.* Grand Rapids: Baker, 1992.

Geivett, R. Douglas, and Gary R. Habermas. *In Defense of Miracles: A Comprehensive Case for God's Action in History.* Downers Grove, IL: InterVarsity Press, 1997.

[why it matters]

THE RESURRECTION OF JESUS AS A PRECURSOR TO HEAVEN

Jesus' resurrection is applicable to far more than Christian evidences or salvation. The New Testament relates this event to many crucial areas of both theology and practice. For example, what details could we know about heaven if our only pointer was the resurrection? Perhaps surprisingly, many truths emerge regarding eternity. Let's look at ten truths.

First, more than any other doctrine, the New Testament asserts approximately twenty times that believers will be raised like Jesus (Acts 4:2; 1 Cor. 6:14), with a body that is similar to his (Phil. 3:20–21; 1 John 3:2). This alone explains much about our heavenly existence as embodied persons.

Second, heaven will be both *real* as well as *substantial*. It makes little sense for real bodies to inhabit a world that consists only of dreams or ideas, or one where we lose our personhood.

Third, the life of heaven is eternal. Just as Jesus would never die again, neither will believers (John 11:25–26; 1 Thess. 4:17; Heb. 10:12–14).

Fourth, Peter explains that Jesus' resurrection ensures that our heavenly inheritance is incorruptible and indestructible, without flaw, and will never lose its glory. Moreover, our heavenly treasure is guarded so as never to be disturbed (1 Peter 1:3–4).

Fifth, Jesus promised that God's kingdom would involve wonderful heavenly fellowship with others (Matt. 8:11), as well as with himself (John 14:1–3). Jesus' followers recognized him (John 20:20) and enjoyed his presence after his resurrection (Luke 24:28–31; John 20:14, 19, 26), and we will know each other then, as well (1 Cor. 13:12).

Sixth, having been raised with Jesus, believers will be exalted with him in heaven (Eph. 2:6). This also involves our glorification (Rom. 8:18, 30).

Seventh, believers before the slain but risen Lamb will enjoy rousing times of worship and service in heaven (Rev. 5:6–14). Earthly worship can only hint at this magnificence and splendor!

Eighth, whenever Paul speaks of the resurrection of the dead, it is always in the plural. Good Jewish theology dictated that this would be a corporate event, to be shared with each other (Rev. 21:21–27).

Ninth, God's creation will be "raised" along with us, being freed from decay and death, once again becoming God's Paradise (Rom. 8:19–23; 2 Peter 3:13). It would certainly seem, then, that believers will enjoy God's new creation.

Tenth, the believer's eternal life actually begins now (John 6:47; 1 John 5:13). Rather than waiting for eternity, some of God's initial blessings are manifest in the present. After all, we are already citizens of heaven (Phil. 3:20–21).

That Jesus' resurrection is such a well-evidenced event makes these guarantees of the believer's eternity even more exciting. With Paul, while living is wonderful, dying is far better (Phil. 1:21, 23)! In light of these truths, we must go to work, with an eye toward eternity (1 Cor. 15:58; Gal. 6:8–10).

—Gary R. Habermas

Gary R. Habermas is distinguished research professor and chair of the Department of Philosophy and Theology at Liberty University, where he teaches in the PhD program at Liberty Baptist Theological Seminary and Graduate School. He has written more than thirty books, including *Did the Resurrection Happen?* with David Baggett and the late Antony Flew. Visit him at www.garyhabermas .com.

CHAPTER 4

Is Darwinian Evolution the Only Game in Town?

Evolution is a fact. Beyond reasonable doubt, beyond serious doubt, beyond sane, informed, intelligent doubt, beyond doubt evolution is a fact. The evidence for evolution is at least as strong as the evidence for the Holocaust, even allowing for eye witnesses to the Holocaust.

—Richard Dawkins

Few issues generate such heated debate as the question of human origins. However, from the perspective of the New Atheists, the debate should have been settled in 1859 when Darwin released *On the Origin of Species*. Both Sam Harris and Christopher Hitchens claim that the evidence for Darwinian evolution is "overwhelming." Richard Dawkins says evolution is a fact that is accepted by all except the "woefully uninformed." He goes so far as to claim that no reputable scientist disputes it.[1]

But is this true? Is Darwinian evolution the only game in town? In 2001, the Discovery Institute began to compile a list of scientists who dissent from Darwin. By signing their names, the scientists indicate their agreement with this statement: "We are skeptical of claims for the ability of random mutation and natural selection to account for the complexity of life. Careful examination of the evidence for Darwinian theory should be encouraged."[2] Since the inception of the list, more than eight hundred PhD-holding scientists from institutions such as MIT, Cambridge, Princeton, and UCLA have made their dissent known. Many world-class scientists doubt Darwin's evolutionary theory—and for good reason.

UNDERSTANDING EVOLUTION

Before we can explain why an increasing number of scientists have come to doubt Darwin's theory, it's important to understand precisely what is meant by the term *evolution*. *Evolution* can mean several things. Darwinists often define evolution as change over time. Another definition is organisms' adaptation to changing environments. For example, thirteen subspecies of finches live in the Galapagos Islands, and beak sizes of the finches have been found to vary as the environment goes through different seasons. This is small-scale evolution, known as microevolution.

The controversial claim is that microevolution inevitably leads to macroevolution (i.e., Darwinian evolution). Macroevolution operates under two assumptions to explain the origin of life and life's diversity. First, all organisms trace their lineage back to a common ancestor, a theory often called "universal common descent" or "common ancestry." Second, the mechanism that drives common descent is natural selection acting on random mutation. According to Dawkins, mutations provide the "raw material" for evolution.[3]

Darwin believed that nature selected the fittest organisms to survive in their environments. The organisms that had a favorable adaption from a random mutation then produced offspring. Given enough time, this undirected process generated all diverse and complex life, without any need for a Creator.

UNDERSTANDING INTELLIGENT DESIGN

Even though it's the most widely held view of biological origins, Darwinian evolution faces a radical challenge from the theory of intelligent design (ID).* Intelligent design's main claim is that nature exhibits patterns that are best explained as the product of intelligent cause (design) rather than an undirected material process (chance and necessity).

Surprisingly, many evolutionists admit that the world looks designed. In *Why Evolution Is True*, Jerry Coyne says, "If anything is true about nature, it is that plants and animals seem intricately and almost perfectly designed for living their lives."[4] According to Dawkins, "Biology is the study of complex things that appear to have been designed for a purpose."[5] In *The Greatest Show on Earth*, Dawkins says organisms look as if they were "meticulously planned."[6] Of course, Dawkins insists that the appearance of design is illusory. In contrast, ID proponents claim the world looks designed because it was designed.

Archaeologists, forensic scientists, and SETI researchers (scientists looking for signs of intelligence from outer space) all do ID research. Design can be seen in such diverse scientific disciplines as biology, cosmology, chemistry, physics, astronomy, and neuroscience (we discuss some of this evidence in chapters 5–9). Consider the most popular biological example—the bacterial flagellum. In public lectures, Harvard biologist Howard Berg has called the bacterial flagellum "the most efficient motor in the universe." The flagellum is a tiny, bidirectional, motor-driven propeller attached to certain bacteria. It spins up to a hundred thousand revolutions per minute, can change direction within a quarter of a turn, and propels a bacterium through its watery surroundings. It is a molecular machine of the highest caliber. The flagellum has multiple, functionally integrated parts (like the parts of a mousetrap), so that the removal of a key part destroys the function of the entire system.

---

* A majority of Americans now reject Darwin's theory in favor of intelligent design. In a 2009 Zogby poll, 52 percent agreed that "the development of life was guided by intelligent design." "In Darwin Anniversary Year, New Zogby Poll Reveals Majority Support for Intelligent Design," June 30, 2009, available at www.evolutionnews.org/2009/06/in_darwin_anniversary_year_new.html.

Darwinists have proposed various explanations for how this little motor came about. All such explanations try to make plausible how systems simpler than the flagellum might have evolved into a flagellum. But systems simpler than a flagellum don't work as a flagellum, so if they evolved into a flagellum, they must have started off doing something else. But what? Darwinists speculate wildly about what those previous systems (known as *precursors* or *intermediates*) might have been. But such arguments from imagination are not evidence. Undirected material processes give no evidence of producing such complex machinelike structures. But intelligence does and can.

The theory of intelligent design does not challenge the definition of evolution as change over time, or even common ancestry.* But it does challenge the Darwinian claim that all life's complexity and diversity can emerge through a blind, undirected process. Intelligent design finds design in the natural world, which leads to the question of who the designer could be. A designer's existence has further implications for the value and purpose of life. This is the controversial aspect of intelligent design.

DOUBTING DARWIN

Scientists are beginning to recognize that natural selection and random mutation do play a minor role in the history of life,

---

* For example, biochemist Michael Behe, author of *Darwin's Black Box* and *The Edge of Evolution*, accepts common ancestry but argues that intelligence is still required. While Behe believes that apes and humans share a common ancestor, he rejects Darwin's claim that random variation and natural selection are sufficient to guide the entire process. Thus, he accepts the first tenet of Darwinism but rejects the second. Many ID theorists, on the other hand, reject common descent. For example, developmental biologist Jonathan Wells, coauthor of *The Design of Life*, sees fossil and molecular data as so full of gaps as to overthrow the gradual pattern of organismal change predicted by Darwin's theory. ID theorists may disagree over whether or not all organisms trace their lineage back to a common ancestor, but they agree that organisms show clear, scientific evidence of design. The primary question for intelligent design is not *how* organisms came to be (though they regard that as an important question also); rather, it is whether organisms demonstrate clear, observable marks of being intelligently caused.

but they are skeptical that this blind, material process can account for all the diversity and complexity of life. And so are we.

Let's look closely at a few of the most common evidences the New Atheists offer in support of evolution.

HIV and Bacterial Resistance

According to Sam Harris, "Viruses like HIV, as well as a wide range of harmful bacteria, can be seen evolving right under our noses." Richard Dawkins writes, "Bacteria offer another priceless gift to the evolutionist."[7]

In one sense, Harris and Dawkins are right. HIV and bacterial resistance provide great examples of natural selection in action. But here is the pivotal question: can we extrapolate minor adaptations within the HIV virus and bacteria (*micro*evolution) to account for the diversification of life (*macro*evolution)? Recent evidence points to the exact opposite of what the New Atheists claim. Let's focus on HIV.

As a virus, HIV has far less genetic information than a typical cell. HIV can mutate extraordinarily fast and is thus a great test case for the limits of the creative powers of natural selection. With millions of infections worldwide, the HIV virus has undergone countless mutations. It is therefore uniquely positioned to help determine whether natural selection is viable, as Darwin surmised.

So, what have these mutations shown? According to biochemist Michael Behe, author of *The Edge of Evolution*, "*very little*. Although news stories rightly emphasize the ability of HIV to quickly develop drug resistance, and although massive publicity makes HIV seem to the public to be an evolutionary powerhouse, on a functional biochemical level the virus has been a complete stick-in-the-mud."[8]

HIV has not gone through the radical changes we should expect if natural selection is the creative force the New Atheists claim. HIV functions exactly the same as when it was discovered fifty years ago. Although minor changes have allowed it to resist certain drugs, no fundamentally new structures or biological information have emerged. This is also true for malaria, *E. Coli*, and all other microorganisms that scientists have studied over the past century. Claiming that HIV or bacterial mutations provide evidence for macroevolution is a leap of faith far beyond the available evidence.

Homology

You may recall your high school biology textbook, which probably had a picture of a human hand next to a bat wing, a porpoise flipper, and a horse hoof. Even though individual bones in each animal have different sizes, shapes, and functions, they share a similar underlying structure. Similar anatomy in different animals is called *homology*. This raises an interesting question: why should your hand have the same structure as the wing of a bat?

Dawkins offers the evolutionary explanation: "The pattern of resemblances among the skeletons of modern animals is exactly the pattern we should expect if they are all descended from a common ancestor, some of them more recently than others. The ancestral skeleton has been gradually modified down the ages."[9] Dawkins suggests that homology provides more convincing evidence for evolution than the fossil record.

We agree that homology makes sense from an evolutionary perspective. But here's the catch: *it also makes sense from the perspective of design.* Think about it. When people design things, such as computers, they begin with a basic concept and then adapt it to multiple ends (such as a desktop, laptop, and hand-held device). Rather than beginning from scratch, designers often reuse effective design patterns. Just as an engineer adapts an effective design pattern to multiple inventions, a designer could adapt the same feature to multiple organisms.

We have two theories that both account for the data of homology: one is evolution and the other is intelligent design. Since the evidence of homology is consistent with both theories, it cannot be used as evidence solely for one.

Biogeography

When Darwin first traveled to the Galapagos Islands, he noticed that species on the different islands closely resembled each other. For example, Darwin found three different species of mockingbirds on separate islands. He noticed that these species were significantly more similar to one another than to mockingbirds found in other parts of the world. From a Darwinian perspective, the similarity in the mockingbirds of the Galapagos Islands is due to their common descent from the same mockingbird species that first migrated to the Galapagos. Dawkins favorably quotes evolutionary geneticist Jerry Coyne, who claims that the biogeographic evidence for evolution is now so powerful that he has never seen a creationist even attempt to answer it.[10]

You may be surprised to learn that we have little problem with Darwin's conclusion about the mockingbirds of the Galapagos. The evidence does seem to indicate that the mockingbirds have adapted to their unique environments. But what we do question is how significant this finding is for Darwin's *grand* claims. Mockingbirds adapting to their environments does little to establish the claim that all creatures trace their lineage back to a common ancestor through the process of natural selection acting on random mutation. Again, the evidence offered to support Darwin's theory is based upon small-scale changes (microevolution), rather than large-scale development of novel features (macroevolution).

Further, many geneticists now believe that variations in species (such as the mockingbird) occur because of a loss of genetic information from populations isolated through migration or some other natural circumstance. Thus, the biogeographic distribution of species is not the result of new biological information appearing in a particular species, which is what macroevolution requires, but the shuffling or elimination of preexisting genetic information.[11] While Darwin's theory can explain minor biological adaptations within existing organisms, it cannot explain how mockingbirds—or any other organism—first appeared. In other

63

words, evolution can explain the survival of the fittest, but not the arrival.

Poor Design

A favorite example of the New Atheists against intelligent design is the alleged poor design in nature. According to Sam Harris, "Nature offers no compelling evidence for an intelligent designer and countless examples of *un*intelligent design."[12] Both Hitchens and Dawkins claim the eye is "ill-designed" and is best understood as the result of an unguided evolutionary process.[13]

However, the New Atheists overlook a basic point: design does not have to be perfect—it just has to be functional. Imperfection relates to the *quality* of design, not its *reality*. Consider successive versions of the iPod. The various versions have minor imperfections, but each clearly was designed; none evolved blindly. Our ability to envision a better design hardly means the object in question lacks design.

What is true for an iPod is equally true in biology. Living systems bear unmistakable signs of design, even if such design is, or appears to be, imperfect. Product designers and engineers know that perfect design does not exist. They work with constraints and thus aim for the best compromise in order to accomplish a function. For instance, a larger computer screen may be preferable to a smaller one, but designers must also consider cost, weight, size, and transportability. Given competing factors, designers choose the best overall compromise—and this is precisely what we see in nature. Dawkins agrees, "Perfection in one department must be bought, in the form of a sacrifice in another department. The lesson applies to all living creatures. We can expect bodies to be well equipped to survive, but this does not mean they should be perfect with respect to any one dimension."[14] Building involves a give-and-take process.

Let's return to Dawkins's critique of the human eye. How do we know that its design could be better? Dawkins suggests the human eye was installed backward.[15] But there are good reasons for its construction, and no one has demonstrated how the eye's function might be improved without diminishing its visual speed, sensitivity, or resolution.[16] The alleged poor design in nature is still functional, and may result from the best design options.

Pseudogenes

The New Atheists consider the existence of so-called "pseudogenes" as compelling evidence for evolution. Pseudogenes are thought to be genes that once did something useful, but have since lost their original function. According to Dawkins, "It stretches even [Creationists'] creative ingenuity to make up a convincing reason why an intelligent designer should have created a pseudogene—a gene that does absolutely nothing and gives every appearance of being a superannuated version of a gene that used to do something."[17]

As with other evidences offered for evolution, pseudogenes do not demonstrate the creative ability of natural selection. At best, their existence provides evidence for microevolution. What's more, pseudogenes could have formed *after* the creation of human beings, representing an example of devolution (loss of information) rather than evolution. But as it turns out, numerous examples have been found in which pseudogenes provide an important function in the cell.[18]

WHY OUR ORIGIN MATTERS

Why is Darwin's theory such a big deal? Why not believe in both God *and* evolution? These are important questions. Our primary concern with the blending of Darwinian evolution (i.e., macroevolution) and Christianity is that we find the evidence for Darwin's theory unpersuasive. If it were true, then we would believe it. But like the eight hundred scientists who have dissented from Darwin, we're just not convinced. Of equal concern, however, is that evolution has become more than a scientific theory—it has become the prime justification for the naturalistic worldview.

Darwin intentionally designed his theory to eliminate any

need for God in the cosmos.[19] He aimed to reduce every aspect of human behavior—whether relationships, art, morality, language, or religion—to its animal origins. Dawkins sums up the Darwinian perspective:

> On his [Darwin's] world-view, everything about the human mind, all our emotions and spiritual pretensions, all arts and mathematics, philosophy and music, all feats of intellect and of spirit, are themselves productions of the same process that delivered the higher animals.[20]

In other words, *everything* in life is the result of the combined forces of natural selection and random mutation. Darwinism leaves no room—anywhere—for a higher intelligence or purpose. In fact, intelligence is the by-product of evolution, not the guiding force that produced it.

Richard Dawkins and other prominent Darwinian scientists have argued that Darwin's theory undermines theism in general and Christianity in particular and makes naturalism more plausible. According to Dawkins, "Darwin made it possible to become an intellectually fulfilled atheist."[21] In *The New Atheism*, physicist Victor Stenger remarks, "Darwinism implies that humanity developed by accident, contradicting the traditional teaching that humans are special, created in God's image."[22] Stenger is right. If Darwinism is true, then human beings are not the intentional creation of a loving, personal God. Rather, we are the accidental outcome of a purely mindless, material process.

ENDOWED BY A CREATOR

In contrast, Thomas Jefferson believed that the universe was intelligently designed. And he saw clearly the implications that followed from it. In 1823, when materialistic evolutionary theories were already circulating, he wrote a letter to John Adams, insisting that the evidence for design was clear: "I hold (without appeal to revelation) that when we take a view of the Universe, in its parts general or particular, it is impossible for the human mind not to perceive and feel a conviction of design, consummate skill, and indefinite power in every atom of its composition."[23] After considering evidence for design in the cosmos and in biological organisms, Jefferson concluded, "It is impossible, I say, for the human mind not to believe that there is, in all this, design, cause and effect, up to an ultimate cause, a fabricator of all things from matter and motion."[24] Jefferson based his convictions on the empirical evidence of nature, not on religious authority.

Stephen Meyer explains how significant this finding was for Jefferson's view of human rights:

> The "ultimate cause" and "fabricator of all things" that Jefferson invoked was also responsible for the "design" of life's endlessly diverse forms as well as the manifestly special endowments of human beings. Moreover, because the evidence of "Nature's God" was publicly accessible to all and did not depend upon a special appeal to religious authority, Jefferson believed that it provided a basis in reason for the protection of individual liberty. Thus, the Declaration of Independence asserted that humans are "endowed by their Creator with certain inalienable rights."[25]

Jefferson believed that design provided a basis in reason for the protection of individual liberty, and he framed the Declaration of Independence accordingly.

If you've only read the New Atheists, then you may think evolution is the only game in town. From their perspective, the evidence for evolution is "overwhelming," "conclusive," and "beyond serious doubt." But this is not the whole story. When examined closely, their most compelling examples turn out to be (at best) evidence for microevolution. Not only is the evidence for Darwinian evolution lacking, compelling evidence for design can be found from the tiniest cell to the origin and structure of the universe. Let's take a closer look.

FOR FURTHER ENGAGEMENT

Dembski, William A., and Sean McDowell. *Understanding Intelligent Design: Everything You Need to Know in Plain Language.* Eugene, OR: Harvest House, 2008.

Wells, Jonathan. *Icons of Evolution: Science or Myth? Why Much of What We Teach About Evolution Is Wrong.* Washington, DC: Regnery, 2000.

EVIDENCE FOR DESIGN AND THE DIFFERENCE IT MAKES

Darwinian evolution is hard to square with Christian faith. People do it, but people also do lots of crazy things, like eat crushed glass. When historian of biology Will Provine describes evolution as "the greatest engine of atheism ever invented," he is on target. That's not to say evolution requires atheism. But the converse is true: atheism requires evolution. To be an intellectually fulfilled atheist demands that one embrace an evolutionary creation story. That's why intelligent design is such a potent antidote to the New Atheism. By undermining the atheists' creation story, on which atheism depends, intelligent design undermines atheism itself.

But what's the evidence for intelligent design and why should we take it seriously? Such evidence of design abounds. The authors have touched on it here in this book. Perhaps the two best places to study such evidence in detail are Stephen C. Meyer's *Signature in the Cell* and my own *The Design of Life* (coauthored with Jonathan Wells). The case for intelligent design has grown considerably stronger in the last decade, and young people are in a much better position to resist the challenge of evolution than when I got into this business thirty years ago. Even with the state of knowledge back then, it quickly became clear to me that material forces such as natural selection had limited creative power and could not adequately account for the complexity and diversity of life.

The sense that unintelligent evolution can't work and that intelligent design is an indispensable requirement for life has served as a ballast in my Christian walk, keeping me from being swayed by materialist arguments that weaken and cheapen the faith. These days, evolution is increasingly used as an ideological weapon to undermine the sanctity of life, traditional marriage, and a host of other long-standing norms by arguing that evolution excludes their permanent validity (after all, everything is evolving, including those norms). Intelligent design, by showing that we are designed to operate within certain constraints (constraints established for our benefit!), has enabled me calmly to embrace the abiding truths of Christianity without worrying whether the newest intellectual fad is going to sweep them away.

Of course, in the end the question is not whether intelligent design allows us to live a more serene Christian life but whether it is true. Precisely because our best scientific evidence confirms its truth, intelligent design supports Christianity in a way that evolution never has or could. Intelligent design, while not the gospel, has in my life proven itself to be a good friend of the gospel.

—William A. Dembski

William A. Dembski is research professor in philosophy at Southwestern Baptist Theological Seminary. He has authored or edited twenty books, including *Intelligent Design Uncensored: An Easy-to-Understand Guide to the Controversy*. To read more of his work, visit www.designinference.com.

CHAPTER 5

How Did the Universe Begin?

As many critics of religion have pointed out, the notion of a creator poses an immediate problem of an infinite regress. If God created the universe, what created God?

—Sam Harris

In September 2009, *Scientific American* devoted a special issue to understanding origins. Writers explored the origin of rubber boots, antibiotics, clocks, LSD, the paper clip, recorded music, the HIV virus, cupcakes, and more. Whether it's a gadget, such as a digital audio player, or the origin of life itself, we are naturally intrigued by the question of where things come from.

While all the topics in the issue were fascinating, one topic seemed to be more pressing and pertinent than all the others—the origin of the universe. The article concludes that the universe began with a big bang 13.7 billion years ago and has been cooling and expanding ever since.[1] Even though other models exist, the standard big bang model is the most widely accepted and reasonable explanation for the origin of the universe. And it raises a crucial question: what led to the big bang? Furthermore, does the big bang undermine or support the biblical doctrine of creation?

In a well-known joke, a group of scientists approach God and claim they can do everything he can. "Like what?" asks God. "Like creating human beings," say the scientists. "Show me," says the Almighty. The scientists say, "Well, we start with some dust, and then—" God interrupts, "Wait a second. Get your own dust." Just as a carpenter relies upon preexisting wood to build a desk, so these scientists were relying on preexisting dust to create a human being.

Where did the dust come from? From stars? And where did the stars come from? From the big bang? And where did the matter in the big bang come from? From a quantum vacuum fluctuation? A quantum vacuum does not contain absolutely nothing. A subatomic vacuum contains energy and is subject to physical laws. So where did the energy come from? At some point such questions must end at an ultimate reality—the source of being of the universe.

For centuries and even millennia, atheists claimed that the universe is uncaused and eternal. On the other hand, theists claimed that God is the uncaused creator of the universe. Scientifically speaking, there was no way to determine who was right. While there were philosophical and theological considerations, the scientific evidence was indecisive. But this began to change in the early part of the twentieth century when Albert Einstein developed the mathematical equations for his general theory of relativity. Like most scientists of his day, he simply assumed the universe was static and eternal. Yet his equations pointed strongly toward a universe that was either expanding or contracting.

The conclusions of his theory deeply irritated the agnostic Einstein. Why? Einstein realized a *beginning* of the universe pointed strongly toward a *Beginner*—a powerful mind that brought the universe into existence. His scientific findings had powerful theistic implications. Yet rather than following the evidence wherever it led, Einstein inserted a fudge factor into his equations called the "cosmological constant" so he could maintain an eternal universe. Einstein later accepted that the universe has a finite past. Why did he change his mind? In 1929 legendary cosmologist Edwin Hubble confirmed the expansion of the universe. He peered through the hundred-inch telescope at the Mount Wilson Observatory in California and viewed galaxies never seen before. Hubble showed that light from distant galaxies shifts toward the red end of the light spectrum. This redshift means that the universe is expanding in all directions.* This provided powerful confirmation of Einstein's findings that the universe is not static but is expanding in every direction.[2]

The implications of these findings are stunning. If we could push rewind on the expansion of the universe, we would see everything contract back to the first moment of existence when space, time, and matter began. In other words, if we go far enough back in time, we reach an initial creation event. This first moment of existence is called the *singularity*, which is an edge or boundary to space-time itself. According to Arizona State University professor Paul Davies, "For this reason most cosmologists think of the initial singularity as the beginning of the universe. On this view the big bang represents the creation event; the creation not only of all the matter and energy in the universe, but also of spacetime itself."[3]

For nearly fifty years, Antony Flew was the world's leading academic atheist. In 2003 Flew made a shocking announcement: he had become a theist, primarily because of scientific advancements regarding the origin and nature of the universe. In his book *There Is a God: How the World's Most Notorious Atheist Changed His Mind*, Flew accounts for how the big bang influenced his conversion:

> When I first met the big-bang theory as an atheist, it seemed to me the theory made a big difference because it suggested that the universe had a beginning and that the first sentence in Genesis ("In the beginning, God created the heavens and the earth") was related to an event in the universe. As long as the universe could be comfortably thought to be not only without end but also without beginning, it remained easy to see its existence (and its most fundamental

---

* For a visual grasp on the expanding universe, suppose that you could attach buttons to a balloon; as the balloon expands, the buttons would move apart from one another in all directions.

features) as brute facts. And if there had been no reason to think the universe had a beginning, there would be no need to postulate something else that produced the whole thing. But the big-bang theory changed all that. If the universe had a beginning, it becomes entirely sensible, almost inevitable, to ask what produced this beginning.[4]

KALAM COSMOLOGICAL ARGUMENT

The twentieth-century developments in cosmology brought renewed focus to a classic argument for the existence of God—the kalam cosmological argument. The name *kalam* may sound sophisticated, but the argument is surprisingly simple.* Since it's easy to learn and memorize, we have shared this argument many times in conversations with nonbelievers. Philosopher William Lane Craig, the most vocal defender of the argument today, states it this way:

1. Whatever begins to exist has a cause.
2. The universe began to exist.
3. Therefore, the universe has a cause.[5]

Given the rules of logic, if the first two premises are true, then the conclusion necessarily follows.

In teaching my (Sean's) students the first premise of this argument, I challenge them to give an example of something coming into existence from nothing. My query is typically followed by silence while the absurdity of such a request sinks in. How could *some*-thing come from *no*-thing? As the ancient Greeks regularly observed, "Out of nothing, nothing comes." Even David Hume, the great Scottish skeptic, said the idea of something arising without a cause is absurd.[6]

---

* "Kalam" is the Arabic word for speech. Christian thinkers developed the kalam cosmological argument to rebut Aristotle's doctrine of the eternity of the universe. Medieval Islamic theologians developed it into an argument for the existence of God. William Lane Craig, *Reasonable Faith: Christian Truth and Apologetics*, 3rd ed. (Wheaton, IL: Crossway, 2008), 96.

We may not always know the cause of a particular event (such as the breaking of a window or the explosion of a super-nova), but it seems reasonable to believe that things that begin to exist have a cause. We have already seen that the big bang theory assumes the universe had a beginning. Einstein's general theory of relativity and the redshift both support this. Let's consider some additional scientific evidence as well.

According to the second law of thermodynamics, processes taking place in a closed system always move toward a state of equilibrium. In other words, unless outside energy is added to a closed system, the usable energy within the system will even-tually run down. For instance, imagine a hot cup of coffee in a room completely sealed off from the outside (no energy or matter can intrude). Eventually the coffee will cool and match the tem-perature of its environment. If the coffee were not yet at a state of equilibrium with the room, if the coffee's temperature were still above that of the room, then you would know definitively that it had not been there forever.

In the atheistic view, the universe is a closed system, since there is nothing beyond it (like our cup of coffee in the sealed room). Given sufficient time, the universe will eventually run out of energy and reach a state of equilibrium known as "heat death." At this stage, all the universe's useful energy will be gone. If the universe had been in existence for an infinite duration, then it would have already run out of energy. Yet, since there is disequi-librium in the temperature of the universe, it must have a finite past. Therefore, the universe had a beginning.

There is also good philosophical evidence for the beginning of the universe. For instance, imagine you went for a walk in the park and stumbled across someone proclaiming aloud, ". . . five, four, three, two, one—there, I finally finished! I just counted down from infinity!" What would be your initial thought? Would you wonder how long the person had been counting? Probably not. More likely, you would be in utter disbelief. Why? Because you know that such a task cannot be done. Just as it's impos-sible to count up to infinity from the present moment, it's equally impossible to count down from negative infinity to the present moment.

Counting to infinity is impossible because there is always (at least) one more number to count. In fact, every time you count a number, you still have infinite more to go, and thus get no closer to your goal. Similarly, counting down from infinity to the present moment is equally impossible. Such a task can't even get started! Any point you pick in the past to begin, no matter how remote, would always require (at least) one more number to count before you could start there. Any beginning point would require an infinite number of previous points.

Here's the bottom line: we could never get to the present moment if we had to cross an actual infinite number of moments in the past. Yet, since the present moment is real, it must have been preceded by a finite past that includes a beginning or first event.[7] Therefore, the universe had a beginning.

ALTERNATE EXPLANATIONS?

The evidence for the big bang is so compelling that Alexander Vilenkin, a leading cosmologist of our day, concludes, "It is said that an argument is what convinces reasonable men and a proof is what it takes to convince even an unreasonable man. With the proof now in place, cosmologists can no longer hide behind the possibility of a past-eternal universe. There is no escape, they have to face the problem of a cosmic beginning."[8] However, given the powerful theistic implications of the big bang model, the New Atheists have been eager to find an alternative explanation.

New Atheist Daniel Dennett agrees that the universe must have had a cause for it to come into existence, but his solution is that the universe brought itself into existence. According to Dennett, in the ultimate "bootstrapping trick," the universe caused itself to exist.[9] While this is an imaginative proposal, it raises the question of why the universe is the only thing that came into existence from nothing.[10] Why don't basketballs and ice cubes have that potential? For something to cause itself to come into being, it must first already exist. But if it first already exists, then it must have a cause outside itself. The idea that something could cause itself is absurd.

This is why the laws of nature cannot plausibly explain the origin of the universe. Natural laws can only act on things that already exist, so they can't be the first cause for the universe itself. The laws came into existence with the big bang, so they can't be the explanation *for* the big bang.

In the 1960s and 1970s some cosmologists postulated an oscillating model of the universe in opposition to the big bang model. According to the oscillating model, the universe has gone through an infinite series of expansions and collapses (i.e., cycles), and thus had no beginning. Like an accordion, the universe is thought to continually spread out and then contract again for all eternity, avoiding any need for an absolute beginning. The oscillating universe theory is plagued with multiple problems. For one thing, no known laws of physics could regulate such a process. Furthermore, rather than slowing down, the expansion of the universe is actually speeding up and shows no signs of slowing. Even Dawkins admits that recent evidence undermines the oscillating universe.[11]

Stephen Hawking popularized a theory that seemingly avoids a beginning to the universe.[12] In Hawking's model, the past can avoid an absolute beginning because time "rounded off" at the final moments before the big bang. To make his scenario work, Hawking introduced "imaginary numbers" into Einstein's equations. The problem is that imaginary numbers don't translate to the real world. In fact, when Hawking converts to using real numbers, the beginning of the universe reappears.

Some atheists, like Bertrand Russell, content themselves with thinking of the universe as eternal, needing no cause or explanation. They believe that the universe simply exists. But if the universe can theoretically be eternal and uncaused, then why can't God? Both theists and atheists agree that there is nothing unreasonable about something being eternal and uncaused. However, what is unreasonable is to suppose that a universe arose, uncaused, from nothing.

WHO MADE GOD?

If everything that begins to exist has a cause, then what about God? According to Richard Dawkins, "The whole argument turns on the familiar question, 'Who made God?'"[13] While rhetorically powerful, this objection misses the point of the argument. The claim is not that everything has a cause. Rather, everything that *begins* to exist has a cause. The universe clearly began to exist, and so it needs a cause. On the other hand, God is the uncaused, self-existent, eternal cause of the universe.

It's impossible to avoid positing an uncaused cause of the universe. Think about it. If God was caused by something else, then that thing would also need a cause, and we would have an infinite regress without a beginning. Yet if there was no beginning, then nothing could exist. The regression only stops with something that is self-existing. This thing cannot be physical because physical matter itself began to exist. A supernatural being is the best explanation of the first cause.

A cosmic beginning is a problem from the atheistic perspective, but it is right at home in the Judeo-Christian worldview. After all, the first line in the Bible, written thousands of years before the advent of modern cosmology, says, "In the *beginning* God created the heavens and the earth."[14]

KALAM AND THE JUDEO-CHRISTIAN GOD

In a book review, Sam Harris critiques the kalam argument: "In any case, even if we accepted that our universe simply had to be created by an intelligent being, this would not suggest that this being is the God of the Bible."[15] We agree with Harris. The kalam argument cannot demonstrate that the Bible is reliable, that Jesus is God, or that Christianity is true. What the kalam reveals is that the universe was made and that someone made it. Further, the kalam helps narrow the range of possible causes to a being that is nonphysical, spaceless, timeless, changeless, and powerful:

- If matter began to exist at the moment of creation, then the matter's cause must be *nonphysical*, or *spiritual*.

- Since space itself came into existence at the big bang, space's cause must be *spaceless*.
- Since time began at the moment of the big bang, time's cause must be *timeless*.
- Since change is a product of time, time's cause must also be *changeless*.
- Given the immensity of energy and matter that comprises the universe, energy and matter's cause must be unimaginably *powerful*.

The best explanation for the origin of the universe is that it was brought into existence through the free will of a personal Creator. Since the universe is the result of a creative act, it is best explained as the result of a mind. Thus, mind is the cause of matter, not the other way around. Philosopher William Lane Craig explains the implications of the kalam argument:

> On the basis of a conceptual analysis of the conclusion implied by the *kalam* cosmological argument, we may therefore infer that a personal Creator of the universe exists, who is uncaused, beginningless, changeless, immaterial, timeless, spaceless, and unimaginably powerful. This, as Thomas Aquinas was wont to remark, is what everybody means by "God."[16]

Paul Draper is an agnostic philosopher who has thought deeply about the kalam argument. While he admits that this argument doesn't get all the way to the Christian God, he recognizes that accepting its conclusions does require the rejection of naturalism.[17] The kalam argument leads to accepting a *supernatural* cause of the universe, and naturalism rejects anything outside the natural world.

In *God and the Astronomers*, agnostic astronomer Robert Jastrow considers whether the big bang points toward a cosmic designer. He closed his book with these famous words, which also seem fitting for the conclusion of this chapter: "For the scientist who has lived by his faith in the power of reason, the story ends like a bad dream. He has scaled the mountains of ignorance; he is about to conquer the highest peak; as he pulls himself over the final rock, he is greeted by a band of theologians who have been sitting there for centuries."[18]

FOR FURTHER ENGAGEMENT

Copan, Paul, and William Lane Craig. *Creation Out of Nothing: A Biblical, Philosophical, and Scientific Exploration.* Grand Rapids: Baker, 2004.

Craig, William Lane. *Reasonable Faith: Christian Truth and Apologetics.* 3rd ed. Wheaton, IL: Crossway, 2008.

[why it matters]

GOD, THE UNIVERSE, AND ME

Who or what created God is about the silliest question a professional scholar could ask, and yet I'm asked this all the time. This question is a diversion from the fundamental question: "How do *you* explain the beginning of the universe?" The only plausible answer is that the universe was caused by something that didn't have a beginning, precisely because it must be timeless and immaterial to create space and time. In short, nothing created God. But if it hadn't been for God, nothing that is created would have been created.

The cosmological argument—which has survived scrutiny for hundreds of years—has never been more compelling than it is now. There is impressive scientific evidence that the universe had a beginning. However, science can take us to the beginning, but not beyond it. Science has no authority to claim that the universe has always existed, or that it came into existence without any help. I can't count on science to answer the profound question of the universe's origin, but I do have a reasonable answer.

Almost everyone has the powerful sense that the physical universe must have been caused. Many people say this is why they believe in something they call a "Higher Power." When people tell me they believe in a Higher Power, I often ask why. Usually, they answer with roughly the same reasons spelled out in the cosmological argument, which are reasons to believe in God! People just can't bring themselves to call this being God.

The explanation, I suspect, is personal. Calling God a "Higher Power" is a way to protect ourselves from accountability to a personal Creator. We can be "spiritual" without being "religious." We can complain about "organized religion" and still acknowledge a vague and mysterious spiritual reality. But the evidence embedded in the cosmological argument tells us that the Creator is more than just some "Higher Power."

Realizing that I owe my existence to God, the Creator of the universe, I must take seriously the possibility that God is part of my world, and hence part of my life—regardless of what I may think or prefer. And since there are such clear signs of God's existence, I should be especially alert to additional evidence that brings my understanding of God into greater focus.

Our universe is not an accident. A personal God created intentionally and purposefully. The point of my life depends on whether this is true. Believing it to be true, I also believe it matters what else God has in mind for me.

—R. Douglas Geivett

R. Douglas Geivett is professor of philosophy in the Talbot Department of Philosophy at Biola University. He is the author of many books, including *Faith, Film, and Philosophy*, as well as many essays for journals and books. Visit him at www.douggeivett.com.

CHAPTER 6

How Did Life Begin?

The origin of life only had to happen once. We therefore can allow it to have been an extremely improbable event, many orders of magnitude more improbable than most people realize.... Once that initial stroke of luck has been granted... natural selection takes over.

—Richard Dawkins

One of our favorite movies is the 1994 comedy *Dumb and Dumber.*[1] The story revolves around two good-hearted but incredibly inept friends in a cross-country extravaganza. At the end of the movie, Lloyd (Jim Carrey) finally asks Mary (Lauren Holly), the object of his affection, if there is any chance they could end up together:

LLOYD: What do you think the chances are of a guy like you and a girl like me... ending up together?

MARY: Well, Lloyd, that's difficult to say. I mean, we don't really—

LLOYD: Hit me with it! Just give it to me straight! I came a long way just to see you, Mary. The least you can do is level with me. What are my chances?

MARY: Not good.

LLOYD: You mean, not good like one out of a hundred?

MARY: I'd say more like one out of a million.

LLOYD: [*Pause*] So you're telling me there's a chance... *Yeah!*

Lloyd obviously missed the point. When Mary said his chances were one in a million, she really meant, practically speaking, he had *no* chance at all.

Chance can explain certain events in the universe. It can explain an occasional lucky roll in Vegas. But can chance explain a hand of four aces at every deal in a poker game? Clearly not. What about deeply improbable events in the universe such as the origin of life? Richard Dawkins seems to think it can. Dawkins believes that chance (he calls it "luck") is a sufficient explanation for how life began.

THE MYSTERY OF THE ORIGIN OF LIFE

The scientific community is virtually unanimous that the problem of life's origin is unsolved. Sam Harris, more in line with the mainstream view, admits that the origin of life is a complete mystery.[2] The problem of how life began has become so difficult that Harvard University recently announced a $100 million research program to address it.[3] As Harvard biologist Andy Knoll said, "We don't know how life started on this planet. We don't know exactly when it started, we don't know under what circumstances."[4] And as origin-of-life researcher Stuart Kauffman concludes, "Anyone who tells you that he or she knows how life started on the earth some 3.45 billion years ago is a fool or a knave. Nobody knows."[5]

Skeptics often like to claim that as science progresses the gaps of scientific knowledge diminish. But this is incorrect. The more we learn about the universe, the wider the "gaps" often become. This is particularly true in the study of the origin of life. The more we have learned about the nature of life, the greater the problem of its origin has become.

For instance, Charles Darwin and many of his colleagues thought the cell was made of a simple gel-like substance called protoplasm. Thus, he suggested that life could have arisen through chemical reactions in a "warm little pond."[6] If cells were simple, as Darwin surmised, then such a scenario might be believable. The problem is that Darwin radically underestimated the complexity of the cell. As scientific knowledge has progressed, it is now clear that the cell's technology goes far beyond what Darwin ever imagined. As we will see, the complexity of even the simplest cell not only poses an unbelievably difficult hurdle for atheism, but it points strongly toward the existence of an immaterial Mind.

TECHNOLOGY AND INFORMATION IN THE CELL

It's incredibly difficult to grasp the astonishing complexity of the cell. A typical cell has roughly 100 million proteins of 20,000 different types, and yet the entire cell is so small that a few hundred cells could fit on the dot of this letter i.[7]

According to geneticist Michael Denton, even the smallest bacterial cell, which weighs less than a trillionth of a gram, is "a veritable microminiaturized factory containing thousands of exquisitely designed pieces of intricate molecular machinery, made up altogether of 100 thousand million atoms, far more complicated than any machine built by man and absolutely without parallel in the non-living world."[8] Nearly every feature of our own advanced technology can be found in the cell.

Biologists today describe the cell using language reminiscent of engineering and computer science. They regularly use terms such as genetic "code," "information-processing system," and "signal transduction." Richard Dawkins writes, "Apart from differences in jargon, the pages of a molecular-biology journal might be interchanged with those of a computer-engineering journal."[9]

With the discovery of the structure of DNA in 1953, scientists learned that information is basic to life. The information for organizing proteins is stored in four nucleotide bases: guanine (G), adenine (A), thymine (T), and cytosine (C). These four bases function as letters of an alphabet, creating meaningful letter arrangements, which is why biologists regularly refer to DNA and RNA as carriers of "information." The amount of information in the human body is outright staggering.

The human body has an average of 100 trillion cells. In a single cell, the DNA contains the informational equivalent of roughly eight thousand books. If the DNA from one cell were uncoiled, it would extend to about three meters in length. Thus, if the DNA in an adult human were strung together, it would stretch from Earth to the sun and back roughly seventy times![10]

But DNA does not just store information. In combination with other cellular systems, it also processes information. Hence Bill Gates likens DNA to a computer program, though far more advanced than any software humans have invented.[11] This is why Arizona State University physicist Paul Davies says, "Life is more than just complex chemical reactions. The cell is also an information storing, processing and replicating system. We need to explain the origin of this information, and the way in which the information processing machinery came to exist."[12]

This quick depiction of cellular life should help clarify the daunting challenge of explaining how life began. *How could a mindless material process spawn a system of such dizzying intricacy and sophistication?*

COULD LIFE HAVE BEGUN BY CHANCE?

Richard Dawkins admits that the existence of life is deeply improbable, but he credits chance (luck) as a sufficient explanation. While it may seem intuitively possible for life to emerge by chance, especially given the size of the universe, the task is much more difficult than it may seem. Consider some of the many probabilistic hurdles that must be overcome for a single functional protein to arise by chance alone.[13]

First, all individual amino acids, the building blocks of a protein, must be connected to each other through the right kind of bond. Proteins can only fold properly (and hence function) with peptide bonds. And yet, when mixtures of amino acids are allowed to freely interact in a test tube, peptide and nonpeptide bonds form with equal probability. How does nature select solely peptide bonds?

Second, amino acids exist in nature in two distinct forms: left-handed (L-form) and right-handed (D-form). Every amino acid found in nature has a mirror image of itself, called an optical isomer. While both forms of amino acids are produced with equal frequency in nature, functional proteins can only tolerate left-handed amino acids. How does nature know to isolate the left-handed amino acids from the right-handed amino acids to form a functional protein?

Third, since amino acids function like letters in a meaningful sentence, sometimes changing one amino acid destroys the function of the entire protein. Amino acids must be in precise locations for a functional protein. What mechanism in nature arranges amino acids into the proper sequence?

Given these constraints, what is the probability that nature could generate a single functional protein by chance alone? According to Stephen Meyer, the odds of getting a functional protein of 150 amino acids by chance is no better than 1 in 10^{164}.[14] Now consider that there are 10^{80} elementary particles in the entire universe. Thus, the probability of finding a functional protein through chance alone is a trillion, trillion, trillion, trillion, trillion, trillion, trillion times smaller than the odds of finding a specific particle in a random search throughout the entire universe![15]

But there's more! A minimally functional cell requires multiple proteins. In 1983, astrophysicist Fred Hoyle (who famously coined the term "big bang") estimated the odds of producing all the proteins necessary for a functional cell by chance to be 1 in $10^{40,000}$, which is why he compared the odds of life originating by chance to a tornado slashing through a junkyard and forming a Boeing 747. Practically speaking, the probability of such a thing happening is zero. For these reasons (and many more), most origin-of-life researchers have abandoned chance theories as an explanation for how life began.

WHAT ABOUT SELF-ORGANIZATION?

Since chance is out of the question, many scientists believe nonliving matter has the inherent capacity to organize itself into life, just as a draining bathtub naturally forms a vortex, or magnetic filings align themselves systematically around a magnet. With the release of the popular textbook *Biochemical*

Predestination, Dean Kenyon became a leading proponent of self-organizational models for the origin of life.[16] Rather than attributing the order in nature to chance, Kenyon believed that forces of attraction exist between life's basic building blocks. Kenyon put it this way: "Life might have been biochemically predestined by the properties of attraction that exist between its chemical parts—particularly between amino acids in proteins."[17]

Yet six years after the publication of *Biochemical Predestination*, Kenyon began to doubt his own theory. One of his students (ironically named Solomon Darwin) pressed Kenyon to explain how his model of self-organization could account for the origin of information in the cell. After much deliberation, Kenyon became convinced that the information content in DNA could not have arisen through natural lawlike processes alone.[18]

While self-organizational models may be able to explain the origin of *order* in living systems, they cannot explain the origin of specified *information*. Drain a bathtub, for instance, and you will see a vortex emerge naturally. But here's the catch: while a vortex may have order, its information content is simple and repetitive. This is a far cry from the specified information in computer code, written language, and DNA.

Moreover, there is no known law of nature that could cause amino acids to link up in the right sequence to produce a functional protein. This is why Kenyon abandoned his theory and became a proponent of intelligent design. His reasoning was clear-cut: *lawlike processes are not capable of generating specified information in the way that intelligent minds are.* Kenyon put it this way, "We have not the slightest chance of a chemical evolutionary origin for even the simplest of cells... so the concept of intelligent design of life was immensely attractive to me and made a great deal of sense, as it very closely matched the multiple discoveries of molecular biology."[19]

RNA-FIRST MODEL

The relationship between protein and DNA has been a persistent paradox for origin-of-life researchers. Here's why: the genetic information in DNA is required for the construction of proteins, but the information of DNA can only be processed with the help of proteins. In other words, DNA requires proteins, yet proteins require DNA. How could two mutually dependent systems emerge separately? This chicken-and-egg problem has confounded scientists for decades.

On the other hand, the puzzle would be solved if the first living organism did not require proteins. This is why the RNA-first model has become a popular theory for how life began. RNA and DNA are both nucleic acids, but they do have structural and functional variations. Some advocates of this theory have proposed that a primitive form of RNA acted as a precursor to both DNA and protein, since it can perform certain features of both. Many scientists consider the RNA-first model the most promising framework for solving the problem of the origin of life. Dawkins suggests RNA may have been the vital ingredient in the emergence of complex life.[20]

Despite its prominence, however, the RNA model has significant problems. Recall that the key feature of life is information. Any valid theory for how life began must be able to explain information's origin. Yet this is precisely what the RNA-first model *cannot* explain. The RNA-first model either presupposes or ignores the origin of information. Here's the bottom line: scientists have no idea how the information in primitive forms of RNA could have formed spontaneously on the early Earth. According to Stephen Meyer, "explaining how the building blocks of RNA might have arranged themselves into information-rich sequences has proven no easier than explaining how the parts of DNA might have done so, given the requisite length and specificity of these molecules."[21]

The odds of a functional, self-replicating RNA sequence arising spontaneously are vanishingly small. And even if one did emerge, it likely would have quickly disintegrated because of destructive forces in the environment. In addition, there are no plausible scenarios for how RNA could have evolved into modern cells. These are a few of the reasons why Scripps biochemist

Gerald Joyce concludes, "You have to build straw man upon straw man to get to the point where RNA is a viable first biomolecule."[22]

SIMULATING THE ORIGIN OF LIFE

A popular means of demonstrating how life began is through the use of computer simulations. Richard Dawkins made the first such attempt in *The Blind Watchmaker*. He aimed to show how natural selection and random mutation could generate biological information. He set up a program with the target sequence being a single line from Shakespeare's *Hamlet*: "Methinks it is like a weasel." Dawkins instructed his computer to randomly change one letter or space at a time and then to preserve the sequences that most closely matched the goal. In a mere forty-three generations, Dawkins's program generated the line from *Hamlet*. According to Dawkins, the same process could work in nature.

The problem, of course, is that Dawkins selected his target in advance. Rather than the computer program generating biological information through a random and unguided search, Dawkins intelligently guided the program to reach a predetermined end. Yet this is the very thing natural processes alone cannot accomplish.

Two recent computer programs, known as Ev and Avida, also attempt to simulate how life began. Such programs take for granted the origin of the information necessary to generate the first self-replicating life form. Evolutionary algorithms only work if they are guided with informational input from a computer scientist. In Avida, for example, virtual "organisms" are preprogrammed with the capacity to self-replicate. What (or Who) programmed nature with the same capacity?

IGNORANCE OR DESIGN?

A common objection to intelligent design is the claim that it is based on an argument from ignorance. In other words, according to critics, intelligent design reasoning looks something like this: "Naturalistic scenarios for the origin of life currently fail, so God must have done it!" But the case for design is not simply inferred from the present ignorance of naturalistic scenarios.

Intelligent design is also positively based on our uniform experience that information always arises from an intelligent mind, not an unguided material process. Computer scientists write computer programs. Authors write books. Young people text their friends. Lovers send messages to their beloved. For every instance in which we are able to trace information back to its source, we find an intelligent mind.

Origin of life research is at a complete standstill. Scientists have no clue how life could have arisen through natural processes alone.[23] And yet there is a promising alternative. Former atheist Antony Flew put it best, "The only satisfactory explanation for the origin of such 'end-directed, self-replicating' life as we see on earth is an infinitely intelligent Mind."[24]

WHAT DNA SHOWS ABOUT THE DESIGNER

Like the evidence for the beginning of the universe, the discovery of the information content in DNA cannot tell us that the Bible is true, that Jesus rose from the dead, or that Christianity is the only means of salvation. But this hardly means intelligent design evidence is trivial. In fact, two important conclusions follow.

First, the DNA evidence poses a serious challenge to the materialistic worldview that has long dominated much of Western culture and civilization. According to the New Atheism, "In the beginning were the particles. Through the combined forces of chance and law, the particles became complex. Eventually the particles formed solar systems, planets, and rocks. Then the particles became alive and formed trees, animals, and people."

The discovery that DNA is a coded instruction manual for living organisms strikes at the heart of this worldview. The organic world is not simply matter; it consists of information that encodes every living thing. Nancy Pearcey summed up the significance of this discovery best:

> It's beginning to look like the key to interpreting the organic world is not natural selection, but information. In science we are hearing echoes of John 1:1, "In the beginning was the Word." ... Modern genetics seems to be telling us that life is a grand narrative told by the divine Word—that there is an Author for the text of life.[25]

The DNA evidence also tells us that some kind of intelligence must have been involved in the origin of life. This raises the question of what we can learn about the designer from creation. While examining the nature of life cannot take us all the way to the Christian God, it can tell us that the intelligence behind life must be personal. After all, only persons can create information of the kind we see in books, computer programs, and DNA. Life is not a cosmic mistake. It's the result of the forethought of an intelligent being. The implications this has for the purpose and meaning of life are staggering.

FOR FURTHER ENGAGEMENT

Meyer, Stephen C. *Signature in the Cell: DNA and the Evidence for Intelligent Design*. New York: HarperOne, 2009.

Rana, Fazale, and Hugh Ross. *Origins of Life: Biblical and Evolutionary Models Face Off*. Colorado Springs, CO: NavPress, 2004.

[why it matters]

MY MOST IMPORTANT DISCOVERY

When asked as a child, "What would you like to be when you grow up?" I usually answered, "I don't know." Yet I knew what I wanted to be—an explorer. Embarrassment kept me from sharing my desire, because I was convinced there were no new territories left to discover and explore.

Upon entering college and taking courses in chemistry and biology, I came to recognize my error. There were untold scientific "lands" to investigate! For me, the most exciting was the molecular world inside the cell.

My fascination with life's chemical systems prompted me to study and eventually pursue a career as a biochemist. I joined a coterie of scientific explorers who—with the aid of sophisticated scientific instruments and an assortment of techniques—opened up vistas on the inner workings of the cell.

From my perspective, the most fascinating discovery made by these scientific pioneers had little to do with the cell's structures or activities. Rather, the captivation lay in the sheer beauty and artistry of the biochemical realm. The elegance and sophistication of life's chemical systems immediately struck me as a young graduate student and prompted questions about how these magnificent systems came to be.

How did the chemical systems that carry out life's most fundamental processes come into existence? How did biochemistry begin? Though not part of my formal course work, I began to study the origin-of-life question whenever I had the chance.

The scenario origin-of-life researchers offered to explain life's initial chemical evolution—the transformation of a complex chemical mixture into living entities strictly through the outworking of chemical and physical events—seemed inadequate to produce the cell's vastly

93

complex, highly sophisticated, tightly orchestrated chemical systems. Based on my experience as a chemist, I knew that chemical systems could self-organize, but the organization displayed by biochemical systems differs qualitatively from the order possessed by crystals and other types of molecular aggregates that form spontaneously. The best chemists typically experience difficulty getting a few chemicals in a flask to do what they want, even when they expend enormous amounts of mental effort and rely on the past work of other chemists. How could random physical and chemical events yield the amazingly elegant and highly integrated biochemical systems found inside the cell?

The elegance, sophistication, and complexity of the cell's chemical systems, along with the inadequacies of evolutionary explanations for the origin of life, convinced me as a biochemistry graduate student that a Creator must exist. Prior to this epiphany, I had fully embraced the evolutionary paradigm and spent little (if any) time considering God.

Once I recognized that a Creator must exist, I began to ask questions like, "Who or what is that Creator?" and "How do I relate to that Creator, if at all?" After a six-month search, I became convinced that the answers to these questions reside in the Christian faith.

—Fazale R. Rana

Fazale R. Rana is vice president of research and apologetics with Reasons to Believe (www.reasons.org). He is the author of *The Cell's Design* and coauthor of *Origins of Life*.

CHAPTER 7

Why Is the Universe Just Right for Life?

A universe with a creative superintendent would be a very different kind of universe from one without.

—Richard Dawkins

Did you know that the laws that govern the universe are delicately balanced to support the emergence and sustenance of intelligent life? Tweak these laws in almost any way, and our universe would be uninhabitable. Like Little Bear's bowl of porridge that Goldilocks enjoyed, the universe is "just right" for life.

Scientists have been struck by how precisely the laws of physics seem to be calibrated for life. "There are many such examples of the universe's life-friendly properties," says Tim Folger in *Discover* magazine, "so many, in fact, that physicists can't dismiss them all as mere accidents."[1] British astronomer Fred Hoyle remarked, "A commonsense interpretation of the facts suggests that a super intellect has monkeyed with physics, as well as chemistry and biology, and that there are no blind forces worth speaking about in nature."[2]

The fine-tuning of the universe raises some troubling questions for the New Atheists: *Why is the universe habitable? Why are the laws so exquisitely calibrated for life?*

A FINE-TUNED UNIVERSE

Fine-tuning is a compelling feature of the universe. Theists see the remarkable fine-tuning of the universe as pointing toward the existence of an Intelligent Designer. Let's look at a couple examples of this exquisite fine-tuning and consider whether or not an Intelligent Designer is the best explanation.

First, the expansion rate of the universe after the big bang had to be just right to support life. "If the balance between gravity and the expansion rate were altered by one part in one million, billion, billion, billion, billion, billion, billion," claim scientists Mark Whorton and Hill Roberts, "there would be no galaxies, stars, planets, or life."[3] How precise is this? If the initial mass of the universe differed by as little as one grain of salt, there would be no universe. Add one grain of salt and the universe would not have expanded; take one grain away and the universe would have expanded too quickly to form galaxies, solar systems, and habitable planets.

Second, each of the four fundamental forces of nature had to be carefully fine-tuned for life: gravity, electromagnetism, the strong nuclear force, and the weak nuclear force. In particular, the ratio of the electromagnetic force to the gravitational force must be delicately balanced to one part in 10^{40} (that's one part in 10,000,000,000,000,000,000,000,000,000,000,000,000,000). If the ratio varied even slightly, then our universe would not have small and large stars, which are both necessary for a planet to sustain life. How delicate a balance is this? Imagine covering one billion continents the size of North America with coins. Stack the coins in columns that reach to the moon. Paint one coin red and place it in one of the columns. Blindfold a friend and have her attempt to pick it out. The odds are roughly 1 in 10^{40} that she will.[4]

Third, recent scientific discoveries confirm that Earth has extremely rare conditions that allow it to support life, even though the vast majority of the universe is uninhabitable. Let's briefly consider a few:

- *Life must be in the right type of galaxy.* Of the three types of galaxies, only spiral galaxies (like the Milky Way) can support life.
- *Life must be in the right location in the galaxy.* We are situated in just the right place in the Milky Way to avoid harmful radiation.
- *Life must have the right type of star.* While most stars are too large, too luminous, or too unstable to support life, our sun is just the right size and age. There is a window of time in which a sun can support complex life. It can't be too young or old.
- *Life must have the right relationship to its host star.* If Earth were slightly closer to or farther from the sun, water would either freeze or evaporate, rendering Earth uninhabitable for complex life.
- *Life needs surrounding planets for protection.* A habitable planet must have large surrounding bodies (such as Jupiter and Uranus) to protect it from incoming comets.
- *Life requires the right type of moon.* If Earth did not have a moon of the right size and distance, it would be uninhabitable. The moon stabilizes the earth's tilt, preventing extreme temperatures and thus creating a stable, life-friendly environment.[5]

What happens when we try to assign a probability to the fine-tuning of *all* the known constants of nature? Oxford physicist Roger Penrose concluded that such a task would be impossible, since the necessary digits would be greater than the number of elementary particles in the universe.[6] This level of precision completely dwarfs human technology and innovation.

The evidence for design is so compelling that Paul Davies, an internationally acclaimed physicist at Arizona State University, has concluded that the biofriendly nature of our universe looks like a "fix." In other words, the universe is so uniquely calibrated to support life that it seems to go beyond the reach of coincidence. He writes, "The cliché that 'life is balanced on a knife-edge' is a staggering understatement in this case: no knife in the universe could have an edge *that* fine."[7] According to Davies, any legitimate scientific explanation must account for this overwhelming appearance of design.[8]

OBJECTIONS TO AN INTELLIGENT DESIGNER

Some argue that since we could not exist in a universe that was not conducive to our existence (i.e., fine-tuned), we should not be surprised that the universe is fine-tuned. This objection is known as the weak anthropic principle.

Imagine you go to a professional football game and find out the two people seated next to you have last names alphabetically close to yours. You probe further and find out the entire stadium is seated in alphabetical order. What would you think? Suppose the person sitting next to you says, "Everybody's gotta be seated somewhere. So you shouldn't be surprised that we all happen to be seated in alphabetical order." Would you accept such a claim? Obviously not! The reason is that you do not need to know *why* each person needs to be seated somewhere. You need to know why each person is seated *particularly in alphabetical order.* The fact that people need to be seated somewhere does nothing to explain how we came to be seated in alphabetical order. Yes, we need a seat somewhere in the stadium, and there are many possibilities. But being seated in alphabetical order conforms to a deeper pattern that demands justification. Claiming that we have to sit somewhere doesn't explain our particularly surprising arrangement. The same is true for the universe. Given all the possible variations of the constants, why do we happen to find ourselves in a universe capable of supporting life? Merely claiming that we could not observe ourselves in any other universe offers no explanation for why we are actually in a fine-tuned universe in the first place.

Philosopher John Leslie expands on this need for explanation in his famous "firing squad" analogy. Suppose fifty trained sharpshooters are lined up to take your life, and they all miss. You could hardly dismiss this occurrence by saying, "If they hadn't all missed me, then I shouldn't be contemplating the matter so I mustn't be surprised that they missed."[9] You should still be surprised that you are alive given the enormous unlikelihood of all the sharpshooters missing their mark. Your survival demands an explanation. And so does the fine-tuning of the laws of the universe.

Richard Dawkins admits that there is presently no naturalistic explanation for the fine-tuning of the universe.[10] But, from his perspective, this hardly counts in favor of God. According to Dawkins, accepting the design hypothesis raises a further question: Who designed the Designer? Thus, the fine-tuning argument fails because it doesn't explain the origin of the Designer.

However, is this how science works? Can scientists only accept explanations that have further explanations? The problem with this objection is that it is always possible to ask for a further explanation. There comes a point, however, when scientists must deny the request for further explanation and accept the progress they have made. If the universe looks designed, why not accept design as the most plausible explanation, even if we can't explain the Designer?

Imagine an archaeologist who discovers an ancient object that looks like an arrowhead or digging tool. She would be fully justified in concluding that it was the product of design, rather than the result of erosion and other natural forces, even if she could not explain the origin or identity of the designer. If the evidence for design was compelling, she would be irrational for *not* accepting the design hypothesis.

Dawkins also suggests that the fine-tuning argument fails because the Designer must be more complex than the universe. Thus, positing God as the explanation for fine-tuning offers no explanatory advantage or advance. However, this assumption is not necessarily true, as we can see in the case of human beings. In *The New Atheism*, Victor Stenger claims that modern computers, created by humans, can do many things faster and more efficiently than the human brain.[11] If so, this is an example of something "simpler" creating something more complex.

Still, Dawkins's objection has even less force against God, for

God does not have a physical body and brain with interworking parts. God is not physically complex like a computer, car, or building. As a nonphysical Mind, God is a rather simple being. A mind might have complex *ideas*, but a mind itself is rather simple. Philosopher William Lane Craig explains why a mind is considered simple: "As a non-physical entity, a mind is not composed of parts, and its salient properties, like self-consciousness, rationality, and volition, are essential to it. In contrast to the contingent and variegated universe with all its inexplicable quantities and constants, a divine mind is startlingly simple."[12]

ARE THERE MANY UNIVERSES?

Given that the fine-tuning evidence seems to imply a cosmic Fine-Tuner, it's not surprising that atheists are eager to come up with an alternative explanation. The most popular alternative to the fine-tuning evidence is the multiverse hypothesis, in which many universes exist and each have their own set of laws and constants. "Short of invoking a benevolent creator," says Tim Folger, "many physicists see only one possible explanation: our universe may be but one of perhaps infinitely many universes in an inconceivably vast multiverse."[13]

Dawkins believes the multiverse theory holds the greatest promise for answering the fine-tuning argument.[14] Yet fellow atheist Bradley Monton points out a flaw in the multiverse theory: "Dawkins is not *certain* that these other universes exist. If appealing to the existence of other universes is the only way Dawkins has of replying to the fine-tuning argument, then under the supposition that the other universes don't exist, the fine-tuning argument is successful."[15]

Does this mean that multiple universes, if they were ever discovered, would undermine God? Absolutely not! We would still be left with the question as to what generated our fine-tuned universe, and any system that generates a habitable universe must itself be fine-tuned. The multiverse hypothesis simply moves the fine-tuning problem up one level, asking why multiple universes are able to sustain life. Robin Collins explains:

To give an analogy, even a mundane item such as a bread machine, which only produces loaves of bread instead of universes, must have the right structure, programs, and ingredients (flour, water, yeast, and gluten) to produce decent loaves of bread. Thus, it seems, invoking some sort of multiverse generator as an explanation of the fine-tuning reinstates the fine-tuning up one level, to the laws governing the multiverse generator.[16]

The multiverse theory is interesting, but is no more than an untested and speculative mathematical exercise. We have no *purely scientific* reason to postulate the existence of multiple universes.[17]

WILL ANY LIFE DO?

Critics of the fine-tuning argument often claim that if the laws of physics were different, then some other non-carbon-based life form could have existed. Besides being entirely speculative, many instances of fine-tuning do not rely upon the assumption that life must be carbon-based. In other words, exquisite fine-tuning would be required for life forms of *any* kind, whether carbon based or not. Philosopher William Lane Craig explains:

> In order for the universe to permit life … whatever form organisms might take, the constants and quantities have to be incomprehensibly fine-tuned. In the absence of fine-tuning, not even atomic matter or chemistry would exist, not to speak of planets where life might evolve![18]

In our universe, however, carbon *is* an essential ingredient for complex life. Science fiction movies often feature non-carbon-based organisms that mirror life on Earth. But this is pure fiction. No other element in the periodic table has the information-storage capacity of carbon or its ability to remain stable through chemical and heat pressures. Carbon is the only element capable of supporting complex life.[19]

In addition to carbon, life also requires a solvent to allow for chemical reactions. As the most abundant chemical compound in the universe, water is uniquely suited for this task. Water has some unusual physical characteristics that make it the perfect solvent for life:

- Water is unique in that it is denser as a liquid than as a solid. This causes frozen water (ice) to float, insulating the water underneath from further heat loss and allowing underwater life to survive in harsh conditions.
- Water has unusually high melting and boiling points. Thus, water helps moderate Earth's climates and allows larger organisms to regulate their body temperatures.
- Water has unusually high surface tension, which enables it to provide better capillary action in trees. This process allows trees to draw water up from its roots, seemingly against the force of gravity.

Water and carbon seem to be perfectly matched for life. Guillermo Gonzalez and Jay Richards explain, "Water appears to be an ideal match for carbon-based chemistry. For starters, organic reactions are optimal over the same range of temperatures that water is liquid at Earth's surface. At low temperatures, reactions become too slow, while at high temperatures, organic compounds become unstable."[20]

If it wasn't for carbon and water, no complex life could exist in the universe. Evolution cannot account for these properties, for evolution is dependent upon their preexistence. Long before Darwinian evolution could have occurred, the chemical elements for life were already in place. *Why were they there? And how did they get there?* Even if Darwinian evolution were true, it could not explain why we have a fine-tuned universe as well as the chemical properties in nature that can support life.

WAS LIFE FINE-TUNED TO THE UNIVERSE?

In *The New Atheism,* physicist Victor Stenger suggests that life is fine-tuned to the universe rather than the universe being fine-tuned for life.[21] It turns out just the opposite is true. The very existence of water, carbon, and other life-permitting compounds depends upon the fine-tuning of the fundamental constants of nature. If these constants were even slightly different, then stars could not have formed. And if stars could not have formed, the elements that are necessary for life could not have formed either. Without stars, it is impossible to see how any elements necessary for life could have arisen. Alister McGrath explains:

> There is an implicit assumption that life would adapt to whatever hand of physical and chemical cards were dealt to it. Yet this is untested and intrinsically questionable.... The capacity of evolution to fine-tune itself is thus ultimately dependent on fundamental chemical properties which in themselves can thus be argued to represent a case of robust and fruitful fine-tuning.[22]

The New Atheists seem to find it unproblematic and un-interesting that our universe has the right chemical materials and fine-tuned physical properties that allow for their theory of Darwinian evolution. In their discussions of evolution, they treat chemistry and physics as irrelevant background information. Yet they fail to see that their theory of biological evolution depends upon the *pre*existence of certain elements that have life-permitting qualities, such as the metal ions manganese, nickel, copper, iron, and zinc.[23] Life itself depends on these elements, which in turn depend upon the fine-tuned constants of nature. In short, no fine-tuning, no elements for life. Once again, McGrath explains:

> This point [that the existence of biologically essential elements requires cosmic fine-tuning] is not negated by suggesting that evolution can fine-tune itself. Chemical reality constrains evolution; these processes can only occur because the chemistry of certain metals, predetermined by quantum mechanical parameters, permits them to do so....

Evolution can only fine-tune itself because of the predetermined properties of chemical elements.[24]

A PRIVILEGED PLANET

Before the sixteenth century, scientists believed that Earth was stationed at the center of the universe. This seemed appropriate, since man is made in the image of God and Earth is our home. In 1543, however, Copernicus argued that Earth revolves around the sun. In doing so, Copernicus didn't just propose a new theory about Earth's orbit. Rather, he sparked an intellectual revolution regarding Earth's significance in the cosmos. Scientists began to think of Earth as an average planet orbiting an average star in an average galaxy. As astronomer Carl Sagan put it, Earth is now viewed as a "pale blue dot" lost in space.[25]

The idea that Earth is ordinary runs deep in our culture. In *The Hitchhiker's Guide to the Galaxy*, novelist Douglas Adams describes the universe's most excruciating torture device imaginable, the Total Perspective Vortex. What makes the device so horrible is that victims are forced to comprehend the vastness of the universe, and, therefore, grasp how meaningless their lives really are. Victims see a microscopic dot with the message "You Are Here" amid the enormity of the universe. The message is clear: human life is an insignificant speck in a massive universe.[26]

New discoveries, however, reinforce the earth's significance. An article in *Discover* magazine captures the current state of the evidence:

> Life, it seems, is not an incidental component of the universe, burped up out of a random chemical brew on a lonely planet to endure for a few fleeting ticks of the cosmic clock. In some strange sense, it appears that we are not adapted to the universe; the universe is adapted to us.[27]

In other words, Earth is not an insignificant speck in a vast, dark, and purposeless universe.

The fine-tuning of the universe, widely considered the greatest problem in physics (at least for those unwilling to consider a nonnaturalistic explanation), points to a Designer.* Whenever we have a fine-tuned system that performs a function, we know that intelligence is involved. Intelligent beings fine-tune musical instruments, computers, planes, and all sorts of things. Since the universe is unmistakably fine-tuned for life, the best explanation is an Intelligent Mind.

FOR FURTHER ENGAGEMENT

Gonzalez, Guillermo, and Jay W. Richards. *The Privileged Planet: How Our Place in the Cosmos Is Designed for Discovery.* Washington, DC: Regnery, 2004.

McGrath, Alister E. *A Fine-Tuned Universe: The Quest for God in Science and Theology.* Louisville, KY: Westminster John Knox Press, 2009.

---

* This is not a god-of-the-gaps argument, in which God is posited for the lack of a naturalistic explanation. Rather, we appeal to God because of our *positive* experience that intelligent agents have the capacity for fine-tuning. The enigma of fine-tuning seems best understood as the work of a Fine-Tuner. Mathematician David Berlinski said it best: "One answer is obvious: It is the one that theologians have always offered: *The universe looks like a put-up job because it is a put-up job.*" *The Devil's Delusion: Atheism and Its Scientific Pretensions* (New York: Basic Books, 2009), 112 (emphasis in original).

THE HEAVENS DECLARE THE GLORY OF GOD

I've always found the fine-tuning arguments in cosmology and physics quite compelling and also inspiring. But on several occasions, fellow Christians have said, "Yeah, but they don't go far enough." My reply is always the same: "Far enough for what?"

The worry is that if an argument drawn from science suggests that there's a Creator but doesn't get people all the way to Jesus, then it's dangerous. After all, somebody might believe in God but end up with all sorts of false ideas about him. As a result, some Christians think that an argument should never end merely with a Creator, but should always point to the Christian God.

I'm all for people getting all the way to Christianity. In fact, I'd love to be able to show that if you accept the law of noncontradiction, then you have to believe all the truths of the Nicene Creed. But alas, that's just not how God has chosen to reveal himself. God's eternal power and divine nature are clearly seen, Paul says, "in the things that have been made" (Rom. 1:20 ESV). That's God's general revelation of himself. We can also learn what God has done through history by special revelation.

Psalm 19 suggests that God reveals himself in this twofold way. The psalm begins by telling of the heavens declaring the glory of "God," of "El" in Hebrew. Israelites and other peoples in the ancient Near East used the word *El* to refer to a Creator. The psalm tells us that the heavens—which are visible to everyone—pour forth speech and display knowledge day and night throughout the world. When the psalm begins to speak of the law, which God gave specially and personally to the Israelites, it speaks of God not as "El," but as the LORD, that is, "Yahweh." "Yahweh" is God's personal name. The psalmist knows God's name only because God has revealed it specially.

The Creator who is revealed clearly through the natural world, but in a limited way, also reveals himself particularly in history, in Scripture, and especially in Jesus Christ.

So, if evidence from physics and cosmology points in the direction of a Creator, then it's going as far as it's supposed to go. We should rejoice if it gets people from blind materialism to theism, even if they still have a way to go in learning that the Creator also loves them and has died for them.

—Jay W. Richards

Jay W. Richards is senior fellow of the Discovery Institute (www.discovery .org). He is the author of multiple books, including *The Privileged Planet* and *Money, Greed, and God: Why Capitalism Is the Solution and Not the Problem.*

CHAPTER 8

Has Science Shown There Is No Soul?

All the evidence points to a purely material universe, including the bodies and brains of humans, without the need to introduce soul, spirit, or anything immaterial.

—Victor Stenger

Recently one of my (Sean's) former students relayed to me a conversation she had on the first day of English class in college. The teacher began the class by reading an article by a science fiction writer who believes computers and technology will produce super-humans that will eventually take over the world by 2030. The teacher was hoping these super-humans would be environmentalists so that they would want to preserve our lesser-evolved selves. My former student raised her hand and asked, "How can a purely material thing spawn consciousness?" The teacher simply laughed and said, "Oh, I suppose you believe in the soul, too?" And the whole class laughed at her.

From the perspective of this teacher, as well as the New Atheists, the evidence for the existence of the soul is so miniscule as to be laughable. After all, hasn't science shown that there is no soul? Many scientists today are naturalists who believe that the physical world is the only reality. Absolutely everything, including thoughts, beliefs, mind, and will, can be explained in terms of the interaction of matter. According to Daniel Dennett, "We now understand that the mind is not... *in communication with the brain in some miraculous way; it is the brain, or, more specifically, a system or organization within the brain....*"[1] Just as God is a delusion created by humankind (according to Richard Dawkins), the mind is an illusion created by the brain.

ADMITTING THE OBVIOUS

The thought that the mind is an illusion of the brain runs contrary to the way we naturally think about ourselves. Take a moment to reflect. Do you consider yourself identical to your body? Or do you think of yourself as one who *has* a body? When asked to give an account of ourselves, most of us assume we are a center of consciousness (an I, self, or soul) that has a body. This is true of everyone, regardless of his or her worldview.

I (Sean) heard a lecture by an outspoken atheist who described himself as a materialist. In his view, the mind does not exist over and above the brain and the soul is not distinct from the body. A human being is entirely physical. Yet, in describing an act he deemed immoral, he said, "I would not do such an act because that would hurt my *brain*, and it would hurt *me*." His language betrayed him. He claimed not to believe in the reality of the soul, yet without even realizing it, he articulated a deeply entrenched belief that the body and the soul are distinct.

Virtually all cultures throughout history have believed in life after death where some type of soul survives the death of the body. Jesus told of a vast immaterial world, filled with God, angels, demons, and souls, which is just as real as the physical world. He said, "Do not fear those who kill the body but are unable to kill the soul; but rather fear Him who is able to destroy both soul and body in hell."[2]

According to the Christian worldview, the material world is not all that exists. God made human beings in his image, and human beings consist of both body and soul. God placed a desire for eternity in our hearts so that even though our bodies decay, we can live in eternal relationship with him.[3]

Dawkins admits that humans have a universal predisposition

toward belief in the soul. He writes, "The idea that there is a me perched somewhere behind my eyes and capable, at least in fiction, of migrating into somebody else's head, is deeply ingrained in me and in every other human being, whatever our intellectual pretensions to monism."[4] In *Letter to a Christian Nation*, Sam Harris says that atheism is "simply an admission of the obvious."[5] If the universal human intuition is to believe in the soul, as Dawkins admits, then shouldn't we follow the "obvious" unless we have some convincing reason to the contrary? When it comes to human nature, materialism is *not* the obvious position. In fact, as Dawkins rightly observes, it's quite counterintuitive. We should require considerable evidence when asked to deny our deep-seated intuitions about the world.

CAN THE SOUL SURVIVE DEATH?

On June 22, 2009, *USA Today* featured a story titled "The God Choice" that was surprisingly favorable to the reality of the soul.[6] The story told of a young woman, Pam Reynolds, who was found to have an aneurism on her brain stem. She was beyond the help of conventional medical procedures and had only one option, an experimental procedure called "cardiac standstill." The surgeons put her under general anesthesia, taped her eyes shut, and placed speakers on her ears that emitted clicks about as loud as a plane taking off. As soon as her brain stopped responding to the clicks, the doctors lowered her body temperature to sixty degrees and drained the blood from her head. With the blood drained, they quickly removed the aneurism, which had collapsed from lack of blood, and sewed her back up.

When the surgery was over, Pam had a surprising story to tell: *she had left her body and witnessed the whole thing from above.* This might seem like a fantastic claim, but she was able to back it up with surprising detail, especially for someone whose heart stopped beating, whose brain waves were completely flat, and who was clinically dead. She was able to describe intimate details of the operating room as well as the number of surgeons. She described the Midas Rex bone saw that cut open her skull, as well as the drill bits and blade container. Pam also overheard specific details of conversation in the room. All the details were confirmed from the official hospital records. Pam's neurosurgeon, Robert Spetzler, said he had absolutely no scientific explanation for how it could have happened.[7]

If this were the only documented case of a near-death experience (NDE), then it might be written off as an aberration. But such cases are unexpectedly common. In *Beyond Death*, Gary Habermas and J. P. Moreland document many NDEs that have been investigated and confirmed. For instance, they report the case of a girl, Katie, whose body was in a comatose state at the hospital after nearly drowning in a pool. Yet upon recovery, she reported following her family home during the time her body was in a comatose state in the hospital. She was able to remember specific, minute details, such as the meal her mom prepared the evening of the accident, how her father reacted to hearing about the accident, the clothing her family members were wearing, and which toys her brother and sister were playing with at the time.[8]

Another fascinating case involves an eight-year-old girl who almost drowned when her hair got caught in a pool drain. It took forty-five minutes of CPR to resuscitate her. She claimed that she floated out of her body and went to heaven. After her recovery, she was able to recount, with remarkable precision, details of the paramedics' arrival and the hospital emergency room.[9]

What is the best explanation for NDEs? From a naturalist perspective, such cases should not simply be rare—they should be *impossible*. We cannot be separated from our bodies because we *are* our bodies. And when our bodies die, we die. But if we don't begin with this naturalistic presumption, then NDEs are very plausible. NDEs strongly imply that consciousness continues after death, and that the body is distinct from the soul.

NDEs cannot be explained away as the result of drug use or a hallucination, because many cases of NDEs have been reported when no drugs were administered to the patients. As for hallucinations, oxygen-deprived, hallucinating brains leave patients confused. But people who experience NDEs tell coherent narratives that include detailed observations of the incident, all while their brains register no activity.

According to neuroscientist Mario Beauregard and journalist Denyse O'Leary, naturalistic explanations such as hallucinations and drug use "do not explain what most needs explaining, that patients report information later verified and recount life-changing experiences from periods when they were known to be clinically dead."[10] NDEs provide compelling evidence for the distinction between body and soul as well as for a continued consciousness in the initial moments of the afterlife.[11]

ARE YOUR CHOICES REALLY FREE?

In 1996, American culture critic Tom Wolfe wrote a succinct essay titled "Sorry, But Your Soul Just Died." He discussed a new imaging technique that enabled neuroscientists to study the brain of a patient during a thought or emotion. He said, "Since consciousness and thought are entirely physical products of your brain and nervous system—and since your brain arrived fully imprinted at birth—what makes you think you have free will? Where is it going to come from?"[12] We agree with the conclusion of Wolfe's argument. If there is no soul, then free will does not exist.

If materialism is true, then a human being is simply a body. If *you* are solely a material system, then you have no inner *self* that has the capacity to freely choose between options. You have no center of consciousness to make reasoned decisions. Physical systems operate completely by external programming, not by inner decision making. Thus, if materialism is true, you do not have any genuine ability to choose your actions.

But this deeply contradicts how we experience the world. We operate as if our minds freely make decisions that are carried out by the circuitry of our brains. For instance, if a stranger stops to open the door for us, we might describe his thought process by saying, "The nice man made up his *mind* to stay a moment longer and hold the door open for us." We would not say, "The circuitry in his brain caused him to turn around and hold the door open."

We assume he *freely* chose to open the door, which is why we would likely express our thanks.

So compelling is the experience of making free choices that people cannot act as though that experience is counterfeit. Philosopher John Searle reminds us that if a waiter presents us with a choice of either pork or veal, we cannot rightly say, "Look, I'm a determinist. I'll just have to wait and see what order happens!"[13]

Denying free will comes at a high price, for it raises troubling questions: How is love meaningful if not *freely* chosen? How can we hold people morally accountable for their actions if they could not have done otherwise? What's the point of punishment? Our experience of free will is one of the best reasons to believe in the reality of the soul.[14]

ARE YOU THE SAME PERSON AS BEFORE?

Imagine taking a wooden desk apart piece by piece and replacing each piece with a plastic part. Now suppose your neighbor took the discarded parts from the wooden desk and rebuilt the desk. Which one would be the original desk—the wooden one or the plastic one? Of course the wooden desk would be the original one. Here's why: if something is made solely of physical parts, then it simply *is* all the parts that make it up. If my current desk is the same as my desk from last year, it must be made out of the same stuff as a year ago. If not, then the desks are not identical.

This raises some interesting questions: Are you the same person you were yesterday? How about a year ago? How about seven years ago? The physical atoms of the body are almost entirely replaced every seven years. Apart from a few neurons in the brain, the physical components of your body—hair follicles, cells, and other microscopic parts—are constantly in flux. Thus, if you were solely your body, then your identity would be constantly changing. *You* would literally not be the same person from moment to moment.

But practically and legally speaking, we know this is not true. I (Sean) get excited about future events, like going on a

113

cruise, even though the strictly material *I* will be an entirely different *I* at that future point. Our criminal justice system is based upon sameness of identity over time. The person who serves the sentence is the same person who committed the crime. Can you imagine a defendant saying to a judge, "I'm innocent. The person who committed the crime disappeared a long time ago!" No reasonable judge would accept such a defense.

One of my (Sean's) former students e-mailed me about a discussion she had in her college philosophy class. Her professor claimed that the few neurons that remain unchanged in the brain sufficiently account for identity over time. Here's the problem I helped her to see: if we transformed a Corvette part by part into a Camaro but maintained the same spark plugs, would we consider it the same car? Of course not. The same is true for a person. Something nonphysical must account for sameness of identity over time, even with a few unchanging neurons in the brain. The soul is the most reasonable explanation.

NEUROSCIENTISTS TO THE RESCUE

Imagine you turn on the news tonight and hear that the top Al Qaeda operative has been captured in Afghanistan. The anchor reports, "Rather than use torture, new techniques will be applied to gather information from the prisoner. Neuroscientists will probe his brain for valuable information to help prevent future attacks." Would you believe such a story? Not likely, because we know people have private access to their own mental life. The terrorist is in a privileged position to know his own thoughts in a way not available to anyone else. No amount of probing his brain can reveal that information unless he tells us—whether freely or coerced.

While mental thoughts are uniquely available to the person who has them, such is not the case for physical property. Physical objects, including the brain, are "public" objects that are available to anyone who views them. A neuroscientist can know more about your brain than you do, but he can't know the content of your mental life unless you tell him.

Some materialists claim that we may reach a point when neuroscientists can know more about a person's mental life than he or she does. After all, by examining the brain, scientists can determine when a person is experiencing anxiety, sadness, anger, and other emotional states. But while certain brain states regularly correlate with certain emotions, there is no way to determine the *content* of the emotion without asking the subject. Questions such as, "Who or what is she angry at?" "Why is he anxious?" and "What brought on the sadness she is experiencing?" could not be answered without asking the subject.

In order to establish a correlation between a thought and a brain state, scientists have to ask the patient what he or she is thinking. This information cannot be accessed without the person revealing it. Brain states are publicly available, but thoughts are not.

MENTAL AND PHYSICAL STATES

Having private access to our own mental life is only one way that mental states are different from physical states. William Lane Craig and J. P. Moreland list a few other aspects of mental states that are not true of physical states:[15]

- Mental states have a raw qualitative "feel" (taste, sound, smell, texture).
- Mental states are *of* or *about* things in the world (e.g., a thought about dinner).
- Mental states are immediately available to the subject (i.e., a person is directly aware of what he or she is thinking).
- Mental states cannot be described in physical terms (i.e., it makes no sense to ask how much a thought weighs, or how long your beliefs could be stretched out).

Here's why this matters. Philosophers talk about the nature of identity, which means that everything is itself and not something else. For instance, Sean McDowell is identical to the husband of Stephanie. If this is the case, then *everything* true of Sean must be true of the husband of Stephanie. For example, they must drive the same car, live at the same residence, like the same ice cream, and wear the same clothes. If even *one* single thing is true of Sean that is not true of Stephanie's husband, then the two are not identical. This may seem obvious, but it has powerful implications for the reality of the soul.

Remember, materialists (such as Daniel Dennett) are committed to the idea that "the mind ... is the brain."[16] If this were true, then everything true of the brain must be true of the mind, and vice versa. But as we just saw, many things about the brain are not true of the mind. For instance, the brain is made of matter that has height, width, and weight. On the contrary, it makes no sense to ask how much a thought weighs or how long it is. Thus, the mind is distinct from the brain, and, by extension, the soul is distinct from the body.

AN INSUPERABLE DILEMMA

The question of how mind could come from matter is a seemingly insuperable dilemma confronting atheists. As my student asked, "How can a purely material thing spawn consciousness?" Dawkins admits that the origin of consciousness may be another gap as improbable as the origin of life.[17] We agree. It's difficult to see how a mind could arise from nonmind through the purposeless, material, mindless process of evolution. It's much easier to see how a Conscious Mind could produce the human consciousness.[18] We conclude with the words of neuroscientist Mario Beauregard and journalist Denyse O'Leary:

> Despite claims trumpeted in the popular media, the new discoveries have *not* explained away basic concepts such as consciousness, the mind, the self, and free will. Hypotheses that reduce the mind to the functions of the brain or deny that the mind exists have remained just that—hypotheses.[19]

FOR FURTHER ENGAGEMENT

Beauregard, Mario, and Denyse O'Leary. *The Spiritual Brain: A Neuroscientist's Case for the Existence of the Soul.* New York: HarperOne, 2007.

Moreland, J. P. *The Recalcitrant Imago Dei: Human Persons and the Failure of Naturalism.* London: SCM Press, 2009.

[why it matters]

SOUL MATTERS: BUILDING UP OUR HUMANITY

Two men enter a room: one suffers from Parkinson's disease and the other makes his living as a triathlete. Who is more valuable? Two women enter a room: one is a bank teller and the other a supermodel. Who is more valuable? If a person was merely a body, we could measure one's value by what a person can do for us. But deep down, we know this system of value is flawed.

In our nonprofit work with Soulation, we remind people that they are not identical to their bodies. Nineteenth-century preacher and novelist George MacDonald wrote in *Annals of a Quiet Neighborhood* that we *are* souls and *have* bodies. The more we disregard the soul, the more we tend to value people for shallow and transitory qualities. We need to beware of any movement or ideology that disinherits us of our souls, for the soul forms the bedrock for the belief that humans are equally valuable.

If people are more than bodies, our perception of them changes. If we pause to see each other beyond our physical qualities (though we remain equally valuable even if our bodies are not perfect), we may discover the man with Parkinson's exercises kindness better than the triathlete. We may find the heart of the bank teller bigger than the supermodel because she's manicured her soul.

Our souls are fertile ground for us to cultivate. As Dallas Willard says in *Renovation of the Heart*, "What you would take care of you must first understand, whether it be a petunia or a nation"—or a soul. We ask ourselves, if the soul exists how are we nurturing it? Do we care enough to examine our beliefs about God, ourselves, our world? Do we cultivate our desires to want goodness and scorn evil? How are we learning to strengthen our wills to choose what is wise and beautiful? Do we judge our neighbors by the package of their bodies or are we taking time to look at them for who they are as souls? Do we treat those who are physically weak or disabled with the same or less attention than we treat the celebrated, powerful, and beautiful? These questions cultivate our souls.

Jesus said it well, "And what do you benefit if you gain the whole world but lose your own soul? Is anything worth more than your soul?" (Matt. 16:26 NLT).

As we roll out of bed every morning, we are reminded that there is more in this world than meets the eye, starting with our unseen core—our souls. In these short years on earth, we get to mold our souls around the truth, beauty, and goodness of God, reflecting him, because forming our souls is the most essential part of what it means to be human.

—Dale Fincher and Jonalyn Fincher

Dale Fincher and Jonalyn Fincher are the founders of Soulation (www .soulation.org), a nonprofit organization dedicated to helping others be appropriately human. Their most recent book is *Coffee Shop Conversations: Making the Most of Spiritual Small Talk.*

CHAPTER 9

Is God Just a Human Invention?

Freud made the obvious point that religion suffered from one incurable deficiency: it was too clearly derived from our own desire to escape from or survive death. The critique of wish-thinking is strong and unanswerable.

—Christopher Hitchens

A lot of people believe in God—*like billions*. Religion is all over the place and growing.[1] So why are humans so religious? Well, there is no shortage of explanations for belief in God. Our intention in this chapter is to walk through some of the most common reasons skeptics think God is a human invention and see if they sufficiently show that belief in God has been rendered unreasonable, or if the reason that so many people believe in God is *best explained* by the fact that he actually does exist. First, however, we need to address a common misunderstanding about approaching the question of God.

Many times it is assumed that the one who believes in God—the theist—bears a special burden of proof when it comes to arguing for God's existence. In other words, in the absence of evidence for God's existence, one should presume that God doesn't exist; this is the famous "presumption of atheism." However, both "God does not exist" and "God exists" are claims to knowledge that are either true or false. Both viewpoints require justification or evidence. The New Atheists don't get a free pass; they must make the case for their worldview too. Yet all of the theories we will discuss in this chapter explicitly or implicitly draw on the presumption of atheism.

If there is a default position, then it is "I don't know if there is a God" (agnosticism), not "there is no God" (atheism).* So why don't we just retreat to the default position of not knowing? Knowledge, as the only firm foundation on which to build a life, is always preferable and should be pursued—*especially* on questions as important as this. Agnosticism can be a virtue for a season of exploration, because we definitely want to avoid being gullible. But as Yann Martel wrote in *Life of Pi*, "Doubt is useful for a while.... But we must move on. To choose doubt as a philosophy of life is akin to choosing immobility as a means of transportation."[2] Moreover, with tongue in cheek, it has been observed that being an *agnostic* (Greek word) sounds much more sophisticated than being an *ignoramus* (Latin word), yet both mean not to know. Saying that one is an "ignoramus with respect to the question of God" just doesn't carry the same punch.

THE PROJECTION THEORY

In *The Future of an Illusion*, Sigmund Freud wrote that religious beliefs are "illusions, fulfillments of the oldest, strongest, and most urgent wishes of mankind.... As we already know, the terrifying impression of helplessness in childhood aroused the need for protection—for protection through love—which was provided by the father; and the recognition that this helplessness lasts throughout life made it necessary to cling to the existence of a father, but this time a more powerful one. Thus the benevolent rule of a divine Providence allays our fear of the dangers of life."[3] In short, we project the existence of God based on a human need

---

* For a more detailed treatment of this issue, see Scott A. Shalkowski, "Atheological Apologetics," in *Contemporary Perspectives on Religious Epistemology*, ed. R. Douglas Geivett and Brendan Sweetman (Oxford: Oxford University Press, 1992). It should be noted that we are intentionally dealing with the "presumption of atheism" as it typically is used, not in the precise sense that Antony Flew originally conceived of it. In the 2009 debate between Christopher Hitchens and William Lane Craig, Craig pressed Hitchens on this point but Hitchens was either unwilling or unable to set forth a positive case for atheism.

for him. Is this hypothesis unanswerable as Hitchens claims in this chapter's epigraph? We think not for the following reasons.

First, it begs the question *against* God. Freud's argument is, essentially, since we know that God doesn't exist, what are psychological explanations of this belief? His argument assumes from the outset that no object of belief exists. This is the presumption of atheism that we discussed above. The New Atheists commonly approach the God question in the same way: "Since God doesn't exist—and we know this, along with every other sane person in the world—why do so many people still believe?"

We have evidence for God's existence (e.g., arguments from origins, design, morality, etc.) and know that God is far from dead in the academy (see chapter 1). In fact, many world-class philosophers and scientists are Christians and are publishing at the highest levels. Yet, as one looks through the bibliographies of the New Atheists, it quickly becomes obvious that they are not interacting with the most sophisticated defenders of Christianity.[4]

Second, another assumption made by those who employ Freud's projection theory is that having beliefs that bring us comfort means that those beliefs are false. But this does not follow logically. Philosophers of religion Paul Copan and Paul Moser observe that "a belief that brings comfort and solace should not be considered necessarily false. We find comfort in human relationships, and this is perfectly normal, reasonable, and healthy, at least in routine cases. It would be implausible to presume that our finding comfort in something is automatically cognitively defective or otherwise wrong."[5]

Third, part of the rhetorical force of Freud's projection theory cited by Hitchens is the *perceived* connection between God being an illusion and Freud's rigorous psychoanalysis. Actually, this connection is what's illusory. Emeritus professor of psychology at New York University and former atheist Paul Vitz writes, "Nowhere did Freud publish a psychoanalysis of the belief in God based on clinical evidence provided by a believing patient," and further that "Freud's general projection theory is an interpretation of religion that stands on its own, unsupported by psychoanalytic theory of clinical evidence."* In other words, there is no psychological basis for his conclusions because he never performed psychoanalysis on people who actually believed in God.

Fourth, the projection theory cuts both ways. If it can be argued that humans created God out of a need for security or a father figure, then it can just as easily be argued that atheism is a response to the human desire for the freedom to do whatever one wants without moral constraints or obligations. Perhaps atheists don't want a God to exist because they would then be morally accountable to a deity. Or maybe atheists had particularly tragic relationships with their own fathers growing up, projected that on God, and then spent most of their adult lives trying to kill a "Divine Father Figure."[6] Consider the heartbreaking childhood of Bertrand Russell (1872–1970), perhaps the leading English atheist of the twentieth century. His mother died when he was two and his father when he was four. An extremely stern Presbyterian woman raised Russell. A loner with no real childhood friends, he would grow attached to nannies and then become inconsolable when they left. We don't mention this to make light of it—it's sad and tragic. We mention it because it's possible that not all of Russell's reasons for rejecting Christianity and God were purely rational or intellectual. Belief is a complex thing.

Finally, perhaps the idea that humans invented God to meet their desires is precisely backward. Perhaps the reason humans have a desire for the divine is because something or someone exists that will satisfy them. C. S. Lewis powerfully articulates this point: "Creatures are not born with desires unless satisfaction for those desires exists. A baby feels hunger: well, there is such a thing as food. A duckling wants to swim: well, there is such a

---

* Paul C. Vitz, *Faith of the Fatherless: The Psychology of Atheism* (Dallas: Spence, 1999), 9. McGrath further states that "while it is a historical truism that Freud was a confirmed atheist long before he became a psychoanalyst, it is important to note that he became a psychoanalyst precisely because he was an atheist. His indefatigable harrying of religion reflects his fundamental belief that religion is dangerous." Alister McGrath, *The Twilight of Atheism: The Rise and Fall of Disbelief in the Modern World* (New York: Doubleday, 2004), 70.

thing as water. Men feel sexual desire: well, there is such a thing as sex. If I find in myself a desire, which no experience in this world can satisfy, the most probable explanation is that I was made for another world. Probably earthly pleasures were never meant to satisfy it, but only arouse it, to suggest the real thing."[7]

THE "GOD GENE" AND NEUROSCIENCE

We are living in the biotech century and genetic information has taken center stage. Humanity will benefit from mapping the human genome (completed in 2003), and we should applaud that progress.[8] But the focus on genetics has some unfortunate by-products. One example is *The God Gene: How Faith Is Hardwired into Our Genes* by Dean Hamer. In this book Hamer explores the impact of genetics on belief in God. The specific gene in question, that everyone has some version of, is $VMAT_2$. Hamer claims that this gene accounts for the spirituality that emerges in some people but not others.

To be fair, Hamer admitted his title was overstated in a later interview and that there "probably is no single gene."[9] But if he knew this going in, then why not change the title of the book? Admissions such as these after the fact never make it on the cover of magazines to correct public misconceptions. The implication to be drawn from his title is that the God question can be reduced to a genetic roll of the dice. Some believe and some don't and it is not a matter of evidence or truth.

None of Hamer's work was subjected to peer review by other geneticists or published in any scientific journals. And the study, upon which the book was based, was never repeated. While *The God Gene* became a *New York Times* best-seller and made the cover of *Time* magazine, the book's main conclusion has been shown to be completely overstated and unreliable. The Human Genome Project director, Francis Collins, states plainly, "There is no gene for spirituality." In an interview, Collins suggested a more appropriate title for Hamer's book, *The Identification of a Gene Variant Which, While Not Yet Subjected to a Replication Study, May Contribute About One Percent or Less of a Parameter*

Called Self-Transcendence on a Personality Test. But then he added, "that probably wouldn't sell many books though."[10]

So we can dismiss Hamer's "God gene," but what about future discoveries? Collins gives us wisdom on what to make of future genetic link discoveries and the implications of those discoveries for certain behaviors, diseases, or belief in God:

> There is an inescapable component of heritability to many human behavioral traits. For virtually none of them is heredity ever close to predictive. Environment, particularly childhood experiences, and the prominent role of individual free choices have a profound effect on us. Scientists will discover an increasing level of molecular detail about inherited factors that undergird our personalities, but that should not lead us to overestimate their quantitative contribution. Yes, we have all been dealt a particular set of genetic cards, and the cards will eventually be revealed. But how we play the hand is up to us.[11]

Similarly, we need to temper our conclusions in neuroscience in the same way Collins encourages in regard to genetics. Neuroscience is a critical field of study that promises to be fruitful in many ways. Much has been made of religious experiences being manipulated, whether through electrodes hooked up to the brain or by taking certain drugs.* But philosopher Keith Ward discusses the inherent limitations associated with neuroscience:

> What neuroscience can do, then, is to clarify the physical basis in the brain of human beliefs and feelings.... What neuroscience cannot do is prove that religious belief or behavior is nothing more than the by-product of brain

---

* Dawkins mentions in passing for cumulative effect: "Visionary religious experiences are related to temporal lobe epilepsy." *The God Delusion* (New York: Houghton Mifflin, 2008), 196. Again, all this would show is that there is a *correlation* between the physiology of the temporal lobe and a certain kind of experience; not that the experience is exhaustively explained by the physiology.

behavior or of our naturally evolved cognitive processes. The question of truth remains primary.... Brain processes come up with truths and falsehoods. But brain processes alone cannot distinguish between them. What can? People with brains can, and they do so by using their brains, not being controlled by them![12]

The mind or soul is clearly *correlated* with certain brain states or chemistry, but the mind or soul is not *identical* or *reducible* to them. We reject as inadequate materialistic accounts of reality that reduce human consciousness, free will, morality, or belief in God to genetics and neuroscience—as important and promising as these fields are.

MEMES

We now turn to Dawkins's account of the root of religious belief: "The fact that religion is ubiquitous probably means that it has worked to the benefit of something, but it may not be us or our genes. It may be to the benefit of only the religious ideas themselves, to the extent that they behave in a somewhat gene like way, as replicators."[13] Dawkins calls these replicators *memes*, which he defines as "units of cultural inheritance."[14] Elsewhere, he compares the spread of memes to a computer virus in which "self-replicating information leaps infectiously from mind to mind."[15] Did you catch his word choice? Obviously viruses are not good. Dawkins candidly admits, "To describe religions as mind viruses is sometimes interpreted as contemptuous or even hostile. It is both."[16]

While Dawkins scores points for creativity by coining the term *meme*, the idea has been subject to severe criticism and is by no means a mainstream view among his peers.[17] First, unlike genes, there is no scientific evidence that memes actually exist. Dawkins reveals as much, "We don't know what memes are made of or where they reside. Memes have not yet found their Watson and Crick; they even lack their Mendel."[18] Next, the gene had to be postulated due to the observational data piling up. Not so the meme, which is explanatorily redundant because anthropologists and sociologists are already exploring beliefs and communal dynamics in human cultures.[19] Or as one book reviewer put it in the *Los Angeles Times*, "Memetics is no more than a cumbersome terminology for saying what everybody knows and that can be more usefully said in the dull terminology of information transfer."[20] Finally, Alister McGrath observes, "Since the meme is not warranted scientifically, are we to conclude that there is a meme for belief in memes? The meme concept then dies the slow death of self-referentiality, in that, if taken seriously, the idea explains itself as much as anything else."[21]

But let's briefly return to the notion that religion is a virus of the mind. How does one decide what is a dangerous idea and what is a beneficial idea? Or to put the matter bluntly, why are the ideas that Dawkins dislikes (e.g., religion or God) viruses of the mind, but others like Darwinian evolution are pure, safe, and beneficial? *All* these ideas would have infectiously leaped from mind to mind. *All* would function as memes in his view. It seems wholly arbitrary and subjective to prefer one set of beliefs and condemn another. As McGrath has pointed out, "Each and every argument that Dawkins adduces for his idea of 'God as virus of the mind' can be countered by proposing its counterpart for 'atheism as a virus of the mind.' Both ideas are equally unsubstantiated and meaningless."[22]

A BY-PRODUCT OF NATURAL SELECTION

Dawkins, in conjunction with his dubious meme theory, turns to the emerging field of evolutionary psychology to explain the roots of religion.[23] Perhaps humans were hardwired to believe in God by the process of natural selection?[24] Maybe this belief was useful for human survival? Many experiments in cognitive psychology strongly suggest that "human minds come into the world with all sorts of 'software' both preinstalled and booted up" and that "some of this software manifests itself right from birth, while other bits of it become operative at specifiable times in human development."[25] This research is fascinating and illuminating, but not very controversial until it is applied to religion.*

Michael Murray describes the sort of cognitive evidence that leads some researchers to conclude that we are hardwired to believe in God:

> We have a mental tool that makes us think there are agents around when we detect certain sounds (bumps in the night), motions (rustling in the bushes), or configurations (crop circles) in nature. This "Hyperactive Agency Detection Device" (or "HADD") leads us to hypothesize invisible agents that, for example, control the forces of nature. And this disposes us to belief in the supernatural.[26]

It needs to be pointed out that one could just as easily interpret the emerging cognitive evidence to mean that the reason that people naturally form beliefs about God is that God actually exists and designed humans to form these kinds of beliefs. Barrett, one of the pioneers of this field, concludes that "belief in gods generally and God particularly arises through the natural, ordinary operation of human minds in natural ordinary environments.... The design of our minds leads us to believe."[27]

If belief in God is indeed an issue of hardwiring, then two possible explanations exist for the design we observe. Either a blind process of natural selection produces religious belief over time as a by-product with some selective advantage, or an Intelligent Mind designed humanity to naturally believe God exists. If the latter is the case, then we are back to our original question—what is the evidence for God? The evidence is what will allow us to make sense of why people seem to naturally believe in God.

---

* Since we talk about the morality question elsewhere, we will only mention here that the corollary of the religion argument would run the same way. If we discover through cognitive psychology that it seems certain moral behaviors are hardwired into properly functioning human beings, then this would fit nicely as well with the biblical notion of God's laws being written on the human heart (see Rom. 2:14–15).

WHAT IF WE WERE DESIGNED TO BELIEVE?

So if, as we have labored to show in this book, it is reasonable to conclude that God exists, then it is also possible to infer that the reason so many humans have desires for and beliefs in the divine points to God's desire to be known. This coheres nicely with the portrait of God we find in the Bible, for as the writer of Ecclesiastes observes, God "has also set eternity in the hearts of men."[28]

FOR FURTHER ENGAGEMENT

McGrath, Alister. *Dawkins' God: Genes, Memes, and the Meaning of Life*. Malden, MA: Blackwell, 2005.

Murray, Michael J. "Belief in God: A Trick of Our Brain?" In *Contending with Christianity's Critics: Answering New Atheists and Other Objectors*, edited by Paul Copan and William Lane Craig, 47–57. Nashville: B & H Publishing, 2009.

[why it matters]

BELIEF IN GOD: NATURAL, YES—BUT IS IT RATIONAL?

Raised in a Christian home, I don't remember *not* believing in Jesus. My best friend in high school was an atheist (in those days, he was the strange one; as a Christian, I was normal), and he and I spent many hours arguing about God. But truth be told, neither of us had very good arguments; mostly we were parroting our parents. Later, in college and graduate school, I did encounter people whose atheism was well thought out. Belief in God, they argued, was wish-projection (Sigmund Freud), the opiate of the masses (Karl Marx), a virus of the mind (Richard Dawkins), a function of the evolved human brain (Dean Hamer and others), or an evolutionarily advantageous adaptive behavior (Stephen Pinker and others). Such arguments needed answers, I thought. If they were successful, I could no more believe in God than in Santa Claus. But I discovered there were powerful answers, both defeaters for the antitheistic arguments and arguments in favor of theistic belief.

I found powerful arguments, strong enough to challenge the brightest minds of this and past centuries, and sufficient to ground belief. People believe things for reasons, and there are good and bad sorts of reasons. Believing in Jesus because my family did may have been a good reason when I was a child, but when faced with good intellectual objections, I needed even better intellectual reasons, and they were there: the ontological argument (to my mind, the most sublime piece of reasoning in Western philosophy); the cosmological, design, and moral arguments; and others as well.

I spent several years as a missionary in France, where I interacted with philosophically sophisticated thinkers; and then I spent fourteen years as a pastor in two churches in college towns, where I interacted with university students reexamining their beliefs and with professors and other professionals who were very much aware of their own beliefs and the grounds for them. I found that people were usually quite surprised that Christianity could withstand intellectual scrutiny, and even more surprised that excellent reasons—arguments—could be given in support of Christian belief. In the years since, during doctoral studies in philosophy and teaching at both secular and Christian universities, I've seen time and again Christians who are surprised—and relieved!—to know that their faith is supported by solid evidence and sound arguments, and atheists who are surprised to find their complacent disbelief gently yet forcefully challenged.

It's often said that you can't argue someone into the kingdom of God. True—but you can't love them into the kingdom either. Faith is ultimately the gift of the Holy Spirit. But in showing that there are excellent reasons for Christian belief, we can lead unbelievers to a place where they may be more open to the Spirit's work. And in showing Christians that there is solid ground for their faith, we increase their confidence and their courage in facing this secular age and the popular gadflies of the New Atheism.

—Garry DeWeese

Garry DeWeese is professor of philosophy at Talbot School of Theology, Biola University. He is the author of *God and the Nature of Time* and coauthor of *Philosophy Made Slightly Less Difficult.*

PART 2

Responding to Moral and Biblical Challenges

CHAPTER 10

Is Religion Dangerous?

Violent, irrational, intolerant, allied to racism and tribalism and bigotry, invested in ignorance and hostile to free inquiry, contemptuous of women and coercive toward children: organized religion ought to have a great deal on its conscience.

—Christopher Hitchens

Religion is not just false, it's dangerous. So say the New Atheists. Sam Harris thinks religion ought to be lumped in with slavery and eradicated.[1] Christopher Hitchens concludes *God Is Not Great* by rallying the troops against the enemy of religion: "It has become necessary to know the enemy, and to prepare to fight it."[2] Richard Dawkins lays all his cards on the table: "I am attacking God, all gods, anything and everything supernatural, wherever and whenever they have been invented."[3] And far more often than not, Christianity is the particular object of his contempt: "Unless otherwise stated, I shall have Christianity mostly in mind."[4]

Many of their arguments for these bold claims revolve around violence. Who can deny that we live in a violent world? But is religion *uniquely* to blame for this? Is there something *inherent* within religion that necessarily—like gravity—leads to evil and violence? If we were to imagine with Richard Dawkins and John Lennon "a world with no religion," would we really all be better off? No more violence, oppression, racism, slavery, poverty, injustice, and war?

DETAILS MATTER WHEN EXAMINING RELIGION

Religion is a nebulous concept, and defining it is a bit like trying to nail Jell-O to the wall. So the first thing we need to do is dispense with the idea that religion, used in some categorical or generic sense, causes *anything*.

In *Is Religion Dangerous?* Oxford philosopher and theologian Keith Ward observes that "saying religion is dangerous is vacuous, unless you have in mind some specific religious institution and you are accusing that of being dangerous, either because its beliefs or practices are dangerous, or because the very existence of the institution itself is dangerous to society."[5] A categorical rejection of all religion is unwarranted and unhelpful. It matters very much which religion the objector has in mind. For example, injustices committed by the Taliban in Afghanistan ought not be used (rhetorically or logically) as part of a cumulative case against religion in general or Christianity in particular.*

Additionally, almost anything can be abused or misused simply because people are involved, and people tend to manipulate, control, or exploit to get what they want. Alister McGrath makes the critical point that "all ideals—divine, transcendent, human, or invented—are capable of being abused. That's just the way human nature is. And that happens to religion as well. Belief in God can be abused, and we need to be very clear, in the first place, that abuse happens, and in the second, that we need to confront and oppose this. But abuse of an ideal does not negate its validity."[6]

Ward contends that the rational and scientific way to engage this issue is to "treat religious beliefs in their best intellectual forms with care and respect and careful analysis, and with due consideration for the many different interpretations that exist."[7] If someone wants to criticize Christianity, he or she must make

---

* In other words, arguments against Islam are not arguments against Christianity. Both are theistic religions, but they are very different theologically. To learn about the differences between the impact of Islam and that of Christianity, see Alvin J. Schmidt, *The Great Divide: The Failure of Islam and the Triumph of the West* (Boston: Regina Orthodox Press, 2004).

an honest and careful examination of the life and teachings of Jesus because he is the founder of Christianity. Is there anything he taught that necessarily leads to violence?

Unfortunately, it becomes apparent with each turn of the page that the New Atheists cite much evidence and many anecdotes that reduce to religious people behaving badly (Hitchens is especially gifted in this tactic). But simply because religion, and for our purposes Christianity, has been abused, does not make it false or inherently dangerous.

RELIGION IS NOT THE PROBLEM—PEOPLE ARE

That violence has been done in the name of religion in general and Christianity in particular will not surprise anyone who has taken a Western Civilization class. The usual suspects are the Crusades, the Inquisition, and witch trials; they get *a lot* of press.[8] But, do they tell the whole story about the *root* causes of violence and war?

When one surveys the conflict and violence throughout the history of civilization, a common denominator emerges—*people*. John Ortberg writes,

> Imagine a society with no religion, no faith, no God.... Does it seem likely that in that society no one is going to covet someone else's money, no one is going to covet someone else's house or someone else's spouse, that people whose skin tones are different are suddenly going to be one another's devoted servants? The problem of "otherness" is suddenly going to be solved? It is hard to imagine that just because religion is done away with, greedy people will become generous, angry people will become merciful, Jerry Springer will be cancelled, and everyone will support PBS and listen to NPR.[9]

Upon reflection, most would agree that *people* are the problem, not *religion*. There are deeper issues at work. The human heart is corrupt.

Throughout history, power has been used in disturbing ways and religious beliefs have been co-opted for personal or political gain. Ward's comments are helpful:

> No one would deny that there have been religious wars in human history. Catholics have fought Protestants, Sunni Muslims have fought Shi'a Muslims, and Hindus have fought Muslims. However, no one who has studied history could deny that most wars in human history have not been religious. And in the case of those that have been religious, the religious component has usually been associated with some non-religious, social, ethnic, or political component that has exerted a powerful influence on the conflicts.[10]

This observation about the history of warfare reinforces the critical point McGrath made above, namely, that *all* ideals, religious or irreligious, are capable of being abused.

But weren't the abuses of Christianity far worse than anything else we've seen in history? Actually, no, they weren't. While the point of this chapter is not to return the favor of the New Atheists by saying that atheism *necessarily* leads to violence, it is simply historically inaccurate to conclude that the worldview of atheism has not contributed to oppression, injustice, and human suffering. We need to set the record straight concerning the death tolls resulting from Christianity because the New Atheists utilize these tragic events to rhetorically bludgeon people into believing that Christianity is the cause of violence and the virus that needs to be irradiated. But when you compare the human suffering associated with atheism versus Christianity, a much different picture emerges.

If you were just to examine the big three atheistic regimes of the twentieth century—Mao in China, Stalin in Russia, and Hitler in Nazi Germany—then you would discover that they are responsible for more than 100 million deaths.* (This number

---

* Whether Hitler's motivations were Christian or atheistic in origin is sometimes disputed. To explore this further and decide for yourself, see Richard Weikart,

does not even include death tolls from other regimes like Pol Pot's mass killings in Cambodia.) Dinesh D'Souza observes,

> Religion-inspired killing simply cannot compete with the murders perpetrated by atheist regimes. I recognize that population levels were much lower in the past, and that it's much easier to kill people today with sophisticated weapons than it was in previous centuries to kill with swords and arrows. Even taking higher populations into account, atheist violence surpasses religious violence by staggering proportions. Here is a rough calculation. The world's population rose from around 500 million in 1450 A.D. to 2.5 billion in 1950, a fivefold increase. Taken together, the Crusades, the Inquisition, and the witch burnings killed approximately 200,000 people. Adjusting for the increase in population, that's the equivalent of one million deaths today. Even so, these deaths caused by Christian rulers over a five-hundred-year period amount to only 1 percent of the deaths caused by Stalin, Hitler, and Mao in the space of a few decades.[11]

D'Souza points out the double standard in play when it comes to violence in history: "If Christianity has to answer for Torquemada [cf. Inquisition], atheism has to answer for Stalin. By the same token, if the ordinary Christian who has never burned anyone at the stake must bear some responsibility for what other self-styled Christians have done on behalf of religion, then atheists who think of themselves as the kinder, gentler type do not get to absolve themselves for the horrible suffering that their beliefs have caused in recent history."[12] It seems the New Atheists want to have it both ways. But if Stalin represents a perversion of atheism, then why can't the Crusades be considered a perversion of Christianity?

All loss of life is tragic, and we are certainly not trying to whitewash the evils done in the name of Christianity. Yet history

---

From Darwin to Hitler: Evolutionary Ethics, Eugenics, and Racism in Germany (New York: Palgrave Macmillan, 2004).

shows that societies in which God has been banished—not Christianity—are responsible for the largest death tolls in history.[13]

IS ATHEISM REALLY THE ABSENCE OF BELIEF?

At this point, the New Atheists yell foul. Dawkins argues that the atrocities mentioned above were not done in the name of atheism, for how can the "absence of belief" cause anything?[14] Again, D'Souza's critique is instructive:

> Dawkins seems to have deluded himself into thinking that these horrors were not produced on atheism's behalf. But can anyone seriously deny that Communism was an atheist ideology?... Not only was Marx an atheist, but atheism was also a central part of the Marxist doctrine. Atheism became a central component of the Soviet Union's official ideology, it is still the official doctrine of China, and Stalin and Mao enforced atheist policies by systematically closing churches and murdering priests and religious believers. All Communist regimes have been strongly anti-religious, suggesting that their atheism is intrinsic rather than incidental to their ideology.[15]

We have discussed one aspect of whether atheism is the absence of belief in chapter 1, but the question takes a different form in this context. Hitchens, in a rather interesting display of logic, asserts, "And here is the point, about myself and my co-thinkers. Our belief is not a belief. Our principles are not a faith."[16] In *The New Atheism*, Victor Stenger defines an atheist as "someone who believes that no gods exist."[17] As we have pointed out elsewhere, the claim that "no gods exist" is just as much a claim to knowledge as the claim that "God exists" (i.e., both require justification). And all claims to knowledge arise from beliefs, from a mental map of the way the world is—in short, a worldview.*

Ronald Nash helpfully defines a worldview as "a conceptual

---

* This is true whether one is aware of it or not, though it is much better when we are aware of our worldviews and can test them for rational consistency, coherence, and explanatory power and scope.

scheme by which we consciously or unconsciously place or fit everything we believe and by which we interpret and judge reality."[18] Moreover, "because people behave as they believe, their worldviews guide their thoughts, attitudes, values, interpretations, perspectives, decisions, and actions."[19] Our writing flows out of a Christian worldview. A careful reading of the New Atheists reveals that their worldviews stem from naturalism and secular humanism. Everyone has a worldview—including Stalin, Mao, and Hitler. For good or ill, worldviews contain ideas and ideas have consequences.

The New Atheists react strongly to the notion that a "cosmic cop" is up in the sky watching everything that people do. But this is an inaccurate caricature of the Christian God—as if he delights in punishing people for breaking trivial rules. However, the New Atheists fail to realize that when people think they are autonomous and ultimately unaccountable, evil and oppression are not far behind. Stenger unintentionally admits as much when he writes, "The atheist has the comfort of no fears for an afterlife."[20] David Berlinski, a secular Jew, observes, "What Hitler did not believe and what Stalin did not believe and what Mao did not believe and what the SS [Hitler's zealous inner circle of soldiers] did not believe … was that God was watching."[21] That just is the nature of secularism, the place where God is not watching.[22] Thus Dostoyevsky's dictum is appropriate, *if God is not, everything is permitted.*

A UNIVERSAL PROBLEM

If the problems of violence and oppression are rooted in the human condition and not religion, then what is the solution? The first option is to rely on the resources of naturalism and atheism. Even if we overlook the fact that ultimate reality consists of "blind pitiless indifference,"[23] it seems all that is left to humanity is unfettered reason in the form of education and science.* However, as we often point out, the reasoning process itself becomes suspect if naturalism accurately describes reality.

---

* Dawkins reminds his readers there is no good, no evil, no soul, no free will, no objective values or duties, and no ultimate purpose or meaning in life.

University of Southern California moral philosopher Dallas Willard frankly observes, "Our social and psychological sciences stand helpless before the terrible things done by human beings.... We are like farmers who diligently plant crops but cannot admit the existence of weeds and insects and can only think to pour on more fertilizer. Similarly the only solution we know to human problems today is 'education.'"[24] Willard continues, "And can we really think that if people only knew what is today generally understood to be the right thing to do, they would do it?"[25] No amount of education or science will remedy the human condition. Science does not have the resources to diagnose the fundamental brokenness of humanity or to provide a positive vision for how people should live.*

The second option recognizes that as helpful as education and scientific discovery are (and we believe them to be very important), this problem cannot be solved with more data, more cold hard facts about reality. Rather, Willard observes that "the greatest need you and I have—the greatest need of collective humanity—is *renovation of our heart*. That spiritual place within us from which outlook, choices and actions come has been formed by a world away from God. Now it must be transformed."[26] This is a distinctively Christian answer to humanity's core problem. In stark contrast to secular humanism, which places its faith in the inherent goodness of humanity, the Christian worldview paints a more realistic picture. It is hopeful, but honest. Jesus of Nazareth offered those who would follow him a new heart along with the real possibility of transformation.[27] Ezekiel the prophet clearly communicates God's intention, "I will give you a new heart and put a new spirit in you; I will remove from you your heart of stone and give you a heart of flesh."[28]

MAKING THE CASE FOR CIVILITY

Tolerance is another word that has become a victim of political correctness—only a shell of its original meaning remains. It

---

* That is, if human behavior is completely explainable in terms of genetics plus social environment.

has come to mean that for an individual to be tolerant, he must accept everything that someone else says or affirm that all beliefs are equally valid or true.* This new tolerance effectively removes ethics, values, and religion from the domain of reality. These are merely privatized and regulated to the nebulous world of "faith." If these areas contain no fact, then of course they can all be tolerated as long as everyone plays nicely together and no one thinks their viewpoint is objectively true. While this approach to knowledge is prevalent, we reject it as inadequate. For as important as science is, it is only *one* source of human knowledge.[29]

As the New Atheists enter the public fray, they argue that no tolerance should be afforded religion—even in the watered-down sense just described. In the words of Dawkins, "As long as we accept the principle that religious faith must be respected simply because it is religious faith, it is hard to withhold respect from the faith of Osama bin Laden and the suicide bombers. The alternative, one so transparent that it should need no urging, is to abandon the principle of automatic respect for religious faith."†
In response to Harris's book *The End of Faith*, Ravi Zacharias asks, "Has it occurred to Sam Harris that his book might sow the seeds for the slaughter of Christians? Has he paused to think of what motivates him to write these things against a group of people? What would he say if two hundred years from now someone says that genocide against Christians can be traced back to the anti-Christian writings of Sam Harris?"[30] Sobering questions to be sure. Can we find a middle way that avoids the eradication of

---

* This is relativism at its worst. While it may seem initially attractive to avoid some potential for conflict, relativism is ultimately unlivable. For evidence supporting this claim, see Francis Beckwith and Gregory Koukl, *Relativism: Feet Firmly Planted in Mid-Air* (Grand Rapids: Baker, 1998).

† Richard Dawkins, *The God Delusion* (New York: Houghton Mifflin, 2008), 345–46. We are not suggesting that terrorists just need to be listened to and no action taken—as Dawkins implies in his discussion. Osama bin Laden has forfeited his seat at the table of discussion and his actions have been rightly condemned. Furthermore, if study of the Qu'ran and Hadith reveals that Islam is rooted in violence, then people need to address Islam specifically, not lump Christianity in with it.

all religion on the one hand and the ultimate trivialization of it on the other?

The best prospect for humanity living with their deep differences lies in recovering a robust sense of tolerance, or as Os Guinness has put it—civility.[31] The American experiment was able to accomplish something remarkable in the history of Western civilization—freedom *of* religion. Much to the chagrin of the New Atheists, the language does not read freedom *from* religion. Vigorous discussion and thoughtful interaction are needed in the public square, and then we let the best ideas win.

From the Christian perspective, the goal isn't a *sacred* public square where only the ideas rooted in Christianity are preferred (or any single religion for that matter). Nor is the goal a *naked* public square where no ideas from various religious traditions are even entertained. The goal, as Os Guinness describes it, is a *civil* public square:

> The vision of a civic public square is one in which everyone—people of all faiths, whether religious or naturalistic—are equally free to enter and engage public life on the basis of their faiths, as a matter of free exercise and as dictated by their own conscience; but always within the double framework, first of the Constitution, and second, of a freely and mutually agreed covenant, or common vision for the common good, of what each person understands to be just and free for everyone else, and therefore of the duties involved in living with the deep differences of others.[32]

DISAGREEMENT IS HERE TO STAY

In this chapter we have tried not only to set the historical record straight regarding the relationship of religion and violence, but, more importantly, to get beyond the statistics to the root issue of the human condition. Moreover, we have suggested a way forward in this global society grounded in the notion of a civil public square. Faith isn't going anywhere and neither is disagreement. We must learn to debate the ideas and the implications of those ideas without affirming that everyone's view is equally valid on the one hand or demonizing those with whom we disagree on the other—this is what is truly dangerous for society. *Persuasion* rather than *coercion* is the only reasonable way forward. We hope that this book is an example of such spirited yet civil interaction.

FOR FURTHER ENGAGEMENT

Guinness, Os. *The Case for Civility: And Why Our Future Depends on It*. New York: HarperOne, 2008.

Ward, Keith. *Is Religion Dangerous?* Grand Rapids: Eerdmans, 2007.

[why it matters]

CHRISTIANITY, TRUTH, AND DANGER

As a freshman in college, I imbibed a heady brew of modern atheism served up by Sigmund Freud, Karl Marx, and Friedrich Nietzsche. Freud claimed that religion was a projection, a figment of wish fulfillment. We desire a heavenly Father to make life tolerable, but the heavens provide no Father. Marx thundered that religion pacified and placated the desire for social justice, since lasting goodness could only be found in a heaven that did not exist. Nietzsche insisted that Christianity was the attempt by the weak to get revenge on the strong and that the truly free can live "beyond good and evil" by creating their own values in the godless, gladiatorial theater of nature.

Having little understanding of Christianity and no awareness of apologetics (the rational case for Christian truth), I viewed traditional Western religion as dangerous to the intellect, while I became attracted to Eastern religions in a vague sense. I stopped praying, tried to meditate, and fancied myself an aspiring intellectual who needed to oppose Christianity.

But something strange happened that first year in college: Christianity began to speak to my condition, despite my antipathy toward it. A philosophy professor assigned some readings by Søren Kierkegaard, the Danish Christian philosopher. After having dismissed Kierkegaard in a paper, I decided to actually read the primary text, *The Sickness unto Death*. I found a profound assessment of the human condition before God. Much to my surprise and dismay, the book began exposing both my rebellion against God and God's offer of grace through Christ. In addition to my reading, I came to know the loving and courageous witness of two Christian women who were involved in the Navigators, a campus group focused on discipleship and evangelism. Through various providential events, many conversations with Christians, and Bible reading, I confessed Christ as Lord in the summer of 1976.

After a difficult summer of trying vainly to believe Christianity without evidence, I discovered the works of Francis Schaeffer, James Sire, C. S. Lewis, Os Guinness, St. Augustine, Blaise Pascal, and many more high-caliber thinkers, who demonstrated that the Christian worldview has nothing to fear in the world of ideas. I eventually switched my major to philosophy and began a grand intellectual adventure that continues to this day. Now, as a professional philosopher, I find some of the best philosophers alive defending Christianity through rational arguments.

In a sense, I have spent the last thirty-three years trying to disprove Christianity—not as an atheist, but as a philosopher who has investigated all the major religions and philosophies on offer. I found that the anti-Christian arguments of Freud, Marx, Nietzsche, and others missed the mark. I have tackled the toughest challenges to Christianity and investigated the case for other worldviews. My years of study, teaching, and writing have convinced me that Christianity is objectively true, rational, wise, and pertinent to all of life. But I still believe it is dangerous—not to the intellect, but to any other worldview that attempts to refute it.

—Douglas Groothuis

Douglas Groothuis is professor of philosophy at Denver Seminary, where he heads the Philosophy of Religion Master's Degree program. He is the author of ten books, including *Truth Decay*, *On Pascal*, and *On Jesus*. Visit him at http://theconstructivecurmudgeon.blogspot.com.

CHAPTER 11

Does God Intend for Us to Keep Slaves?

Consult the Bible and you will discover that the creator of the universe clearly expects us to keep slaves.

—Sam Harris

Let's be honest. The first time we come across a verse like, "Slaves, obey your earthly masters with respect and fear, and with sincerity of heart, just as you would obey Christ,"[1] who doesn't squirm a little bit? After all, I thought the Bible taught kindness and love, but slavery? Does this mean that Sam Harris and the other New Atheists are right to conclude that the Bible is morally and socially regressive, even dangerous?

That is what we want to explore in this chapter. By now you will not be surprised to learn that our answer is no, the biblical God does not think it is a good idea to keep slaves. But to show this, we need to take a step back and really understand the context and how the Bible, as an ancient book, works.

Appearances can be deceiving. Unfortunately, the New Atheists' approach to the Bible and Christian theology reveals that they are far more interested in gathering ammunition against Christianity than in truly understanding it. We are not alone in this assessment. Secular critic and agnostic Terry Eagleton observes,

Card-carrying rationalists like Dawkins, who is the nearest thing to a professional atheist we have had since Bertrand Russell, are in one sense the least well-equipped to understand what they castigate, since they don't believe there is anything there to be understood, or at least anything worth understanding. This is why they invariably come up with vulgar caricatures of religious faith that would make a first-year theology student wince. The more they detest religion, the more ill-informed their criticisms of it tend to be. If they were asked to pass judgment on phenomenology or the geopolitics of South Asia, they would no doubt bone up on the question as assiduously as they could. When it comes to theology, however, any shoddy old travesty will pass muster.[2]

That is why it is so important to develop a thoroughly Christian understanding of human dignity and the issue of slavery.

CHRISTIANITY DID NOT INVENT SLAVERY

I (Jonathan) remember sitting through a U.S. history class in college while my teacher went off on the Bible and Christians for advocating slavery in the Old Testament. The unspoken implication was that if there had been no Bible, there would have been no slavery. This is a common, yet mistaken, understanding of history. As Dinesh D'Souza observes, "slavery pre-dated Christianity by centuries and even millennia. It was widely practiced in the ancient world, from China and India to Greece and Rome, and most cultures regarded it as an indispensable institution, like the family. For centuries slavery needed no defenders because it had no critics."[3] Orlando Patterson's *Slavery and Social Death* surveys sixty-six different societies that practiced slavery, indicating that slavery has been a part of human history from early tribal cultures to modern times.[4]

This observation is instructive because it reminds us that slavery was a universal phenomenon that *predated* Christianity. More importantly, slavery didn't have any critics before

Christianity came on the scene. Therefore, we need to understand Christianity as entering into an existing situation—not creating it. If we do this, then we will see just how revolutionary and countercultural the message of the Bible really was during the time it was composed. The reality is that slavery is not God's intention; it is a consequence of life in a broken and sinful world. This will become increasingly clear as we go along.

WE MUST PUT THE BIBLICAL DISCUSSION IN ITS CULTURAL CONTEXT

The topic of slavery is emotionally charged and rightly evokes in us repugnant images that remind us of a shameful chapter in American history. When we watch a movie like *Amistad*, we are sickened. For the sake of historical accuracy and getting at the truth of the matter, we need to put the biblical discussion of slavery in its ancient Near Eastern context. Old Testament scholar Christopher J. H. Wright reminds us that the slavery found in ancient Israel was

> qualitatively vastly different from slavery in the large imperial civilizations—the contemporary ancient Near Eastern empires, and especially the latter empires of the Greeks and Romans. There the slave markets were glutted with captives of war and displaced peoples, and slaves were put to degrading and dehumanizing labour. And, of course, Israelite slavery was even more different from the ghastly commercialized and massive-scale slave trade that Arabs, Europeans and Americans perpetrated upon Africa.[5]

In drawing attention to this fact, we are by no means trying to justify slavery, absolve Christians for their participation in it, or mitigate the dehumanization that occurred in the African slave trade; our point is merely that slavery in ancient Israel and the laws pertaining to it recorded in the Old Testament need to be understood within an ancient Near Eastern context because they were different.

Before we can proceed any further, we must understand a

critical principle of interpretation: *Israel as described in the Old Testament is not God's ideal society.** To use an analogy from the computer industry, they were God's people 1.0 because they were a work in progress (just like you and I are). From the Christian perspective, all of humanity is made in God's image—that is God's ideal. When sin entered and perverted the good world God created, that ideal was violated and the ancient world was from then on perpetually plagued by war and poverty. It was within the volatile world of the ancient Near East that God *began* the process of restoration and redemption through the people of Israel (who, by the way, would have been just like everyone else in that culture were it not for God's grace and revelation). Needless to say, there was no United Nations or diplomacy over high tea in this violent culture. Against this backdrop, we are in a better position to assess laws in the Old Testament books of Exodus and Deuteronomy regulating slavery within the nation of Israel. The fact that it was regulated *at all* is striking given the moral poverty of surrounding nations.

The two biggest causes of slavery in the ancient Near Eastern world were war and poverty. The prevalence of these realities made slavery a complex issue both individually and socially. War produces winners and losers, and the winners had to do something to protect themselves from future retaliation by those they conquered. Moreover, poverty often led people to use their labor as a way to provide for their family: people lacking resources put themselves up for collateral in order for their family to survive. This idea is implicit in the Hebrew term for slave, which is more precisely translated "bonded worker."[6]

Concerning the Old Testament, it is beyond dispute that slaves in Israel had a "degree of status, rights, and protection unheard of elsewhere."[7] Scholars universally recognize this fact. Slaves were included in religious life, were granted a weekly Sabbath rest (i.e., had a day off), had to be set free if they were

---

* In saying this, we do not mean to imply that Israel's example is to be applied as merely "what not to do" (see 2 Tim. 3:16–17).

inflicted with bodily harm, had the opportunity for freedom every seven years, and were promised asylum as runaway slaves from other masters.[8] Remember, Israel was intimately acquainted with what slavery was like because they had experienced its brutal and unregulated reality for four hundred years in Egypt.

In addition to these remarkable improvements, Job recognized that his bondservants were created by God just like he was, and therefore he would have to answer to God if he mistreated them.[9] This gets back to God's original design of humankind in his image before sin corrupted everything.[10]

Our modern sensibilities still bristle at a world that has slaves at all, so let's ask a different question to get some perspective on the reality and complexities of economics in the ancient world (and our own). How long has poverty been around and how long has humanity been trying to deal with it? Think of America's power, wealth, and influence, and yet, consider that poverty still exists in spite of all the resources we have. Now imagine a country slightly smaller than New Jersey with limited resources and nestled in the middle of ancient superpowers; this was the nation of Israel. They had few resources and even less power to instigate any wide-scale change.

Influence takes time and moral progress is often painfully slow.* In addition to these realities, consider that God's unfolding plan of redemption works through free moral agents who can either conform to his design or rebel against it. It becomes clear how God can't just eradicate slavery all at once and still retain human freedom. To make it more personal, think of how long real and lasting change takes in your own life. Multiply that by all the people around you and we can start to understand that, despite our ideals, reality is far more complicated than the New Atheists admit.

---

* This is not to say that God's morality is evolving or his standards are changing; rather when people are involved, their capacity to accept and implement a higher vision of morality is often painfully slow (e.g., divorce was allowed due to the stubbornness of their hearts, but was not God's creational ideal; see Mark 10:2–9).

CHRISTIANITY TOLERATED SLAVERY UNTIL IT COULD BE ABOLISHED

The New Testament continues the countercultural trajectory initiated in the Old Testament. To say slavery was a major component of the ancient world is almost an understatement: it is estimated that 85–90 percent of the people in the Roman Empire during the first and second centuries were slaves or of slave origin.[11] Within this context Paul uttered the radical words, "There is no longer Jew or Gentile, slave or free, male or female. For you are all one in Christ Jesus."[12] Society may still segregate and sort according to these classes, but Christianity would not.

In his letter to Philemon, Paul applied the radical idea to the recently converted Onesimus; he should be viewed "no longer as a slave, but better than a slave, as a dear brother. He is very dear to me but even dearer to you, both as a man and as a brother in the Lord. So if you consider me a partner, welcome him as you would welcome me."[13] Think of it—Paul, an apostle, told Philemon to receive Onesimus as he would himself! Paul Copan summarizes that "biblical writers offer, in seed form, the basis for societal transformation—especially by affirming that slaves are equal to their masters before God and, if believers, are in the same spiritual family."[14] These seminal ideas provided the impetus for Christians to eventually abolish slavery—William Wilberforce in England and Christian abolitionists in the United States.

The truth revealed in the Bible challenged Christians to swim against the current of world opinion on the issue of slavery. We must also remember that it takes time for controversial ideas to take root and for people and societies to change. Therefore, when the Bible is properly interpreted and applied, we see that, far from enthusiastically endorsing slavery, the truth is that God's people *tolerated* it with unheard of compassion and humanity until it could finally be abolished.[15]

WHY WAS JESUS SILENT ON THE ISSUE OF SLAVERY?

Sam Harris claims, "There is no place in the New Testament where Jesus objects to slavery."[16] Actually, Jesus did speak to the issue of slavery, but he went after the root of physical slavery: spiritual slavery. Spiritual slavery has led to and continues to lead to immense misery. When Jesus began his public ministry, he stood in the synagogue to read the following passage: "The Spirit of the Lord is upon me, because he has anointed me to proclaim good news to the poor. He has sent me to proclaim liberty to the captives and recovering of sight to the blind, to set at liberty those who are oppressed."[17]

What a mission statement! Jesus came to set captives free, restore, heal, and transform—that is the good news of the kingdom of God. The good news of the kingdom of God is when "up there" comes "down here" and begins to be embodied by a new community.[18] Given the reality of sinful humans and corrupted institutions, Jesus knew the best way to end slavery was first to liberate the hearts and minds of humanity. The truth sets people free. As Ravi Zacharias poignantly frames the question, "Slavery is now illegal, but is *racism* gone?"[19] Simply passing a law doesn't transform the brokenness in the human heart. If obscure Bible passages were really the problem, then why in the twenty-first century are we confronted with the horrible reality of human trafficking and the sex-slave trade?

DOES ATHEISM NATURALLY LEAD TO HUMAN DIGNITY AND EQUALITY?

As we admitted at the beginning of this chapter, a superficial reading of the Bible could lead one to conclude that God has a positive view of slavery. However, we have discovered a much different perspective by engaging the historical context and relevant theological issues. The Bible unequivocally teaches universal human dignity and equality because *all* are made in the image of God.

What is often forgotten is that atheism rose to prominence only after centuries of Judeo-Christian ethic and thought had shaped modern civilization. Atheism did not lay the groundwork for inherent human dignity and equality; it borrows that from a Judeo-Christian worldview. If you remove God from the equation, you also remove inherent human dignity and equality. Atheistic philosopher Friedrich Nietzsche (who was carefully read by Adolf Hitler) explains:

> Equality is a lie concocted by inferior people who arrange themselves in herds to overpower those who are naturally superior to them. The morality of "equal rights" is herd morality, and because it opposes the cultivation of superior individuals, it leads to the corruption of the human species.[20]

History stubbornly does not let us forget that ideas have consequences. Which idea do you think is more dangerous: that *all* people are created in the image of God and possess inherent dignity and value, or that the concept of equal rights leads to the corruption of the human species?

Some may argue that if there had been no Bible, advocates (including preachers!) of colonial slavery couldn't have (apparently) justified the practice. Perhaps. But by this line of reasoning, we would also have to say that if there were no physics—if E didn't equal MC^2—then there would have been no atomic bomb. When you think about it this way, the common denominator that emerges yet again is *people*. What is most needed is the transformation of the human condition. And that, in stark contrast to the worldview of atheism, is exactly what Jesus of Nazareth offers.

FOR FURTHER ENGAGEMENT

Schmidt, Alvin J. "Slavery Abolished: A Christian Achievement." Chap. 11 in *How Christianity Changed the World*. Grand Rapids: Zondervan, 2004.

Wright, Christopher J. H. *Old Testament Ethics for the People of God*. Downers Grove, IL: InterVarsity Press, 2004.

[why it matters]

SLAVERY AND SCRIPTURE: SOME PERSONAL REFLECTIONS

Over the years I've developed a strong interest in the Civil War era, and I'm very much an Abraham Lincoln enthusiast. The Lincoln era is fascinating in many ways, but let's consider slavery. Throughout the Lincoln-Douglas debates of 1858 and during Lincoln's presidential tenure, he regularly appealed to America's founding document—the Declaration of Independence—to ground his position against slavery. Though his primary reason for engaging the South militarily was to preserve the Union, he repeated the theme that "all men are created equal"—including black slaves.

Today, many mistakenly associate the word *slave* in the Old Testament with antebellum Southern plantations and the ruthless treatment of slaves as depicted in former slave and abolitionist Frederick Douglass's writings and in Harriet Beecher Stowe's *Uncle Tom's Cabin*. As I've thought about slavery and Scripture, I've found it helpful to consider the following three points.

First, the existence of a good God helps make the best sense of our moral intuitions about human rights and dignity. The Bible begins with a declaration of *dependence*—that is, the dependence of human dignity and worth on God's uniquely creating us in his image (Gen. 1:26–27). If such a dignity-endowing Creator doesn't exist and if nature is all there is, it's hard to make sense of the rights assumed by our legal system and historic moral reforms (e.g., apartheid, the Civil Rights movement). If we are just dancing to our DNA (as Richard Dawkins declares), then we're not morally responsible agents with dignity and worth; we're just the products of mindless, valueless, deterministic processes that don't have the capacity to produce valuable, rights-bearing beings. A good Creator offers a more plausible context.

Second, key texts and major themes of Scripture should guide our understanding of slavery in Scripture. Former Chrysler CEO Lee

Iacocca is famous for saying, "The main thing is to keep the main thing the main thing." This applies to our reading of Scripture; we should begin with key "framework" texts before dealing with the less-clear ones:

- Being made in God's image (Gen. 1) has huge implications regarding the spiritual and moral status of every human being.
- God's deliverance of Israel from Egypt (Exod. 14) was a formative event for Israel—an ongoing model for how God's people should treat aliens/outsiders in their midst.
- Jesus' own ministry was directed at freeing those in bondage (Luke 4:18).
- Paul considered slaves and masters on the same spiritual and moral level (Gal. 3:28).

Third, slavery in the Old Testament was far different from Western slavery. It was *voluntary*, not forced—a form of contracted labor. In rough economic times, people without available resources would "sell themselves" until they were released in the seventh year. "Selling oneself" doesn't mean property. Think of a professional athlete who is "sold"; think of a team's "owner"; think of a government's "ownership" of those joining the military for a certain period of time. Three Mosaic commands instructed Israelites to harbor/protect runaway slaves from their masters (Deut. 23:15–16); not to engage in kidnapping (Deut. 24:7); and to release injured "slaves" from service/debt (Exod. 21:27). Though nineteenth-century Northerners and Southerners read the same Bible, the Southerners' paying attention to these three stipulations would have rendered antebellum slavery a virtual nonissue.

—Paul Copan

Paul Copan is professor and Pledger Family Chair of Philosophy and Ethics at Palm Beach Atlantic University. He is author of various books, including *True for You, But Not for Me* and *When God Goes to Starbucks: A Guide to Everyday Apologetics*. Visit him at www.paulcopan.com.

CHAPTER 12

Is Hell a Divine Torture Chamber?

If you think that Jesus taught only the Golden Rule and love of one's neighbor, you should reread the New Testament. Pay particular attention to the morality that will be on display when Jesus returns to earth trailing clouds of glory.

—Sam Harris

Hell. It's one of those topics you don't bring up in polite conversation. Yet, according to a 2004 Gallup poll, 70 percent of Americans believe in hell.[1] What exactly they believe about hell is not spelled out, but you can be sure that lots of colorful ideas are out there. Unfortunately many of them originate from urban legends, spittle-spewing "fire and brimstone" preachers, and B-grade horror films (or some unfortunate combination of the three).

New Atheists like Christopher Hitchens and Richard Dawkins have ideas about hell too. Hitchens claims that "not until the advent of the Prince of Peace do we hear of the ghastly idea of further punishing and torturing the dead.... Nothing proves the man-made character of religion as obviously as the sick mind that designed hell."[2] He further describes how the doctrine of hell is used to frighten children with "pornographic depictions of eternal torture."[3] Dawkins concludes, "The extreme horribleness of hell, as portrayed by priests and nuns, is inflated to compensate for its implausibility. If hell were plausible, it would only have to be moderately unpleasant in order to deter. Given that it is so unlikely to be true, it has to be advertised as very very scary indeed."[4] Are Dawkins and Hitchens correct?

Talk of hell makes people uncomfortable. This is partly because some have abused the Bible's teaching on hell by using it to manipulate and scare people into "getting saved" (this seems to be a chief complaint of Hitchens and Dawkins). Also, people don't like to think about the fact that each one of us will die someday, and if God really does exist, then so does the possibility of judgment. When approaching an emotionally charged issue like hell, we need to think clearly about it because only then can we arrive at the truth of the matter, and knowledge of the truth allows us to successfully navigate life.

If you are reading this book, then you have enough years under your belt to know that how you feel about reality does not make you capable of changing it. Reality is painfully indifferent to our feelings. So, if someone's initial aversion to the existence of hell can be reduced to "I don't like hell" and "it makes me uncomfortable and sad," then we agree. We don't like the idea of hell either and honestly it does make us uncomfortable and sad. But it doesn't follow from this sentiment that hell, properly understood from a biblical perspective, is false, inhumane, unjust, outdated, incoherent, or implausible. Nor does the grievous fact that people have distorted this doctrine to manipulate others demonstrate that hell doesn't exist.

In what follows, we invite you to consider a Christian understanding of hell that takes both the Bible and our deepest questions seriously. We also want to point out that our aim is primarily a defense of the Christian view of hell. It is not a positive case for why someone ought to pursue the joy of eternal life with God. So, whether you are new to Christianity or have read the Bible for years, we want to be crystal clear that the point of Christianity is not to avoid hell, but to enjoy the presence of God now and forevermore.*

---

* "Now this is eternal life: that they may know you, the only true God, and Jesus Christ, whom you have sent" (John 17:3). "The concept of eternal life in the New Testament is not primarily one of living forever in heaven, but of having a new

THE MOST VIRTUOUS MAN WHO EVER LIVED TAUGHT THE REALITY OF HELL

Do you know who talked more about hell than anyone else in the Bible? It was the same individual many regard as the most virtuous person who ever lived ... *Jesus*. The same man who taught people to do unto others as they would like to have done to themselves and who so courageously embodied selfless love while calling others to do the same did not balk or stutter when it came to the topic of hell. He saw no contradiction between the offer of love and forgiveness on the one hand and the reality of hell as a place of eternal punishment on the other. Whatever your ultimate verdict on Jesus as the Son of God, the fact that he practiced what he preached is beyond reasonable doubt, giving him substantial moral credibility.

We can capture Jesus' teaching on hell in three vivid images. First, he spoke of "eternal fire" and "eternal punishment."[5] On another occasion, he spoke of hell as a place of "darkness, where there will be weeping and gnashing of teeth."[6] Finally, he talked of the destruction of the soul.[7] Considering the limited time that Jesus had to get his message out (i.e., only three years of public ministry), the fact that he frequently taught on the reality of hell should cause the modern reader to take notice. He obviously thought hell was too important to leave unaddressed.*

IS HELL A FIERY TORTURE CHAMBER?

Is hell a fiery torture chamber? Will people be endlessly burning alive? We'll return to the issue of divine torture below,

---

kind of life now. This new kind of life is so different that those without it can be called dead, truly. This is a life of human flourishing; a life lived the way we were made to function; a life of virtue; character, and well-being lived like and for the Lord Jesus" (J. P. Moreland and Klaus Issler, *The Lost Virtue of Happiness: Discovering the Disciplines of the Good Life* [Colorado Springs, CO: NavPress, 2006], 29).

* The Bible is clear on this point: hell is real, it is eternal, and it is permanent. For a thorough investigation of the biblical issues, see Christopher W. Morgan and Robert A. Peterson, eds., *Hell Under Fire: Modern Scholarship Reinvents Eternal Punishment* (Grand Rapids: Zondervan, 2004).

but for now let's talk about the fire. In order to do this, we need to remember a fundamental principle of communication: *every medium of communication has rules and must be understood within the context of those rules if the message is going to be accurately interpreted.* We don't read the sports page and conclude that the Tennessee Titans *actually* killed the Dallas Cowboys—they just scored a lot more points. Nor when someone says, "You're driving me crazy!" do we infer that the person is *actually* having a mental breakdown at that very moment. Because we are familiar with the ways people communicate in our culture, we understand these to be examples of figurative language or figures of speech.

Unfortunately, the New Atheists don't bring this same level of cultural understanding to the Bible and seem to forget that their interpretations should be governed by the normal rules of literature. To illustrate this, let's take one of Jesus' favorite ways of communicating to his first-century Jewish audience—*hyperbole*, or exaggeration. Hyperbole is effective because it jolts people into paying attention and grasping the big idea. If you read Jesus' statement, "If anyone comes to me and does not hate his father and mother, his wife and children, his brothers and sisters ... he cannot be my disciple"[8] in a woodenly literal manner, you are really going to miss his point. Jesus didn't want us to hate anyone. His followers were to love their parents and even take the more radical step of loving their enemies. His point here was that a person's most important relationship in life was to be with God; it was a matter of priority.

You may wonder why we are making you have flashbacks of your college English class. Our point is simply this: we can take the Bible seriously without having to read it in an overly rigid or hyperliteral way and still be faithful to the text. You may disagree with the teaching of the Bible at the end of the day (you are certainly free to do so), but intellectual honesty and the principle of charity compel us to play by the rules of language. For whatever else the Bible may be, it is *at least* great literature.

So what about the fire? George Ladd is representative of

contemporary New Testament scholarship when he concludes that images like "fire" and "darkness" are "metaphors used to represent the indescribable."[9] It is important to see that this is not a cop out, but that it flows from the normal use of language.*

It would be tempting, then, to think that hell may not be that bad after all since actual fire isn't there, but that would be a mistake because the reality is far worse than the symbol. Fire speaks to the eternal, spiritual decomposition of a person.[10] So, if heaven is where people become fully human, then hell is the ultimate disintegration of what it means to be human.

The darkness refers to the complete absence of relationship in hell. Because we have been so bombarded with images of flames and devils with pitchforks, we fail to see that the essence of hell is relational.[11] The apostle Paul, who was well tutored in the Hebrew Scriptures and a careful student of Jesus' teachings, taught that hell is a place where people "pay the penalty of eternal destruction, *away from the presence of the Lord* and from the glory of His power."[12] The source of anguish is the awareness that floods in from the absence of this fundamental relationship.

Tim Keller observes that thinking of hell in relational terms is foreign to most people:

> Modern people inevitably think hell works like this: God gives us time, but if we haven't made the right choices by the end of our lives, he casts our souls into hell for all eternity. As the poor souls fall through space, they cry out for mercy, but God says "Too late! You had your chance! Now you will suffer!" This caricature misunderstands the very nature of evil. The Biblical picture is that sin separates us from the presence of God, which is the source of all joy and

---

* "The images of darkness and fire appear contradictory, but they should be regarded as symbols pointing to a reality more horrific than either symbol can convey by itself. In fact, biblical images of hell leave many details to the imagination, perhaps because no picture is capable of doing justice to the reality." *Dictionary of Biblical Imagery*, s.v. "hell," ed. Leland Ryken, James C. Wilhoit, and Tremper Longman III (Downers Grove, IL: InterVarsity Press, 1998), 377.

indeed of all love, wisdom, or good things of any sort. Since we were originally created for God's immediate presence, only before his face will we thrive, flourish, and achieve our highest potential.... To lose his presence totally, that would be hell—the loss of our capability for giving or receiving love or joy.[13]

Getting past the caricatures helps us put hell into a context that begins to make sense to us. But more can be said because Jesus taught on hell not just to *inform*, but also to *deter* his audience from a certain way of life.

EVERYONE IS BECOMING SOMETHING

As the famous quote goes, "Sow a thought and you reap an action; sow an act and you reap a habit; sow a habit and you reap a character; sow a character and you reap a destiny." That has never been truer than when applied to the topic of hell. C. S. Lewis vividly paints a picture of this progression:

Hell begins with a grumbling mood, always complaining, always blaming others ... but you are still distinct from it. You may even criticize it in yourself and wish you could stop it. But there may come a day when you can no longer. Then there will be no you left to criticize the mood or even to enjoy it, but just the grumble itself, going on forever like a machine. It is not a question of God "sending us" to Hell. In each of us there is something growing, which will be Hell unless it is nipped in the bud.[14]

The simple fact of the matter is that everyone is becoming something. We are either becoming a lover of self or a lover of God. We make our choices and then our choices make us.

Earlier we spoke of what the metaphorical images of eternal fire, darkness, and destruction point to—*decomposition* and *disintegration*. But that can still seem abstract to us. Again Keller is instructive:

Even in this life we can see the kind of soul disintegration that self-centeredness creates. We know how selfishness and self-absorption leads to piercing bitterness, nauseating envy, paralyzing anxiety, paranoid thoughts, and the mental denials and distortions that accompany them. Now ask the question: "What if when we die we don't end, but spiritually our life extends on into eternity?" Hell, then, is the trajectory of a soul, living a self-absorbed, self-centered life, going on and on forever.[15]

But if God sees where this train is headed, couldn't he stop us? Put differently, couldn't God block the natural consequences of our actions so that we couldn't eventually end up in hell? He could, but only if he removed meaningful freedom and consequently human dignity. The purpose of creation was relationship with our Creator. And the possibility of relationship requires the choice to love or not to love.

We now have the resources to help us make sense of another perplexing question: *Who in their right mind would knowingly choose hell?* The sobering reality is that people are asking for hell every day—though they call it distance from God. They want to be left alone and to live life on their own terms. And in this cry for autonomy, we hear the echoes of Eden reverberating all around us.[16]

C. S. Lewis summarizes the human condition: "There are only two kinds of people in the end: Those who say to God, 'Thy will be done' and those to whom God says, in the end, '*Thy will be done.*' All that are in hell, choose it."[17] People often say that hell isn't fair, but honestly, what could be fairer than giving people the outcome they choose?

ANSWERING SPECIFIC OBJECTIONS

Did God Create Hell?
Everything that God originally created was good—the way it was supposed to be. But when God created people with the

ability to choose, he also created the possibility of evil and by extension the possibility of hell. As philosopher J. P. Moreland puts it, hell was God's "fallback" position. He explains, "When people founded the United States, they didn't start out by creating jails. They would have much rather had a society without jails. But they were forced to create them because people would not cooperate. The same is true for hell."[18] Hell is the logical outworking of God's decision to create humans in his image with freedom.*

Does God Torture "Dead People" in Hell?

Hitchens seems to have a picture of God as a divine sadist.[19] However, as we have already seen, people won't be roasting over open flames in hell. But does God actively inflict pain on those in hell for eternity? No place in the Bible indicates that he does. In fact, the image of God as a divine torturer is utterly inconsistent with the clear teaching of Scripture: "Do I take any pleasure in the death of the wicked? declares the Sovereign LORD. Rather, am I not pleased when they turn from their ways and live? . . . I take no pleasure in the death of anyone."[20]

God no more inflicts torture on people in hell than a judge ruling on a case actively inflicts torture on his prisoners. A judge sentences criminals to life in prison for *what they choose to do*. A criminal misuses the freedom that comes with being a member of society, so the just punishment is the removal of that person from society. In the same way, those who find themselves in hell have actively sought to be away from the presence of God. And God ultimately gives them their wish. They are as Lewis said, "successful rebels to the end."[21]

It is accurate to say that God created the space for hell and that God sustains human existence because everything is contingent upon God. But the anguish people experience in hell

---

* Since this chapter deals primarily with the question of humans and hell, we chose not to introduce another theological layer to this discussion which includes that hell is also spoken of as a place prepared for Satan and his angels (Matt. 25:41). In some sense, they had freedom that they abused, for which they were and will be judged.

is completely of their own design; flows out of their own characters, actions, and regrets; and is proportional to their choices given the information they had in life.[22] The punishment of spiritual death is people's experience of their self-centered trajectory extended into eternity (i.e., "the wages of [their] sin"[23]). But it needs to be emphasized that God is not punishing people while in hell because his presence has been finally and fully withdrawn. Hell is defined by what is not there and can never be again.

Does God Send Children to Hell?

Dawkins and Hitchens implicitly raise the issue of whether children are in hell. While no Bible verses explicitly say "there are no children in hell," at least two compelling theological reasons point to no children in hell. First, there is biblical precedent for believing in an "age of accountability" in which children who die go directly to God's presence. Isaiah 7:16 mentions a period before a child is morally accountable to God, before the child "knows enough to reject the wrong and choose the right."

Second, we get a glimpse into God's heart for children by seeing what Jesus says of them: "'Let the little children come to me, and do not hinder them, for the kingdom of God belongs to such as these. I tell you the truth, anyone who will not receive the kingdom of God like a little child will never enter it.' And he took the children in his arms, put his hands on them and blessed them." On another occasion Jesus says, "It is not the will of your Father who is in heaven that one of these little ones perish."[24] So from a Christian perspective, we have good reason to affirm that no children will be in hell.[25] Ultimately, we trust in the revealed character of God: "Will not the Judge of all the earth do right?"[26]

If God Is Loving, Then Why Can't He Just Forgive Everyone?

If God is all-loving and all-powerful, then why can't he just forgive everyone so there wouldn't have to be a hell at all? This question gets to the heart of one of the most common objections to the idea of hell. The answer lies in what it means for God to be perfectly good. In *The Problem of Pain*, C. S. Lewis addresses this objection by observing the important distinction between condoning evil and true forgiveness: "To condone an evil is simply to ignore it, to treat it as if it were good. But forgiveness needs to be accepted as well as offered if it is to be complete: a man who admits no guilt can accept no forgiveness."[27] The goodness of God would be violated if he just looked the other way. Theologian J. I. Packer helps us see this:

> Would a God who did not care about the difference between right and wrong be a good and admirable being? Would a God who put no distinction between the beasts of history, the Hitlers and Stalins (if we dare use names), and his own saints, be morally praiseworthy and perfect? Moral indifference would be imperfection in God, not a perfection. But not to judge the world would be to show moral indifference. The final proof that God is a perfect moral being, not indifferent to questions of right and wrong, is the fact that he has committed himself to judge the world.[28]

Since all of us expect this level of moral integrity and consistency from human judges, shouldn't we at least expect the same from God?

Closely related is the issue of how to understand God's wrath as described in the Bible. How can wrath be consistent with love? And why is God *so* angry at sin? Many conceive of God as a kindly old grandfather with a gray beard who is largely passive. Ironically, people have no trouble imagining other famous elderly graybeards—like Gandalf the Grey and Albus Dumbledore—having a wrathful response to evil and particularly to the violation of the people they love. But if love and wrath can seem to coexist in fictional characters like Gandalf and Dumbledore without contradiction, then how much more so for the greatest of all possible beings?

Let's make it a bit more personal. Have you ever seen someone you loved—friend, child, spouse—taken advantage of or harmed? What was your response? If we are functioning properly as humans, then when we come face-to-face with situations of corruption, abuse, or neglect, our anger is justified and our desire for justice is good. In the same way, "God's wrath is not a cranky explosion, but his settled opposition to the cancer of sin which is eating out the insides of the human race he loves with his whole being."[29]

In contrast to Hitchens's conception of a capricious and sadistic God, if you carefully examine the narrative of Scripture in context and grant that humans have been given significant freedom with which to do good or evil, then God's wrath is consistent with his other attributes of love and justice.*

IT DOESN'T HAVE TO BE THIS WAY

Any discussion of hell from a Christian perspective would be incomplete and inadequate without acknowledging that Jesus experienced hell on earth. It was not a theoretical exercise that he pontificated on from an ivory tower; his life's mission was on a collision course with it. And when we hear of Jesus crying out, "My God, my God, why have you forsaken me?"[30] while being crucified, we suddenly realize that what he endured on that cross was the awful pain of separation from God the Father. The physical agony was excruciating, but it was nothing compared to the torment he felt from being out of the presence of God. This self-sacrificial act deepens our understanding of God's love for humanity and the just expression of wrath poured out on Jesus.†

---

* *Why does hell have to last forever?* Biblical teaching does not allow for the two responses of annihilationism and universalism, which both run into conceptual difficulties. So if hell is forever (as Jesus taught), then why? How can someone sinning in a finite lifetime earn an eternity in hell? The punishment doesn't seem to fit the crime. Two reasonable explanations have been offered. First, people continue to sin in hell. Their rebellion has not ceased; they still don't want God and thus incur further punishment. Or second, their rebellion against an infinite God warrants an eternal debt to be paid. For more, see Michael J. Murray, "Heaven and Hell," in *Reason for the Hope Within*, ed. Michael J. Murray (Grand Rapids: Eerdmans, 1999), 315–17.

† *Is it just for God to punish an innocent person?* James Taylor has a helpful comment on this: "Since Jesus is God the Son, he is not merely an innocent human being who was sacrificed in place of the guilty. He is the one wronged by human

The cross stands as a constant reminder that hellish existence is not the only option for people; it doesn't have to be this way. We can turn around; we can change our mind. Jesus' word for this was repentance. The gospel is a universal declaration that hell is not God's desire for anyone.*

Lewis once admitted that, "I would pay any price to be able to say truthfully 'All will be saved.' But my reason retorts 'Without their will, or with it?'"[31] No matter what your circumstances may be, you always have a choice. No one is ever "too far gone." Not Richard Dawkins, not Christopher Hitchens, and not any of us.

Jesus always taught for a response, and the topic of hell was no exception. His intention was clear, "I tell you the truth, whoever hears my word and believes him who sent me has eternal life and will not be condemned; he has crossed over from death to life."[32]

FOR FURTHER ENGAGEMENT

Lewis, C. S. *The Great Divorce*. San Francisco: HarperSanFrancisco, 2001.

Murray, Michael J. "Heaven and Hell." In *Reason for the Hope Within*, edited by Michael J. Murray, 287–317. Grand Rapids: Eerdmans, 1999.

---

sinners. As such, it is his prerogative to choose mercifully to endure the penalty owed to him by those who wronged him. Moreover, as a human being who lived a life of complete obedience to the Father, Jesus is the perfect one to represent the entire human race in paying the penalty of sin. Therefore, it is both that justice was served (the penalty was paid by someone who had the right to pay it) and that the sacrifice was effective (since Jesus paid the penalty, those who trust in Christ are saved from having to pay it themselves)." *Introducing Apologetics: Cultivating Christian Commitment* (Grand Rapids: Baker, 2006), 231.

* "This is good, and pleases God our Savior, who wants all men to be saved and to come to a knowledge of the truth" (1 Tim. 2:3–4). Also, "The Lord is not slow in keeping his promise, as some understand slowness. He is patient with you, not wanting anyone to perish, but everyone to come to repentance" (2 Peter 3:9).

WHY HELL IS LOVING AND NECESSARY

I have often doubted the existence of hell. The concept of eternal punishment bothers me. But upon reflection, hell, like many other Christian doctrines, seems not only fair, but also necessary. How so? Let me ask you a couple questions: Have you ever been abused, exploited, or insulted? Have you ever been mistreated, lied to, or victimized in any way?

We all have to some degree. It feels horrible enough, but how much worse do you feel when the culprits get away with it—when the guilty escape justice? I don't know about you, but that makes my blood boil. I want justice! In fact, I demand it.

If there is no afterlife, then there is no ultimate justice. People who committed some of the most horrific acts in history go to their grave without ever getting punished for their deeds. After murdering at least six million people, Hitler died in the comforting arms of his mistress and experienced nothing else. After murdering more than twice that many, Stalin died in bed after shaking his fist one last time at God. And millions of unknown murderers, rapists, and child abusers throughout history never got their just deserts during their lives on earth.

If there is a God—and there is much convincing evidence that there is—then hell is necessary for people like this. But what about your average nonbelievers? Why hell for them?

I've debated atheist Christopher Hitchens a couple of times. I can tell you that he isn't a Hitler or Stalin. He's a sinner just like you and me. But Hitchens admits that he doesn't want to go to heaven, even if it exists. Why not? Because heaven would be "hell" to him. He doesn't want to be in God's presence here on Earth, so why would he want to be with God in eternity? He wants to be separated from God, and separation from God is ultimately what hell is.

God gives us the free will to reject him and his offer of forgiveness. Free will means even God can't force us to love him. Love, by definition, must be freely given; it cannot be coerced. So God doesn't send people to hell—people send themselves there. (A loving God certainly will not force people into *heaven* against their will.) He respects our choices and separates himself forever from those who don't want him.

But why forever? First, it wouldn't be right of God to annihilate unbelievers. Hitchens is made in the image of God just like everyone else. God cannot annihilate his own image. That would be an attack on himself. So he quarantines those who reject him. Second, a crime can take only seconds to commit, but the punishment is typically much longer (especially a crime against an eternal being). Third, it may be that those in hell go on sinning in the next life, thereby continuing their rebellion against an eternal God. Finally, since God is perfectly just, everyone will receive the perfect degree of punishment in hell or reward in heaven.

So despite my doubts, since God is just and loving, hell is necessary. In fact, hell is the main reason Christ came (see Mark 10:45). If there is no hell, what is he saving us from? If there is no hell, an innocent Christ died a brutal death for nothing. Guess I ought to start doubting my doubts and let everyone know about what Christ has done! How about you?

—Frank Turek

Frank Turek is founder and president of CrossExamined.org and coauthor of *I Don't Have Enough Faith to Be an Atheist*. He presents evidence for Christianity on college campuses and hosts a weekly TV and radio program.

CHAPTER 13

Is God a Genocidal Bully?

What makes my jaw drop is that people today should base their lives on such an appalling role model as Yahweh—and even worse, that they should bossily try to force the same evil monster (whether fact or fiction) on the rest of us.

—Richard Dawkins

To read the New Atheists' treatment of the Bible and its moral vision, one would think that obedience to Jesus means killing your neighbors rather than loving them. As we noted in chapter 11, the goal of the New Atheists is decidedly not understanding Christianity, but stockpiling ammunition to employ against it. But the fact remains that the Bible records many events that are confusing—especially in the Old Testament—and that honestly make the modern reader uncomfortable to say the least. Perhaps the most shocking example is the alleged genocide perpetrated against the Canaanites:

> In the cities of the nations the LORD your God is giving
> you as an inheritance, do not leave alive anything that
> breathes. Completely destroy them—the Hittites, Amo-
> rites, Canaanites, Perizzites, Hivites and Jebusites—as
> the LORD your God has commanded you. Otherwise, they
> will teach you to follow all the detestable things they do
> in worshiping their gods, and you will sin against the
> LORD your God.[1] Deut 20:16-18

How could God command such a thing? Were the Israelites morally superior? Is God arbitrarily and violently playing favorites? Is he some sort of cosmic bully?

The language of genocide and ethnic cleansing are emotionally charged and are employed with rhetorical flourish by the New Atheists. But these words are not accurate descriptions of what really happened in what scholars refer to as the "conquest narratives." While we are not going to try to make these events seem nice or sanitized (there is nothing nice or sanitized about war of any kind—even if justified or necessary[2]), we do want to set the discussion within a biblical framework and the cultural context of the ancient Near East.

It would be impossible to say everything that could be said on the controversial subject of God and the question of genocide in one chapter.[3] Indeed, experts in ancient Near Eastern culture and linguistics who are committed to the authority and reliability of the Bible have legitimate differences of opinion concerning how best to interpret these passages. After studying the relevant texts in light of the broader biblical narrative, we offer some observations, clarifications, and principles that have helped us better understand (again, not "make nice") the question of God and the Canaanites.[4]

THINGS ARE NOT THE WAY THEY OUGHT TO BE

It is sad, but unfortunately not surprising that the history of the world is riddled with violence. The simple fact that it took until the Geneva Convention in 1949 (after World War II) to regulate humane treatment in war only serves to reinforce one of the main undercurrents of this book—despite all of human progress, the heart is in desperate need of transformation.

War was not God's idea; he didn't invent it. Rather, God's ideal in creation can best be expressed in the Hebrew word *shalom*. Cornelius Plantinga beautifully captures the word's full meaning:

The webbing together of God, humans, and all creation in justice, fulfillment, and delight is what the Hebrew prophets call *shalom*. We call it peace, but it means far more than mere peace of mind between enemies. In the Bible, shalom means *universal flourishing, wholeness, and delight*—a rich state of affairs in which natural needs are satisfied and natural gifts fruitfully employed, a state of affairs that inspires joyful wonder as its Creator and Savior opens doors and welcomes the creatures in whom he delights. Shalom, in other words, is the way things ought to be.[5]

But Plantinga goes further to help us understand God's justice and wrath in response to the vandalizing of shalom:

> God is, after all, not arbitrarily offended. God hates sin not just because it violates his law but, more substantively, because it violates shalom, because it breaks the peace, because it interferes with the way things are supposed to be.... We may safely describe evil as any spoiling of shalom, whether physically (e.g., by disease), morally, spiritually, or otherwise.[6]

Any discussion of events regarding war, injustice, or humanity's evil intentions and actions must take this backdrop seriously.

The New Atheists consider the question of God and genocide an *internal* problem for Christianity. (We have already discussed good, independent, *external* evidence for belief in God in part 1.) As such, Christians are justified in incorporating the relevant biblical resources in response. We are also right to point out that the New Atheists' condemnation of God's actions and commands makes use of an objective moral standard they have been unable to adequately justify, an idea we will explore in chapter 15.

All historians agree that the ancient Near Eastern world was exceedingly violent. It was a kill-or-be-killed world. In the midst of this violent culture, Israel stood out in that it had general guidelines for warfare: they were to offer terms of peace to distant cities before attack (i.e., not attack them without warning), as well as care for any women and children that had not fled.* The context and guidelines are worth keeping in mind as we move forward.

ISRAEL WAS A THEOCRACY AND YAHWEH SANCTIONED PARTICULAR WARS

The most accurate way to describe what occurs in the conquest narratives is "Yahweh wars." The nation of Israel, during this time of its history, had no human king. Yahweh was "commander and chief," which makes Israel a theocracy (the Christian church today is not[7]). Thus, enemies of Israel were enemies of Yahweh in a unique sense during this period.

The technical term for this particular type of warfare, practiced by other ancient Near Eastern cultures as well, is *hērem* or "ban." Wars under *hērem* conditions were dedicated to the gods. All the spoils or plunder from these wars belonged to God and the nation was not to profit from it.

---

* See Deuteronomy 20:10–15. Old Testament scholar Eugene Merrill offers some important insight here: "Military policy is the subject of vv. 10–15, specifically that pertaining to war against 'distant' cities. In the context this refers to any places outside the parameters of the land the Lord had promised to Israel as an inheritance (cf. v. 16). These peoples were not subject to *hērem* [see above], but many of them would constitute a threat to Israel from time to time and so had to be preemptively or defensively attacked; in addition, all were hostile to the purposes of God and so were subject to his punitive wrath. Nevertheless, the Lord's policy toward them was merciful and redemptive. If they surrendered to him and submitted to his sovereignty, they could be spared. Such leniency was impossible toward the hopelessly unrepentant Canaanites." *Deuteronomy*, The New American Commentary (Nashville: Broadman & Holman, 1994), 285.

A disturbing reality of the conquest is that some children who were in the wrong place at the wrong time became collateral damage because of the wickedness of their parents. As we will see with the possibility of exaggerated language of ancient Near Eastern warfare (pp. 179–81), they were either not targeted specifically for destruction or would have likely fled before Israelite soldiers arrived (e.g., Jer. 4:29 tells us, "At the sound of the horseman and bowman every city flees; they go into the thickets and climb among the rocks; every city is forsaken, and no man dwells in them" NASB). There are differing interpretations as to whether only combatants in the fortified cities were targeted by the "ban" or if that "ban" extended to noncombatants as well. Undoubtedly, some children would have died at the hands of the Israelites during the conquest, but all the children who were killed would wake up in God's presence (see our discussion of children in chapter 12).

The divinely given command to Israel of *hērem* concerning the Canaanites was unique, geographically and temporally limited, and not to be repeated. Old Testament scholar Christopher J. H. Wright is worth quoting at length here:

> The conquest was a single episode within a single generation out of all the many generations of Old Testament history. Of course it spans a longer period than that if one includes the promise and then completion. The conquest of Canaan was promised to Abraham, anticipated as the purpose of the exodus, delayed by the wilderness rebellion, accomplished under Joshua, and brought to provisional completion under David and Solomon. Even including all this, though, it was limited in the specific duration of the warfare involved. Although the process of settling and claiming the land took several generations, the actual invasion and destruction of key fortified cities took place mostly within a single generation. And it is this event, confined to one generation, which constituted the conquest.... Some ... other wars also had God's sanction—especially those where Israel was attacked by other nations and fought defensively to survive. *But by no means are all the wars in the Old Testament portrayed in the same way as the conquest of Canaan.* Some were clearly condemned as the actions of proud and greedy kings or military rivals. It is a caricature of the Old Testament to portray God as constantly on the warpath or to portray it as "typical" of the rest of the story.... So the conquest of Canaan, as a unique and limited historical event, was never meant to become a model for how all future generations were to behave toward their contemporary enemies.[8]

That last point needs to be especially reiterated: the conquest of Canaan is not analogous to Islamic jihad and was inappropriately used to justify wars like the Crusades that involved Christians.[9] We draw attention to this because the New Atheists tend to equate Islam and Christianity for rhetorical effect in their writings and public debates.[10]

GENOCIDE AND ETHNIC CLEANSING ARE INACCURATE TERMS FOR THE CONQUEST OF CANAAN

Contrary to the bombastic claims of Christopher Hitchens, the Canaanites were not "pitilessly driven out of their homes to make room for the ungrateful and mutinous children of Israel."[11] While he cites Israel's sins of ingratitude and mutiny, he conveniently leaves out the long list of Canaanite depravity—idolatry, incest, temple prostitution, adultery, child molestation and sacrifice, homosexuality, and bestiality.[12] Each of these has been extensively documented, but let's look at the despicable practice of child sacrifice:

> Molech was a Canaanite underworld deity represented as an upright, bull-headed idol with human body in whose belly a fire was stoked and in whose arms a child was placed that would be burnt to death. It was not just unwanted children who were sacrificed. Plutarch reports that during the Phoenician (Canaanite) sacrifices, "the whole area before the statue was filled with a loud noise of flutes and drums so that the cries and wailing should not reach the ears of the people."[13]

We could multiply descriptions of their depravity, but we think this sufficient to make the point. They were not an innocent group of people.

The conquest of the land of Canaan "is repeatedly portrayed as God acting in judgment on a wicked and degraded society and culture—as God would do again and again in Old Testament history, *including against Israel itself.*"[14] God had given the Canaanites four hundred years to change their ways, but their wickedness finally reached the tipping point for God to judge.*

---

* "God said to Abram, 'Know for certain that your descendants will be strangers in a land that is not theirs, where they will be enslaved and oppressed four hundred years. But I will also judge the nation whom they will serve, and afterward

In his providence, God used this occasion of judgment to secure the land promised to Abraham, Isaac, and Jacob. In the biblical narrative, the actions of the Israelites are not cast as imperialistic oppression, but rather as God's human means of punishment.[15] God as the creator of life has the right to take life, and during this unique occasion of judgment, that prerogative was *temporarily* extended to the people of Israel since Yahweh was their king (e.g., a theocracy).

Moreover, God using Israel had nothing to do with their moral superiority. Deuteronomy 9:5 says, "It is not because of your righteousness or your integrity that you are going in to take possession of their land; but on account of the wickedness of these nations, the LORD your God will drive them out before you, to accomplish what he swore to your fathers, to Abraham, Isaac and Jacob." What is often overlooked in the discussion of the Canaanites is the fact that God later used the nations of Assyria and Babylon to judge Israel for their wickedness and idolatry with even more severity than what occurred in the conquest.[16] So God is not arbitrary and Israel is not without sin.

While *hērem* was carried out by Israel against a specific people—the Canaanites—it was *not* motivated by racial superiority or hatred. Therefore the language of ethnic cleansing and genocide is inaccurate. Idolatry, not ethnicity, is the issue here. In fact, Rahab, the first Canaanite we meet in the conquest narrative, converts to faith in Yahweh and is spared.[17] Moreover the New Testament views Rahab as an example of courageous faith; and, even more surprising, she ends up in the lineage of Jesus Christ.[18] While the Israelites at the time were unaware of this future development, any lingering doubts that the Bible teaches the conquest of Canaan was motivated by racial impurity are removed by Rahab's inclusion in the genealogy of the Messiah (for, if that were the concern, a Canaanite would have contaminated Jesus' pure bloodline).

---

they will come out with many possessions. As for you, you shall go to your fathers in peace; you will be buried at a good old age. Then in the fourth generation they will return here, for the iniquity of the Amorite [i.e., Canaanites] is not yet complete'" (Gen. 15:13–16 NASB).

WE MUST ALLOW FOR THE POSSIBILITY OF RHETORICAL GENERALIZATION IN ANCIENT NEAR EASTERN "WAR LANGUAGE"

A brief word on taking the Bible literally. Richard Dawkins, at the end of one of his frequent rants against the Bible, asks in frustration, "By what criterion do you *decide* which passages are symbolic, which literal?"[19] This is actually a good question. Contrary to what some may think, taking the Bible literally is not code for reading a passage in the most ignorant way possible. Scholars who propose nuanced and sophisticated interpretations of biblical passages are not automatically guilty of special pleading.* Certainly, interpreting an ancient document comes with its share of challenges when you take into consideration distance in time, culture, and language. But we can discover the meaning of ancient texts if we follow reliable and responsible methods.

So, when Jesus says, "I am the gate,"[20] we don't understand him to be composed of oak or iron. Taking this passage literally requires interpreting it metaphorically. As we have mentioned elsewhere in this book, the goal is to take the Bible *seriously*. Readers need to approach passages and events in the context in which they were written according to the type of literature the biblical authors were writing. And this means making the standard of accuracy what the original readers or hearers would have understood, not our modern conceptions of how the biblical writers should or shouldn't have communicated. In other words, we need to play by the rules when we read the Bible, allowing for normal literary features such as hyperbole, estimation, exaggeration, and metaphor.[21]

What are we to make of the command in Deuteronomy 7:1–2 and 20:16 to destroy everything that breathes? First, we need to remember that other ancient Near Eastern nations practiced

---

* Here is a helpful definition of biblical inerrancy: "The Bible (in its original writings) properly interpreted in light of which culture and communication means had developed by the time of its composition will be completely true (and therefore not false) in all that it affirms, to the degree of precision intended by the author, in all matters relating to God and His creation." David S. Dockery, *Christian Scripture: An Evangelical Perspective on Inspiration, Authority, and Interpretation* (Nashville: Broadman & Holman, 1995), 64.

hērem. "Texts from other nations at the time show that such total destruction in war was practiced, or at any rate proudly claimed, elsewhere. But we must also recognize that the language of warfare had a conventional rhetoric that liked to make absolute and universal claims about total victory and completely wiping out the enemy... which often exceeded reality on the ground."[22]

Accordingly, this ancient Near Eastern rhetorical generalization allows for exaggerated language and "enables us to allow for the fact that descriptions of destruction of 'everything that lives and breathes' were not intended literally."[23] Observe this passage:

> When the Lord your God has delivered them over to you and you have defeated them, then you must destroy them totally. Make no treaty with them, and show them no mercy. Do not intermarry with them. Do not give your daughters to their sons or take their daughters for your sons, for they will turn your sons away from following me to serve other gods, and the Lord's anger will burn against you and will quickly destroy you. This is what you are to do to them: Break down their altars, smash their sacred stones, cut down their Asherah poles and burn their idols in the fire.[24]

Notice the tension. This passage speaks of total destruction and showing no mercy, but then proceeds to instruct the Israelites regarding treaties and intermarriage. But if no Canaanites are going to be around anymore, then why even bother including this? Or think of Rahab the Canaanite. If strict obedience meant showing no mercy to *anyone* or *anything*, then why is the first Canaanite person we encounter allowed to convert to Yahweh,[25] spared from destruction, and shown mercy? It is no accident that her story shows up at the beginning of the conquest narrative in Joshua.

Or notice this summary passage in Joshua 10:

> Thus Joshua struck *all* the land, the hill country and the Negev and the lowland and the slopes and *all* their kings. He left no survivor, but he utterly destroyed *all* who breathed,

just as the LORD, the God of Israel, had commanded. Joshua struck them from Kadesh-barnea even as far as Gaza, and *all* the country of Goshen even as far as Gibeon. Joshua captured *all* these kings and their lands at one time, because the LORD, the God of Israel, fought for Israel.[26]

As we saw above, the "all" in this passage can't mean everyone because we know at least Rahab and her family survived. Wright observes, "the key military centres—the small fortified cities of the petty Canaanite kingdoms—were wiped out. But clearly not *all* the people, or anything like *all* the people, had in actual fact been destroyed by Joshua."[27]

The conquest narratives are filled with tensions like this.[28] This rhetorical generalization is even applied to the people of Israel if they forsook Yahweh.[29] Furthermore, Old Testament scholar Gordon Wenham points out that even in the context of legitimate judgment for the Canaanites' wickedness, "it is evident that destruction of Canaanite religion is much more important than destroying the people."[30] This observation helps us transition to putting the issue of the Canaanites in its ultimate biblical context.

GOD'S PROMISE OF BLESSING FOR ALL THE NATIONS

A careful reading of the Old Testament will reveal that Israel was chosen by God to be a blessing to *all* nations.[31] We see Paul in the New Testament reiterate this theme as well: "The Scripture foresaw that God would justify the Gentiles [all other nations] by faith, and announced the gospel in advance to Abraham: 'All nations will be blessed through you.'"[32] According to Revelation 5:9, the population of the new heavens and new earth will include people from every tribe, language, people, and nation.

Rebellion, depravity, and the violation of shalom had become so rampant among all the nations of the earth that God decided to work his plan of redemption through one nation.[33] But it was never because Israel was "better" than the other ancient Near Eastern people; it was simply God's sovereign choice in love.[34] So much more could be said about God's redemptive plan for the nations,[35] but we want to highlight one final flicker of redemption even in this dark story of God's righteous judgment.

The Jebusites are one of those names we often speed past in the Bible to get to the more important stuff. But Wright makes a remarkable observation about them. The Jebusites moved from "being among the nations destined for destruction" and "came to be included within the covenant people as a clan in Judah." This offers "another little piece of evidence that the conquest was not uniformly destructive and that not only individuals but whole peoples could change sides."[36] It also further reiterates the fact that idolatry was the issue, not ethnicity.

FINAL THOUGHTS ON A DIFFICULT SUBJECT

It will not do, as some have done when approaching this topic, to make the God of the Old Testament a God of judgment and the Jesus of the New Testament a God of love. God is both loving and just.[37] Nor should passages about judgment in either testament be relegated to allegory.

We have tried to face the uncomfortable realties of this narrative head-on using a sound interpretive approach according to the language of the day and within the context of the ancient Near East. Do we wish the Canaanite conquest wasn't in the Bible? Honestly, yes. Are there things we don't understand? Yes again. But we also wish that the realities accurately described in the biblical narratives of wickedness, war, depravity, pain, death, and the darkness of the human heart didn't occur also. We live in a desperate and broken world that groans for redemption.[38] But even in this narrative of God's righteous judgment we see glimmers of God's redemption offered and accepted, and we see the promise of *ultimate* shalom.

FOR FURTHER ENGAGEMENT

Copan, Paul. *Is God a Moral Monster? Making Sense of the Old Testament God*. Grand Rapids: Baker, forthcoming.

Wright, Christopher J. H. *The God I Don't Understand: Reflections on Tough Questions of Faith*. Grand Rapids: Zondervan, 2008.

[why it matters]

THE CANAANITES: WHAT I LEARNED

Over the years, several things affected me deeply while studying the Canaanites and their destruction. The first was that they were, indeed, desperately wicked. How else do we describe a culture whose very worship involved sex with prostitutes, and whose people engaged in rampant incest, adultery, child sacrifice to Molech, homosexuality, and bestiality? Years ago when I first read that their god, Baal, had sex with his sister while she was in the form of a calf, "seventy-seven, even eighty-eight times," I was repulsed for days. For weeks I thought I wouldn't repeat it to anyone, but then I realized that if we don't tell people what actually happened, they won't understand God's true reasons for their destruction.

Second, I was struck by the seductive and corrosive nature of their sins. God warned Israel to utterly destroy the Canaanites or they would be likewise seduced. But Israel didn't destroy them and Israel was seduced. Even King Solomon was seduced and built a temple to the gods of all his foreign wives. He even built a temple for Molech!

Third, I saw the truth of God's fairness. He warned Israel that if they committed the sins of the Canaanites the land would likewise vomit them out (Lev. 18:28). True to his warning, when they committed the same sins they were all but completely destroyed by their enemies—first by Assyria in 722 B.C. and then by Babylon in 586 B.C.

Fourth, it impressed me that God hates sin because sin leads to disease, deformed children (a product of incest), broken marriages, child rape, the murder of children, perversion, and then even more perversion. If we let sin loose in our lives, then we will all plunge into sins that will destroy us and those around us. Anyone who has tried to eradicate lust from his or her life soon realizes that even a little lust isn't okay.

183

Fifth, I'm truly amazed at the Canaanization of our own culture. When I was a boy in the 1960s, the censors wouldn't let a TV program show even a woman's belly button! Now, via the Internet, hard-core pornography is only one click away from almost everyone.

Sixth, and probably worst of all, I've learned that not all Christians are terribly bothered about these sins. Not long ago a Christian student asked me why God ordered the destruction of the Canaanites. When I told her their sins, she gave me a Homer Simpson stare and waited for me to answer her question.

Seventh, I'm sobered that the Bible is unambiguous that God *always* judges those who refuse to repent of their sins. Consider Revelation 1:7: "Look, he is coming with the clouds, and every eye will see him, even those who pierced him; and all the peoples of the earth will mourn because of him. So shall it be! Amen."

Finally, I am more aware of the seriousness of my own sins and I can hardly describe the wonder I have when I consider that Jesus died for me! Truly, there but for the grace of God, go I.

—Clay Jones

Clay Jones is assistant professor of Christian Apologetics at Biola University. A popular speaker on various apologetic issues, he hosted *Contend for Truth*, a nationally syndicated, call-in talk-radio program, and is currently writing a book on the problem of evil.

CHAPTER 14

Is Christianity the Cause of Dangerous Sexual Repression?

> One could write an entire book that was devoted only to the grotesque history of religion and sex, and to the holy dread of the procreative act and its associated impulses and necessities, from the emission of semen to the effusion of menstrual blood.
>
> —Christopher Hitchens

Let us make one thing unmistakably clear from the start. *God is pro sex!* That's right, God created sex and thinks it's beautiful when enjoyed within the proper context.

This may come as a surprise to you, and we realize you may need some convincing, especially if you've been reading the New Atheists. In *God Is Not Great*, Christopher Hitchens argues that religious faith is both the result and cause of dangerous sexual repression.[1] Richard Dawkins claims prosperous democracies have higher rates of STDs, teen pregnancy, and abortion primarily because of the influence of religion.[2] And in *Letter to a Christian Nation*, Sam Harris levels a common critique against Christian sexual morality:

> You [Christians] believe that your religious concerns about sex, in all their tiresome immensity, have something to do with morality. And yet, your efforts to constrain the sexual

behavior of consenting adults—and even to discourage your own sons and daughters from having premarital sex—are almost never geared toward the relief of human suffering. In fact, relieving suffering seems to rank rather low on your list of priorities. Your principal concern appears to be that the creator of the universe will take offense at something people do while naked.[3]

Are the New Atheists correct? Have religious views of sex been a source of repression and harm? Is it absurd to think, as Harris suggests, that a Creator would even care what we do with our bodies? In other words, why is sex such a big deal? Isn't sex just a recreational activity we do for fun?

In *Smart Sex*, Dr. Jennifer Roback Morse demonstrates the absurdity of this way of thinking.[4] Consider her thought-provoking example. She looks closely at the phenomenon of date rape on campus, which can rightly be considered a crisis. According to Morse, it's a puzzle why date rape should be such a big deal. When people go on dates, they frequently find themselves participating in many activities they don't particularly want to do. Why is it a crisis, she asks, to get forced into sex, but not a crisis to get forced into eating Chinese food when you really wanted Mexican? Why aren't there "basketball game date crisis centers" for students to visit after being dragged to a basketball game they didn't want to attend?

Raising this absurd comparison between unwanted sexual activity and other kinds of activities—such as eating Chinese food and going to a basketball game—helps us see that there really is something unique about sex. The whole premise of the sexual revolution (which the New Atheists heartily embrace) is that sex is just another recreational activity. But the proliferation of date rape crisis centers deeply undermines this assumption. Morse explains:

> Either sex is a big deal, or it isn't. If it is really no big deal, then "unwanted sexual activity" shouldn't be particularly

traumatic. Colleges ought to save themselves some money, shut down the date rape crisis centers, and tell co-eds to grow up and get over it. If sex really is a big deal, then we can't very well say that sex is just another recreational activity. And every serious person knows which of these is true.[5]

Sex *is* a big deal. And we all acknowledge this, if we are being honest.

THE BIBLICAL CASE FOR SEX

We agree with the New Atheists that *some* religions have been the source of sexual repression and harm.* But we vehemently disagree that this criticism applies particularly to Christianity. In fact, we believe Christian morality provides the surest avenue to experiencing real sexual freedom and fulfillment. Since we are defending Christian sexual morality, we will use more Scripture in this chapter than in most others.

As we said earlier, the Bible portrays God as pro sex. Proverbs says, "Take pleasure in the wife of your youth. A loving doe, a graceful fawn—let her breasts always satisfy you; be lost in her love forever."[6] The phrase "wife of your youth" refers to the lifelong commitment of marriage. Another Old Testament book, Song of Solomon, also speaks of the beauty and power of sexual intimacy.[7] Sex, as God designed it, is a wonderful thing. God designed sex for three reasons: procreation, unity, and recreation.

Procreation. It should come as no surprise that sex is about making babies. Genesis 1:28 makes this clear, as God says, "Be fruitful and increase in number; fill the earth." It's worth noting that this is actually a *command* from God. We have yet to hear someone complain about this command!

Unity. One of the most powerful aspects of sex is its ability to bond people together. Genesis 2:24 says, "For this reason a man

---

* For example, Christopher Hitchens correctly notes in *God Is Not Great* that Islam has often been a cause of sexual repression in young men and mistreatment of women (see p. 24).

will leave his father and mother and be united to his wife, and they will become one flesh." Sex is not merely a spiritual act; it involves a physical and even neurochemical connection (as we will see below).

Recreation. So many people think God is a cosmic killjoy when it comes to sexuality. But they fail to realize that God is the one who created sex so enjoyable in the first place. God could easily have made sex boring and provincial—a duty we must perform, like taking out the trash or changing the oil in our car. But instead he made it one of the most exhilarating of all human experiences.

What would the world be like if everyone followed the biblical plan for sex, engaging in sexual activity for procreation, unity, *and* recreation in a committed, lifelong relationship? Would there be more suffering as Harris suggests? Or would there be less? Would we have more intact marriages, or more broken homes? Would STDs, teen pregnancies, and abortions increase or decrease? The answers are quite obvious. Following the biblical pattern would not increase harm, as Dawkins and Harris suggest, but would clearly result in fewer STDs, unwanted pregnancies, and abortions.

BOUNDARIES FOR SEX: GOOD OR BAD?

We have not been able to find a single verse in the Bible that disparages sex as sinful, unclean, or wrong. Such verses don't exist. Rather, Scripture condemns the *misuse* of sex—sexual activity expressed outside a lifelong, committed marriage between one man and one woman.

So, why does God put limits on the expression of human sexuality? From the biblical perspective, God's limits are an expression of his love.[8] In Ephesians 5:28–29, Paul says that love involves providing and caring for another, which suggests the idea of nurturing and protection. Parents put boundaries on their children to protect and provide for them. Similarly, God gives commands in the Bible to protect and provide for us. Even the negative commands in the Bible ("Thou shall not") exist for our provision and protection. Harm comes when we ignore God's design for sex—*not* when we follow it. Let's consider a specific example.

As we have seen, one of the purposes of sex is to unite two people together for life.[9] Science has recently confirmed that this bonding takes place on a neurochemical level. A key neurochemical important to healthy sex and bonding is oxytocin. The release of oxytocin generates bonding and trust with another person. In fact, sniffing oxytocin during a game involving finances caused people to be more trusting with their money.[10]

While oxytocin occurs in both genders, it is most prominent in women. A woman's body is flooded with oxytocin during labor and breast-feeding. The presence of oxytocin produces a chemical impact on the mother's brain that a woman experiences as the "motherly bond" with her child. A woman's body is also flooded with oxytocin during intimate physical touch and sexual activity, causing her to desire touch again and again with the man to whom she has bonded, generating an even stronger connection.[11] Oxytocin helps build the trust that is essential for a lasting, healthy relationship.

Few women realize that during each sexual encounter, oxytocin floods their brain and creates a partial bond with each person they have sex with. In *Hooked: New Science on How Casual Sex Is Affecting Our Children*, authors Dr. Joe McIlhaney (founder of the Medical Institute of Sexual Health) and Dr. Freda McKissic Bush explain the devastating affects of promiscuous sex:

> An individual who is sexually involved, then breaks up and then is sexually involved again, and who repeats this cycle again and again is in danger of negative emotional consequences. People who behave in this manner are acting against, almost fighting against, the way they are made to function. When connectedness and bonding form and then are quickly broken and replaced with another sexual relationship, it often causes damage to the brain's natural connecting or bonding mechanism.[12]

The scientific evidence supports the biblical view of sex: appropriate sexual boundaries before marriage provide for healthy human functioning.

Sam Harris is wrong—encouraging people to avoid sexual activity before marriage *is* about relieving human suffering. When people have had sex before marriage, they are more likely to divorce when they do marry later.[13] Promiscuous sex among young people is a leading cause of depression and suicide.[14] The loving thing to do for a young person (or really, *any* person) is to help him or her avoid the harm that comes from ignoring God's guidelines for sex.

But God's plan for sexuality is more than simply avoiding harm; it's about helping people experience the abundant life Jesus proclaimed.[15] In other words, Christianity is not fundamentally about what we have to say no to; it is defined by what we get to say yes to.

WHO'S HAVING THE BEST SEX?

The New Atheists unashamedly bash Christianity as the source of sexual repression and harm. Christians spoil all the fun because they have so many rules about sexual conduct. Surprisingly, just the opposite is true.

A number of years ago an article titled "Aha! Call It the Revenge of the Church Ladies" appeared in *USA Today* and took the perspective of the New Atheists to task.[16] The author of the study, William Mattox, compiled the results from the largest and most accurate sex surveys yet conducted. He wanted to find out who is having the most sex (quantity) and who is having the best sex (quality). In many circles, the findings could only be described as *shocking*. He concluded that Christian men and women in monogamous marriages are among the most sexually satisfied people on the face of the earth. This goes against everything proclaimed in our culture, whether in magazines, movies, TV shows, many chat rooms, or the writings of the New Atheists. Nevertheless, Mattox gave four reasons for the findings.

Reason #1: Saving Sex for Marriage Pays Considerable Dividends

Our society broadcasts the idea that sex before marriage (and outside of marriage) is the expected norm. But as this article demonstrated, people who preserve themselves sexually until marriage experience the greatest sexual satisfaction. The article put it this way: "Several studies show that women who engage in early sexual activity and those who have had multiple partners are less apt to express satisfaction with their sex lives than women who entered marriage with little or no sexual baggage."[17]

Reason #2: People Benefit from a Commitment to Marital Fidelity

The idea of being faithful to one person for life seems old-fashioned. How can I possibly be expected to remain committed to one person for life? Wouldn't this lead to boredom? Isn't variety the spice of life? These are common beliefs today. And yet, the *USA Today* article showed a powerful link between monogamous marriage and sexual satisfaction.

Why is this so? Because sexual enjoyment flourishes in the context of a committed relationship. When you are able to get to know someone with true intimacy, sex becomes far more than a mere physical activity that brings pleasure. Rather, it becomes a sacred connection of two souls on the deepest possible level. When two souls are committed together in such a union, the pleasures of sex can be indescribable.

The authors of *Hooked* concur: "But now, with the aid of modern neuroscience and a wealth of research, it is evident that humans are the healthiest and happiest when they engage in sex only with the one who is their mate for a lifetime."[18]

Reason #3: God's Design Offers Far Greater Sexual Freedom

Although it may seem counterintuitive, following God's pattern for sexuality provides the greatest sense of freedom. How so? In the committed, lifelong context of marriage, there is genuine freedom without fear of consequences. You don't have to

191

worry about a defective condom, feelings of guilt, contracting an STD, unhealthy emotional attachments, unwanted pregnancy, and many other dangers. Once again, the *USA Today* article says it best, "Part of the reason church ladies are having so much fun is that they don't have to worry about many of the fears commonly associated with sexual promiscuity, such as AIDS and other sexually transmitted diseases, pregnancy, fear of rejection, and fear of getting caught."[19]

Reason #4: People Benefit from Believing God Created Sex

This last point may come as the greatest surprise, but it's true—people appear to benefit from the belief that God created sex. Beliefs powerfully shape how we live, especially in the realm of sexuality. Think about how radically different the biblical view of sex is from the atheistic view of sex. If God does not exist, then sex exists simply as a means to pass on our genes to the next generation, to foster the "survival of the fittest." There is no transcendent, deeper meaning to sex. It's simply a part of our animal nature that we ought to enjoy to the fullest. But from the biblical perspective, God designed sex as a beautiful act that binds a lover and his beloved in a lifelong spiritual, emotional, and physical union. Sex is meant to be pleasurable, but it also symbolizes a deep union of two people who have committed themselves together for life. According to this study, believing the latter will actually benefit *you*.

The author of the study concludes his article with these piercing words: "Now these religious teachings are apt to come as a shock to those who believe God is a cosmic killjoy when it comes to sexuality."[20] The New Atheists could not be more wrong. Biblical guidelines are not the cause nor the result of sexual repression. Rather, they are the means to experience true sexual freedom.

WHY ALL THE FUSS?

Why do the New Atheists level such bitter criticisms against Christian sexual morality? What's the big deal? After all, any honest observer would recognize that attacks on the credibility of Christian morality are way out of proportion to any real threat it poses to anyone's freedom.

Answering this question involves looking more deeply at the most attractive element of the sexual revolution: the promise of guilt-free sex. According to the sexual revolution, sex can be morally neutral, offering people the prospect of sex with anyone, anywhere, anytime, in any fashion, without a shred of guilt. The only concern should be the experience of pleasure. Thus, all sexual behavior is valuable, worthy of respect, and no cause for shame.

A "live and let live" attitude is not enough for the New Atheists, however, which is clearly evidenced by their malicious attacks against Christian morality. Jennifer Roback Morse explains why Christian morality cannot be tolerated:

> If the goal is guilt-free sex, then mere legality of an activity is not and never will be sufficient. Anyone who voices moral objections has to be silenced. For that person's ideas and arguments might influence others and cause them distress about their actions. That distress might cause them to feel guilty about what they are doing. They might decide that, on balance, they don't want this anymore. They might have to reform their behavior.[21]

The assaults on Christian morality only make sense if the goal is guilt-free sex. The New Atheists wish Christians (and their sexual morality) would be silent. But this is not an option for the genuine believer. Love motivates Christians to stand up for the biblical view of sex.

Sure, Christians do not always act in love. We personally apologize for Christians who have proclaimed the truth in a harsh, vindictive, and unloving manner. They are not following Paul's advice to speak the truth in love.[22] But this doesn't nullify the truth of what they proclaim—those who follow the biblical framework experience the most fulfilling sex lives on the planet.

True freedom is found not in throwing off Christian morality, but in embracing it wholeheartedly. We conclude with the words of Dr. McIlhaney and Dr. Bush:

> Perhaps the most damaging philosophy about sex in recent years has been the attempt to separate sex from the whole person. Neuroscientific evidence has revealed this approach to be not only false but also dangerous. Popular culture would have you believe that young people should become involved in sex when they feel "ready" and that to not become involved sexually at that point in their lives will cause them to be sexually naïve and repressed ... the facts tell a different story.[23]

FOR FURTHER ENGAGEMENT

McIlhaney, Joe S., and Freda McKissic Bush. *Hooked: New Science on How Casual Sex Is Affecting Our Children*. Chicago: Northfield, 2008.

Morse, Jennifer Roback. *Smart Sex: Finding Life-Long Love in a Hook-Up World*. Dallas: Spence, 2005.

[why it matters]

THE RIGHT VIEW OF SEX

Whether you look into the Bible or recent studies, you will find abundant evidence that abstinence before marriage and fidelity within marriage is best. The Christian faith does not lead to sexual repression, but rather a full experience of what God intended for human sexuality.

Let's start with the obvious. Abstinence prevents pregnancy. Growing evidence shows that teaching abstinence actually does postpone a young person's first sexual encounter. It changes behavior and, of course, reduces the teen pregnancy rate in a community.

Abstinence prevents sexually transmitted diseases (STDs). After more than three decades, the sexual revolution has taken lots of prisoners. Before 1960, doctors were concerned about only two STDs: syphilis and gonorrhea. Today 12 million Americans are newly infected each year with more than thirty significant STDs, ranging from the relatively harmless to the fatal. Two-thirds of these new infections are in people under twenty-five years of age.

Abstinence also prevents emotional scars. Abstinence speakers relate numerous stories of young people who wish they had postponed sex until marriage. Sex is the most intimate form of bonding known to the human race, and it is a special gift to be given to one's spouse. Unfortunately too many people throw it away and are filled with feelings of regret.

One study found that sexually active girls age fourteen to seventeen have rates of depression three times higher than those who have not been sexually active. Sexually active boys are more than twice as likely to be depressed as those who are not sexually active.

Saving sex for marriage not only prevents pregnancy, STDs, and emotional scars; it also contributes to a strong marriage. Many studies have found that cohabiting unions are much less stable than unions that begin as marriages.

Additionally, fidelity within marriage leads to better sex. A University of Chicago survey of Americans between the ages of eighteen and fifty-nine found that monogamous married couples register the highest levels of sexual satisfaction. According to the survey, nearly nine in ten of all monogamous married couples report that they are "extremely" or "very" physically satisfied by their sexual relationship. The least satisfied sexually (both physically and emotionally) were those singles and married couples who had multiple partners.

Religious commitment also seems to be an important ingredient in a good marriage and a good sex life. A study of more than a hundred thousand women by *Redbook* magazine found that strongly religious women are less likely to engage in sexual behavior before marriage and are more likely to describe their current sex lives as "good" or "very good" than moderately religious or nonreligious women.

Christianity doesn't lead to sexual repression. It leads to strong marriages and the best sex.

—Kerby Anderson

Kerby Anderson is the national director for Probe Ministries (www.probe .org) and host of the radio talk show *Point of View.* He holds master's degrees from Yale University and Georgetown University, and is the author of more than a dozen books, including *Christian Ethics in Plain Language* (2005).

CHAPTER 15

Can People Be Good Without God?

Many religious people find it hard to imagine how, without religion, one can be good, or would even want to be good.

—Richard Dawkins

Sometimes Christians say that atheists cannot lead what most would consider moral lives. This is not true. Atheists do not automatically become like Ted Bundy, a murderer and rapist. The crucial question in this chapter is not "Can we be good without *belief* in God?" but "Can we be *good* without God?" The latter is the more fundamental question.

Atheists can live moral lives and discover moral facts about our world. In a Judeo-Christian worldview, this is not only consistent with proper human functioning but also anticipated in the Bible:

> Even Gentiles, who do not have God's written law, show that they know his law when they instinctively obey it, even without having heard it. They demonstrate that God's law is written in their hearts, for their own conscience and thoughts either accuse them or tell them they are doing right.[1]

Can goodness exist in the world if God does not exist? To say that an action is right or wrong is a moral judgment. To say that a moral judgment is *objectively* good or evil is to say that it is good or evil independent of what people think, believe, or agree on. (A *subjective* claim would depend on what people think, believe, or agree on.) For example, "to say that the Holocaust was objectively wrong is to say that it was wrong even though the Nazis who carried it out thought it was right, and it would have still been wrong even if the Nazis had won World War II and succeeded in brainwashing everybody who disagreed with them so that it was universally believed that the Holocaust was right."[2]

In this chapter, it is important to mention that what we are after is an ontological grounding of objective morality, not an epistemological explanation of how we know what is right and wrong. Ontology deals with ultimate reality, with the question of what is real. In the theistic view, objective moral laws are grounded in the reality of a Moral Lawgiver. So what grounds morality in a world without God?

MORALITY WITHOUT GOD

What if, as the New Atheists contend, God does not exist? On what basis can people be good without God? Objective morality would have to be grounded in naturalism because Darwinian evolution becomes the only explanation.

In *The End of Faith*, Sam Harris sets out to offer "A Science of Good and Evil." This is an interesting chapter title since Richard Dawkins writes in *A Devil's Chaplain* that "Science has no methods for deciding what is ethical. That is a matter for individuals and for society."[3] Regardless, Harris is no relativist.[4] For him, "questions of right and wrong are really questions about the happiness and suffering of sentient creatures."[5]

How he seeks to ground this statement as an objective ethic is unclear because he does not really define what he means by happiness. Does he mean the satisfaction of personal desire or a deeper account involving human flourishing? If the latter, then he has not only to explain objective morality, but also human flourishing, which implies human functioning in accordance with a designed plan or purpose. But there is no purpose in natural selection; there is no "end game." Harris offers no solid ontological or metaethical grounding of his assertion that there is right and wrong.* If the former, the "it feels good to me" mentality is fraught with problems, not the least of which is when my personal desires bump up against your personal desires. There is no standard of virtue or goodness above us to decide the question.

Does Dawkins fare any better? He at least attempts to explain altruism in terms of evolutionary thought and in reliance on humans' "selfish genes."† Dawkins, who sees genes as operating at a different level than the organism, writes, "There are circumstances ... in which genes ensure their own selfish survival by influencing organisms to behave altruistically."[6] Dawkins goes on to say,

> We now have four good Darwinian reasons for individuals to be altruistic, generous or "moral" towards each other. First, there is the special case of genetic kinship. Second, there is reciprocation: the repayment of favours given, and

---

* Harris states, "The fact that our ethical intuitions must in some way supervene upon our biology does not make ethical truths reducible to biological ones." *The End of Faith: Religion, Terror, and the Future of Reason* (New York: W. W. Norton, 2005), 226. While this is a more technical point, the reader will notice he doesn't explain how this "supervenience" works. Craig is instructive here, "If there is no God, then it is hard to see any ground for thinking that the property of moral goodness supervenes on certain natural states of such creatures. If our approach to metaethical theory is to be serious metaphysics rather than just a 'shopping list' approach, whereby one simply helps oneself to supervenient moral properties or principles to do the job, then some sort of explanation is required for why moral properties supervene on certain natural states or why such principles are true. It is insufficient for the naturalist to point out that we do, in fact, apprehend the goodness of some feature of human existence, for that only goes to establish the objectivity of moral values and duties, which the theist is ready to affirm." William Lane Craig, "This Most Gruesome of Guests," in *Is Goodness Without God Good Enough? A Debate on Faith, Secularism, and Ethics,* ed. Robert K. Garcia and Nathan L. King (New York: Rowman and Littlefield, 2009), 180.

† Dawkins also tries to demolish the connection between morality and God by introducing a selective reading of the Bible's commands on ethics as a red herring intended to draw attention away from his ethical theory's shortcomings. We address Dawkins's moral objections to the Bible throughout part 2.

the giving of favours in "anticipation" of payback. Following on from this there is, third, the Darwinian benefit of acquiring a reputation for generosity and kindness. And fourth... there is the particular additional benefit of conspicuous generosity as a way of buying unfakeably authentic advertising.[7]

Before our critique, we'll let Harris take the first shot. He observes that

fields like game theory and evolutionary biology, for instance, have some plausible stories to tell about the roots of what is generally called "altruistic behavior" in the scientific literature, but we should not make too much of these stories.... Nature has selected for many things that we would have done well to leave behind us in the jungles of Africa. The practice of rape may have once conferred an adaptive advantage on our species—and rapists of all shapes and sizes can indeed be found in the natural world (dolphins, orangutans, chimpanzees, etc.).... To say that something is "natural," or that it has conferred an adaptive advantage to our species, is not to say that it is "good" in the required sense of contributing to human happiness in the present.[8]

In other words, selective advantage is inadequate to ground why rape is objectively wrong. Something more is needed. Paradoxically, Dawkins seems to share the same sentiment, "I am not advocating a morality based on evolution.... Be warned that if you wish, as I do, to build a society in which individuals cooperate generously and unselfishly towards a common good, you can expect little help from biological nature. Let us try to *teach* generosity and altruism, because we are born selfish."[9]

While Harris and Dawkins do a fine job of undermining their own attempts at grounding objective morality, there are additional reasons that evolutionary accounts of morality fail to explain objective morality. First, evolutionary ethics are descriptive, not prescriptive. Dawkins offers us a description or story of the human population at this point in evolutionary history—how humans now behave. But this has nothing to do with objective morality. For example, we can't say that a murderer's genes *misfired* because that assumes a way they should have been expressed. They only fired *differently*—not better or worse—than other people. The fundamental point that Darwinist explanations miss is that "morality is not about how we do act but about how we should act."[10]

Furthermore, the four reasons Dawkins lists for altruism are *accidental* to history. Nature's laws (e.g., gravity) or logical necessity did not prescribe how altruism evolved. Therefore, William Lane Craig is correct to conclude, "If the film of evolutionary history were rewound and shot anew, very different creatures with a very different set of values might well have evolved."[11] What Darwinian evolutionists call good or evil today is ultimately arbitrary.

Finally, why should we trust our moral intuitions and reasoning if everything about us was selected for adaptive advantage or survival and not for the discovery of the truth? Beings capable of rationality and moral reflection make perfect sense if there is a Mind behind all matter. But if all there is and ever has been is matter, why trust our reasoning abilities if all the real action is occurring at the genetic level?[12] In chapter 2, we noted Dawkins's observation that our senses cannot be fully trusted since they are the product of natural selection. A Darwinian explanation of ethics leaves us with no plausible way to talk about objective morality.

Despite attempts to objectively ground ethics in evolutionary accounts, all explanations reduce to the same basic reality if God does not exist. The New Atheists are left with Dawkins's revealing statement that "nature is not cruel, only pitilessly indifferent. This is one of the hardest lessons for humans to learn. We cannot admit that things might be neither good nor evil, neither cruel nor kind, but simply callous—indifferent to all suffering, lacking all purpose."[13] The New Atheists want to say more than this about morality. Indeed, they appeal to some standard when they condemn religion as evil and dangerous. But physics, chemistry, and natural selection are all they have to work with. Michael Ruse, philosopher of biology at Florida State University, puts the point bluntly:

> Considered as a rationally justifiable set of claims about an objective something, ethics is illusory. I appreciate that when somebody says "love thy neighbor as thyself," they think they are referring above and beyond themselves. Nevertheless, such reference is truly without foundation. Morality is just an aid to survival and reproduction.... Any deeper meaning is illusory.[14]

Will Provine, professor of history of biology at Cornell University, reflects on the grim implications of Darwinian evolution: "No gods, no life after death, no ultimate foundation for ethics, no ultimate meaning in life, no free will—are all connected to an evolutionary perspective. You're here today and gone tomorrow and that's all there is to it."[15]

Where can this grim view of the world lead? The following is an excerpt of a recorded conversation between Ted Bundy, who raped and murdered at least thirty women, and one of his victims before he killed her:

> Then I learned that all moral judgments are "value judgments," that all value judgments are subjective, and that none can be proved to be either "right" or "wrong." I even read somewhere that the Chief Justice of the United States had written that the American Constitution expressed nothing more than collective value judgments. Believe it or not, I figured out for myself—what apparently the Chief Justice couldn't figure out for himself—that if the rationality of one value judgment was zero, multiplying it by millions would not make it one whit more rational. Nor is there

any "reason" to obey the law for anyone, like myself, who has the boldness and daring—the strength of character—to throw off its shackles.... I discovered that to become truly free, truly unfettered, I had to become truly uninhibited. And I quickly discovered that the greatest obstacle to my freedom, the greatest block and limitation to it, consists in the insupportable "value judgment" that I was bound to respect the rights of others. I asked myself, who were these "others"? Other human beings, with human rights? Why is it more wrong to kill a human animal than any other animal, a pig or a sheep or a steer? Is your life more than a hog's life to a hog? Why should I be willing to sacrifice my pleasure more for the one than for the other? Surely, you would not, in this age of scientific enlightenment, declare that God or nature has marked some pleasures as "moral" or "good" and others as "immoral" or "bad"? In any case, let me assure you, my dear young lady, that there is absolutely no comparison between the pleasure that I might take in eating ham and the pleasure I anticipate in raping and murdering you. That is the honest conclusion to which my education has led me—after the most conscientious examination of my spontaneous and uninhibited self.[16]

Bundy's chilling confession is unpleasant to say the least. Any properly functioning human being should be able to say that what Ted Bundy did is wrong, immoral, and evil. From what we have gathered from their writings, Harris, Dawkins, and Hitchens would all condemn Bundy as well. But the pivotal detail here is not that we agree—for we all would want to say far more than what he did was simply *illegal* in the United States—but that naturalism has no way to call Ted Bundy's actions objectively wrong or immoral. In atheism, morality is illusory.*

---

* We hasten to add again that we are not saying that every atheist will end up like Ted Bundy. But we do want you to carefully consider Bundy's own line of reasoning and how he understood his actions to be the logical outworking of certain ideas.

OBJECTIVE MORALITY PROVIDES GOOD EVIDENCE FOR GOD

We believe that the existence of objective right and wrong, good and evil, are powerful reasons to think that God exists. Even Dawkins grants the strength of this intuition: "It is pretty hard to defend absolutist morals on grounds other than religious ones."[17] Putting this belief in terms of a formal argument for God's existence would look like this:

- Premise 1: If God does not exist, objective moral values and duties do not exist.
- Premise 2: Objective moral values and duties do exist.
- Conclusion: Therefore, God exists.[18]

Now if the premises of this argument are true, the argument is sound.* In other words, if either premise 1 or 2 cannot be denied reasonably, then the conclusion follows logically—kind of like intellectual gravity.†

---

* This would be in contrast to Richard Dawkins's central argument against God in *The God Delusion* (see pp. 188–89). Dawkins strings together six claims he seems to believe lead one to conclude that "God almost certainly does not exist." Philosopher William Lane Craig observes, "This argument is jarring because the atheistic conclusion that 'Therefore, God almost certainly does not exist' seems to come suddenly out of left field. You don't need to be a philosopher to realize that that conclusion doesn't follow from the six previous statements. Indeed, if we take these six statements as premises of an argument intended to logically imply the conclusion 'Therefore, God almost certainly does not exist,' then the argument is patently invalid. No logical rules of inference would permit you to draw this conclusion from the six premises." See Craig, "Dawkins' Delusion," in *Contending with Christianity's Critics: Answering New Atheists and Other Objectors*, ed. Paul Copan and William Lane Craig (Nashville: B & H Publishing, 2009), 3.

† Just so we're not misunderstood, we need to clarify what can be expected from an argument like this. We do not claim that the argument cannot be denied or that it is 100 percent certain, or that it proves God's existence. Knowledge doesn't work this way. Precious little in our world—beyond theoretical mathematics—can be 100 percent proven. Rather, we are making the more modest claim that it's more plausible to affirm these two premises than deny them, and that given the reality of objective moral values and duties, it follows that God is the best explanation for them. Also, it is important to recognize that an alternative explanation is not a refutation of these premises. This often comes in the form of a "you could say that…" statement. And you could *say* anything

Let's start by examining premise 2, "objective moral values and duties do exist." When it comes down to it, we all know there is objective good and evil. There is an objective moral difference between Hitler and Mother Teresa. We know that self-sacrifice is good and we also know that what Ted Bundy did was evil. A properly functioning human being does not need an argument or a scientific experiment to determine that child molestation is objectively evil because he or she simply grasps the self-evident fact about reality. For example, if your vision is working correctly, then you will be able to recognize when a tree is in front of you. Our moral faculties work in a similar fashion when we "see" that a great evil or injustice has been done.

So even if everyone in America agreed that what Ted Bundy did was good, it would *still* be objectively evil. Dawkins does not seem comfortable going this far; he thinks "morals do not have to be absolute."[19] However, Harris, in a debate with pastor Rick Warren, clearly states, "I think there is an absolute right and wrong."[20] But as we have seen, Harris has no foundation for absolutes or objective morality. He cannot even say that Hitler was evil. (Hitler would have argued that he was following good Darwinian science to ensure the survival of the strong and the elimination of the weak. Hitler saw the Holocaust as the rational and logical outworking of evolutionary and utilitarian ethics.[21]) Dawkins recognizes the dilemma and is hesitant to affirm moral absolutes.

We recognize that moral relativism is fairly common today. But we would invite you to consider what kind of world it would be if all moral truths were really relative. "It would be a world in which nothing was wrong—nothing is considered evil or good, nothing worthy of praise or blame. It would be a world in which justice and fairness are meaningless concepts, in which there would be no accountability, no possibility of moral improvement,

---

you want. But saying something—telling some different story—is not the same as providing evidence for your claim. This idea is drawn from the helpful discussion in Gregory Koukl, *Tactics: A Game Plan for Discussing Your Christian Convictions* (Grand Rapids: Zondervan, 2009), 59–60.

no moral discourse. And it would be a world in which there is no tolerance."[22] This is not a pretty picture.

Most debate occurs around premise 1, "if God does not exist, objective moral values and duties do not exist." The New Atheists affirm the first part of the statement, and depending who's asked, affirm or deny the second part. But we have seen that objective morality does exist. If God exists, then objective morality is a natural and reasonable inference to make. There seems to be a natural connection between the idea of God as a moral lawgiver and the fact that there is an objective moral law that humans can either violate or obey. Because God created humans, they have dignity and are inherently valuable. The New Atheists have not provided a reasonable naturalistic account of objective morality. Dawkins candidly admits that the concept of objective morality arising from Darwinian evolution is counterintuitive: "On the face of it, the Darwinian idea that evolution is driven by natural selection seems ill-suited to explain such goodness as we possess, or our feelings of morality, decency, empathy, and pity. Natural selection can easily explain hunger, fear, and sexual lust, all of which straightforwardly contribute to our survival or the preservation of our genes."[23] Therefore, it is reasonable to conclude that God exists as the foundation of objective moral values and duties.[24]

SOME THOUGHTS ABOUT HUMAN RIGHTS

In 1948 the United Nations released a declaration of human rights affirming that "All human beings are born free and equal in dignity and rights. They are endowed with reason and conscience and should act towards one another in a spirit of brotherhood."[25] Curiously absent from this document is any reference to a moral basis for these noble ideals. We have certainly seen no reason to believe that Darwinian evolution has endowed humans in these ways. One could rightly ask, who says so? The United Nations? Because they got together and took a vote? What if someday they disagree and amend this document?

In stark contrast, observe the language of the Declaration of

Independence written in 1776: "We hold these truths to be self evident, that all men are created equal, that they are endowed by their Creator with certain unalienable Rights, that among these are Life, Liberty and the pursuit of Happiness." Either humans are just another species with nothing particularly special about them or they are endowed by their Creator with inherent dignity.[26]

FOR FURTHER ENGAGEMENT

Beckwith, Francis J., and Gregory Koukl. *Relativism: Feet Firmly Planted in Mid-Air.* Grand Rapids: Baker, 1998.

Copan, Paul. "God, Naturalism, and the Foundations of Morality." In *The Future of Atheism: Alister McGrath and Daniel Dennett in Dialogue*, edited by Robert B. Stewart, 141–162. Minneapolis: Fortress Press, 2008.

[why it matters]

TURNIPS AND TAXICABS

G. K. Chesterton observed in *Orthodoxy* that a person is only partially convinced of the truth of something if he has managed to latch onto "this or that proof of the thing." One is *fully* convinced only if he finds that *everything*—even turnips and taximeter cabs—proves it.

Some of our convictions are not so much the objects of our conscious thought—much less the conclusions of rigorous arguments—as they are the lens through which we see and think about everything else. Until this moment, I have never consciously entertained the idea that it is better to read bedtime stories to my grandchildren than it is to kick them down the stairs. Nor am I sure how to go about arguing for this, as, now that I think about it, the proposition is far more evident than whatever premises I might try to marshal in its favor. And were I to be found dwelling on a list of reasons why I should refrain from punting my progeny, this might be taken as evidence that I was losing my conviction—and my mind with it.

And so, when it comes to belief in God, perhaps there is something just a bit artificial about isolating "the moral argument"—as I myself have done—and urging it as reason for belief in God. My conviction precedes my philosophy, and, as I see it, *everything* proves it, and does so in a way that need not invoke numbered propositions arranged in neat syllogisms. The case is chiefly cumulative and pretheoretical. Atheists find the existence of God too incredible to be taken seriously. I think *my* existence is too incredible to be taken seriously. It is a wonder that there is a world, and that something such as myself—a living, conscious, rational, and moral agent—is on the scene to wonder about it. And the suggestion that causes "with no prevision of the end they were achieving," as Bertrand Russell has written, managed to produce either life or consciousness or rationality or morality or agency from big bang debris places too great a demand upon my credulity.

Still, for all of my adult life I have found varieties of the moral argument compelling. I believe that it *really is* better to care for my grandchildren than to kick them, and that an adequate explanation for this fact is not afforded on naturalism. The consistent naturalist might tell me that I think my grandchildren precious because I prize them, and that I prize them because of the reproductive advantage to be had in doing so. I, on the other hand, prize them because I think them precious. But on naturalism, the sort of preciousness—or inherent worth—that is implied here is nonsense on stilts. I can make sense of what seems to me self-evident only on the supposition that they are bearers of God's image and, as such, are to be valued, treated, and loved accordingly.

—Mark D. Linville

Mark D. Linville teaches philosophy at Clayton State University. He is author of "The Moral Argument" in *The Blackwell Companion to Natural Theology*, co-author of *The Moral Argument* (with Paul Copan), and coeditor of *Philosophy and the Christian Worldview* (with David Werther).

CHAPTER 16

Is Evil Only a Problem for Christians?

If God exists, either He can do nothing to stop the most egregious calamities, or He does not care to. God, therefore, is either impotent or evil.... There is another possibility, of course, and it is both the most reasonable and least odious: the biblical God is a fiction, like Zeus and the thousands of other dead gods whom most sane human beings now ignore.

—Sam Harris

You won't be surprised to learn that one of the most powerful reasons people struggle with the idea of God is evil—tsunamis, human trafficking, child abuse, rape, famine, war, murder, disease, and death. Even typing these words and knowing these things still occur is uncomfortable. The writings of the New Atheists aim to put God, especially the God of Christianity, on trial for evil. This diversionary tactic is often effective because it draws attention away from their own view of the world and they are rarely forced to grapple with the gravity of the problem of evil on their terms. But everyone, from the Christ-follower to the most militant unbeliever, must deal with evil and suffering. No one gets a free pass; evil is everyone's problem.

It would be easy to fill page after page with the New Atheists' complaints against God. But reading the latest headlines would have the same effect because examples of evil are easy to find. So what do we do with it? How do we make sense of it all? If there is a God, is he to blame? Is God good? Impotent? Before we address these inescapable existential questions, we need to be clear on exactly what the New Atheists offer as explanations for evil.

BLIND PITILESS INDIFFERENCE

A common practice of the New Atheists is using objective moral language to decry the atrocities of religion; it's not just that they don't like religion—they think it is actually bad for people. But this is self-contradictory because they are appealing to Darwinian accounts of morality—which *at the very best* can only describe the way things are up to this point in history but cannot prescribe why anyone should be moral tomorrow (see chapter 15). New Atheists like Sam Harris accuse God for failing to do something they think he *ought* to have done. From what moral high ground or according to what standard do they criticize God?

Here is what Richard Dawkins says you can expect from evolutionary and naturalistic accounts of reality:

> In a universe of blind physical forces and genetic replication some people are going to get hurt, other people are going to get lucky, and you won't find any rhyme or reason in it, nor any justice. The universe we observe has precisely the properties we should expect if there is, at the bottom, no design, no purpose, no evil and no other good. Nothing but blind pitiless indifference. DNA neither knows nor cares. DNA just is. And we dance to its music.*

---

* Richard Dawkins, *River Out of Eden: A Darwinian View of Life* (New York: Basic Books, 1995), 133. Dawkins fails to interact with any scholarly discussion of evil. Instead, he dismisses any attempts at addressing the problem of evil and suffering in a paragraph on page 135 of *The God Delusion* (New York: Houghton Mifflin, 2008).

Or consider Harris's view, "The child born without limbs, the sightless fly, the vanished species—these are nothing less than Mother Nature caught in the act of throwing her clay."[1] Not something you will find in *Chicken Soup for the Soul*, but illuminating nonetheless.

According to the New Atheists, in the end there will be no ultimate justice, no making things right, and no punishment for the wicked. Clever criminals will "get away with it." Worse still, there will be no solace. All the bitter tears shed in human history are unwitnessed and unobserved. They are ultimately meaningless biological reflexes to keep the evolutionary gene pool moving forward—not toward anything, mind you—just forward. So let's be clear: the New Atheist response to evil reduces to tough luck, that's just the way it goes, nature taking its course.

We don't think the New Atheists are correct and have offered reasons throughout this book of why we find naturalism to be an inadequate explanation of reality. But more to the point, when your world falls apart, when tragedy strikes, when death or cancer comes knocking, will you be turning to *The God Delusion* or *The End of Faith* for comfort, hope, and answers? Will you be content to simply accept the illusion of evil as it dances to DNA's music? Will you find rest in evolutionary history blindly and mercilessly grinding ahead?

We don't claim to have everything figured out or pretend to know the answers to all the "whys" in life. Far from it. Evil is not like a complicated math problem to be solved. But contrary to the claims of Harris and the hasty dismissals of Dawkins, Christianity offers substantive hope that is reasonable in the midst of pain, suffering, and evil, even if we are without an ultimately satisfying answer to all of our questions.

INTELLECTUAL ARGUMENTS AGAINST GOD

Before we go any further, we must define evil. Christian theism affirms the existence of a good and all-powerful God and the reality of evil. Evil was not God's intention for the world. According to Genesis 1, everything that God created was good;

evil entered the world through sin.* Evil is not an illusion, but neither is it a "thing." Evil is a departure from the way things ought to be. It is a corruption of good, a parasite. Just as rust cannot exist without iron, and adultery is impossible without the good of marriage, so evil is what it is in virtue of what it steals and corrupts from good.

It is here that the *intellectual* problems of evil come in. If God is all-good, all-knowing, and all-powerful, then he would want to get rid of evil. He would be powerful enough to get rid of evil; yet evil exists. There seems to be a contradiction in the Christian conception of God and the reality of evil.

When you encounter the vast literature on evil, two intellectual problems of evil emerge. First, it is *logically contradictory* for the Christian God and evil to coexist, and second, given the magnitude, duration, and intensity of evil in the world, it is *highly improbable* that God exists. (If these seem rather cold and detached from our personal *experience* of evil, they are. But they are necessary for our arriving at a more holistic understanding.)

Thanks to Alvin Plantinga's famous free will defense in *God, Freedom, and Evil*, professional philosophers widely regard the idea of God and evil as logically compatible. (Logically *incompatible* would be like saying that "square circles" exist.) All that is needed, in order to avoid the objection that the existence of God and evil are logically incompatible, is a possible morally sufficient reason that God allows evil.† Plantinga offers such an explanation:

---

* Evil entered the world through *natural* and *moral* sin. For one perspective of this, see William Dembski, *The End of Christianity: Finding a Good God in an Evil World* (Nashville: B & H Publishing, 2009).

† To know how God and evil can coexist without contradiction is an intellectual or theoretical question and should be addressed as such. A hug and a Bible verse is not the way to satisfy this intellectual struggle. On the other hand, many times we wrestle with the personal or existential problem of evil and thus have different needs. Sophisticated philosophical answers and rigorous analysis will come across as cold, sterile, and unhelpful. What we need is the ministry of presence by others' prayer, love, and hope. A time may come after the storm when a person desires more explanation. Also, when dealing with the problem of evil, it is helpful to distinguish between a *theodicy* and a *defense*. A defense

A world containing creatures who are significantly free (and freely perform more good than evil actions) is more valuable, all else being equal, than a world containing no free creatures at all. Now God can create free creatures, but He can't cause or determine them to do only what is right. For if He does so, then they aren't significantly free after all; and they do not do what is right freely. To create creatures capable of moral good, therefore, He must create creatures capable of moral evil; and He can't give these creatures the freedom to perform evil and at the same time prevent them from doing so. As it turned out, sadly enough, some of the free creatures God created went wrong in the exercise of their freedom; this is the source of moral evil. The fact that free creatures sometimes go wrong, however, counts neither against God's omnipotence nor against His goodness; for He could have forestalled the occurrence of moral evil only by removing the possibility of moral good.[2]

Implicit in Plantinga's argument is that God did not create evil and is not implicated in the evil humans actualized when they misused their freedom. By way of analogy, think of car manufacturers: they make cars, but no one holds them morally responsible for the deaths of innocent people by drunk drivers. The driver of the car is responsible even though the car made the accident possible.[3]

But maybe the issue is that the amount and intensity of evil in the world make it *improbable* that God exists. This objection deals formally with probability theory. While probability theory is not terribly exciting, we must remember that whenever the probability of an event is calculated, it is always done relative to a certain amount of background information (see chapter 3). Now, Christians can admit that God's existence might be im-

merely attempts to show that there is a logical reason behind why a good, all-powerful God would allow evil—the goal being to show that God and evil are not logically contradictory. A theodicy is more ambitious in that it seeks to say what God's reasons *actually* are for allowing evil.

probable *if only the evidence from evil is factored into the equation.* But if other evidence is factored in as well, then this second intellectual objection also fails. As philosopher of religion William Lane Craig makes clear, the Christian

> will insist that we consider, not just the evil in the world, but all the evidence relevant to God's existence, including the ontological argument for a maximally great being, the cosmological argument for a Creator of the universe, the teleological argument for an intelligent Designer of the cosmos, the noological argument for an ultimate Mind, the axiological argument for an ultimate, personally embodied Good, as well as evidence concerning the person of Christ, the historicity of the resurrection, the existence of miracles, plus existential and religious experience. When we take into account the full scope of evidence, the existence of God becomes quite probable.... Indeed, if he includes the self-authenticating witness of the Holy Spirit as part of his total warrant, then he can rightly assert that he knows that God exists, even if he has no solution to the problem of evil.[4]

Furthermore, everyone has to deal with the problem of evil, but the atheist also has to deal with the "problem of good." As theologian N. T. Wright put it in a "blogalogue" with Bart Erhman, author of *God's Problem*, "The other side of the coin of 'the problem of evil' is, after all, 'the problem of good': if there is no God, no good and wise creator, why is there an impulse to justice and mercy so deep within us? Why is there beauty, love, laughter, friendship, joy?"[5]

As to the extent of evil in our world, humans are simply in no position to judge how much would be "necessary" were we to know God's reasons for allowing it. This is not a cop-out, just an honest assessment of our limited cognitive abilities and historical perspective. Given that God would be infinitely wiser than humans, we would expect his reasons for allowing evil to be beyond our grasp. As Tim Keller puts it, "If you have a God great and transcendent enough to be mad at because he hasn't stopped evil and suffering in the world, then you have (at the same moment) a God great and transcendent enough to have good reasons for allowing it to continue that you can't know. Indeed you can't have it both ways."[6] Atheists often say the existence of evil is evidence that there is no God. But if there is no God, what is evil?

OUR GOD HAS WOUNDS

But evil doesn't stay locked up in dusty philosophical journals to be dispassionately pontificated about—it hits us in the face every day. Eastern pantheism regards evil as an illusion and thus fails to take the problem seriously. Atheism, with nature's blind and pitiless indifference, offers no substantive explanation or hope either. But Christianity is not silent. In fact, it offers hope in the most unexpected way. Not by God standing from afar and eradicating evil like some divine exterminator, but by entering the story.

The incarnation of Jesus demonstrates that God is not aloof or uninvolved in our world. He stepped into our existence, experienced all that we have ever experienced and more, and was crucified in our place to conquer death and evil, to redeem all of creation, and to make all things new. An innocent man went through an unjust trial so that we would not have to go through a just one. The evil in human hearts nailed Christ to that cross. But God took our evil and redeemed it for good, the salvation of all who would trust him. The Bible teaches that God made him who knew no sin to become sin on our behalf. And on that dark day, Jesus cried out, "My God, my God, why have you forsaken me?"[7] His cry of desperation was met with the silence of the Father. That is not blind and pitiless indifference.

Ravi Zacharias helps put God and the Christian response to evil in perspective: "Jesus did not conquer death in spite of pain and suffering, He conquered through it."[8] Christianity boasts the only God who has wounds. Evil and sin have been conquered at the cross and await final destruction at Christ's return; evil will not have the final word. As Alister McGrath reminds us:

> Experience cannot be allowed to have the final word—it must be judged and shown up as deceptive and misleading. The theology of the cross draws our attention to the sheer unreliability of experience as a guide to the presence and activity of God. God is active and present in His world, quite independently of whether we experience Him as being so. Experience declared that God was absent from Calvary, only to have its verdict humiliatingly overturned on the third day.[9]

As N. T. Wright points out, it is almost as if the entire story of the Bible is God telling us what he is doing about evil at personal, social, political, and cosmic levels, and the culmination of that story is the person of Jesus Christ.[10]

LESSONS ON PAIN AND SUFFERING

The Bible does not deal with life in the abstract. It is at the same time redemptive and realistic. Page after page reveals God's providential hand in a messed-up world. The three biblical narratives that follow teach important lessons that can help us endure suffering from a distinctively Christian perspective.

Joseph, whose story is told in Genesis 37–50, encountered evil and betrayal at the hands of his brothers. Injustice after injustice afflicted Joseph at every turn. Yet he trusted God in the midst of it all. In the end, God gave him the grace to be able to say, "As for you, you meant evil against me, but God meant it for good in order to bring about this present result, to preserve many people alive."[11] *God's providence may be mysterious—even inscrutable—but it is not without purpose.*

Few have suffered like Job. He lost everything—family, wealth, and finally his health. He challenged God and demanded to know why—what had he done to deserve this? In Job 38–42, God responded with no answers but lots of questions. The point was clear: God is God and Job is not. There is a more subtle and pastoral point to this. The questions were about all the mysteries of Job's world, and yet he could not answer them. Job was asking God why evil and suffering had been allowed in his life. But if Job could not make sense of natural events, then how would God's answer of why evil exists make any sense at all? God was in essence saying, "I am God and you are just going to have to trust me." Although *"why" may be unknowable, God is knowable and he is good.*

The story of Lazarus in John 11 is remarkable at many levels. We want to highlight one aspect of this story as it relates to how Jesus interacted with Lazarus and his family. The gist of the story is that Lazarus, who was loved by Jesus, died before Jesus arrived. Jesus could have arrived before Lazarus's death but intentionally didn't. Martha and Mary, Lazarus's sisters, criticized Jesus for this. Jesus' interaction with evil, suffering, and death in this passage is instructive: *Jesus allowed Lazarus's death even though he was able to prevent it, was grieved by what he allowed, and did something about it in the end (i.e., raised Lazarus from the dead and secured his ultimate resurrection).*

One of the mysteries in this broken world is that people can face the same kinds of suffering and pain but respond differently. Some will draw closer to God through suffering and others will withdraw. History is full of examples of people who have faced horrendous circumstances and yet still love God and look to him for strength. Randy Alcorn observes that in 2005 the *Washington Post* conducted a major survey of Hurricane Katrina survivors who wound up as refugees in Houston. When asked about their faith in God, "Remarkably, 81 percent said the ordeal has strengthened their belief."[12] Even the worst evils did not lead to the wholesale rejection of God by the very people who experienced them.

When the storms of life hit, remember that God is always with us in the midst of whatever evil we encounter; he will never leave us or forsake us. Moreover, God will redeem the evil he allows in our life for good, even if we don't see it immediately or at all.[13] Finally, suffering is temporary and leads to increased faith now and glory in the future.[14] The cross is the greatest reminder of God's goodness and love.* He knows, he cares, and he is with us in the midst of it.

According to the Bible, a day will come when every broken heart will be mended, every illness healed. God will set the world right. Death will not have the final word—Jesus Christ made certain of that. One day, perfect love will eclipse all of our fears. One day, God will no longer have to count the tears we cry, because they will all have been wiped away.[15]

HOW LONG, OH LORD?

The honesty of the psalmist when he sang, "How long, oh Lord?" resonates with even the most devout believer. Why does evil persist? Why hasn't God dealt with it already? What is he waiting for? I think Peter helps us answer *some* of that question:

> Do not let this one thing escape your notice, that a single day is like a thousand years with the Lord and a thousand years are like a single day. The Lord is not slow concerning

---

* In debates with both Dinesh D'Souza and William Lane Craig, Christopher Hitchens has raised the question of why it took God so long to save humanity. The argument is rhetorically powerful. The gist of it is that if *homo sapiens* have been on the planet for 98,000 years or so (according to conventional dating), then why did God wait so long to send Jesus? Was he asleep at the wheel? D'Souza cites Erik Kreps of the Survey Research Center of the University of Michigan's Institute for Social Research in his reply to Hitchens: "The Population Reference Bureau estimates that the number of people who have ever been born is approximately 105 billion. Of this number, about 2 percent were born before Christ came to earth.... So in a sense, God's timing couldn't have been more perfect. If He'd come earlier in human history, how reliable would the records of his relationship with man be? But He showed up just before the exponential explosion in the world's population, so even though 98 percent of humanity's timeline had passed, only 2 percent of humanity had previously been born, so 98 percent of us have walked the earth since the Redemption" (quoted in Dinesh D'Souza, "An Absentee God?" http://news.aol.com/newsbloggers/2008/07/09/an-absentee-god/ [accessed October 25, 2009]. Our thanks to William Lane Craig for helping us track down this source.) This observation fits nicely with what the apostle Paul said in his letter to the Galatians, "But when the fullness of the time came, God sent forth His Son" (4:4 NASB).

his promise, as some regard slowness, but is being patient toward you, because he does not wish for any to perish but for all to come to repentance. But the day of the Lord will come like a thief; when it comes, the heavens will disappear with a horrific noise, and the celestial bodies will melt away in a blaze, and the earth and every deed done on it will be laid bare.[16]

For the Christian, we must remember that we are not called to run to the hills and isolate ourselves until Jesus returns; rather, we are called to embody in our relationships and in the world the healing and restoration of Jesus' atonement on the cross. We share the good news concerning the availability of life with God and practice good works in the midst of whatever cultural situation we find ourselves.

God, being good, patiently waits for all who would turn to him in faith. Atheist John Loftus contends, "The dilemma for the theist is to reconcile senseless suffering in the world with her own beliefs (not mine) that all suffering is for a greater good. It's an internal problem for the theist, so it doesn't matter what the beliefs are for the person making this argument."[17] However, pain and suffering, whatever else may be said of them, awaken us all to the brevity and frailty of life and the universal need for redemption and wholeness. As C. S. Lewis observes, "God whispers to us in our pleasures, speaks in our conscience, but shouts in our pain: it is His megaphone to rouse a deaf world."[18] As much as we would like to believe otherwise, our greatest good is not the absence of pain or the satisfaction of all of our desires; it is to know God. And God waits patiently for people to know him. The passage in Peter, however, shows us that the patience of God will run out someday as the time of salvation passes and the time of reckoning evil will commence.

Where does this leave us? With all our questions answered and all tensions resolved? Not really. Craig puts language to the messiness of life we all feel this side of the new heavens and new earth: "Paradoxically, then, even though the problem of evil is the greatest objection to the existence of God, at the end of the day God is the only solution to the problem of evil. If God does not exist, then we are lost without hope in a life filled with gratuitous and unredeemed suffering. God is the final answer to the problem of evil, for He redeems evil and takes us into the everlasting joy of an incommensurable good: fellowship with Him."[19]

FOR FURTHER ENGAGEMENT

Alcorn, Randy C. *If God Is Good: Faith in the Midst of Suffering and Evil.* Colorado Springs, CO: Multnomah, 2009.

Howard-Snyder, Daniel. "God, Evil, and Suffering." In *Reason for the Hope Within*, edited by Michael J. Murray, 76–115. Grand Rapids: Eerdmans, 1999.

[why it matters]

DOES GOD REALLY CARE ABOUT MY PAIN?

Often we Christians act as if we're not supposed to experience pain and suffering. But God says, "Do not be surprised at the painful trial you are suffering, as though something strange were happening to you. But rejoice that you participate in the sufferings of Christ, so that you may be overjoyed when his glory is revealed" (1 Peter 4:12–13).

We define our good in terms of what brings us health and happiness; God defines it in terms of what makes us more like Jesus.

Years ago I sat in a courtroom as a defendant, listening to abortion-clinic employees tell lie after lie, all under oath. Even though we had engaged in totally peaceful, nonviolent civil disobedience in order to rescue the lives of unborn children, I heard a judge tell the jury they *must* (it was a directed verdict) find us guilty and impose severe financial punishments on us. Yet despite the hardship and injustice it involved, what God did in that situation was wonderful. During the thirty-day court trial, I often recited to myself God's Word, including the assurance that the Judge of all the earth will do right (see Gen. 18:25). Like Jesus, I needed to entrust myself to a faithful Creator who will work all things together for good. (I have subsequently seen amazing ways he has done just that, none of which I could see at the time.)

As an insulin-dependent diabetic I've seen both my body and my mind fail me. I suffer under the curse enough to know just what I want—a new body and a new mind, a transformed heart without sin, no suffering or disability. Every passing year increases my longing to live on the resurrected earth in my resurrected body, with my resurrected family and friends, worshiping and serving the resurrected Jesus.

God uses my weakness and inadequacy not only to build my

character, but also to manifest his strength and grace to me and through me. That's why I see his goodness in giving this weakness to me to accomplish his good purposes (see Paul's thorn in the flesh in 2 Cor. 12:7–10). Not only will I celebrate those purposes in eternity, I am celebrating them now.

In researching my book *If God Is Good,* I interviewed dozens of people who underwent intense suffering, yet testified of a profound and abiding joy that people who have lived easier lives seldom experience. We would do well to spend our days preparing to worship God in the hard times he has promised we will face.

If you know Jesus, then the hand holding yours bears the calluses of a carpenter who carried a cross for you. When he holds out his hand, you see the gnarled flesh of the nail scars on his wrists. When you think he doesn't understand your pain, realize that you don't understand the extent of his pain.

All the evils and suffering that we tell him he never should have permitted, he willingly inflicted upon himself, for us. Love him or not, he has proven he loves you.

In your most troubled moments, when you cry out to God, "Why have you let this happen?" picture the outstretched hands of Christ, forever scarred... for you.

Do those look like the hands of a God who does not care?

—Randy Alcorn

Randy Alcorn is director of Eternal Perspective Ministries (www.epm.org) and author of numerous books, including *Safely Home, The Treasure Principle, Heaven,* and *If God Is Good.*

CHAPTER 17

What Good Is Christianity?

Religion poisons everything.
—Christopher Hitchens

Can you imagine life without computers, cell phones, or refrigerators? Every one of us—believer or not—takes these types of things for granted. We simply get used to having the modern conveniences of life around us. But these conveniences didn't always exist. Someone somewhere invented the cultural goods we enjoy. Yet most of us wouldn't get very far on *Who Wants to Be a Millionaire* if we had to name their inventors. The same is true for foundational ideas and institutions in the modern world.

The truth of the matter is that many cultural ideas and goods would not exist had there never been Christianity—women's rights, protection for infants and the unborn, child labor laws, separation of church and state, liberty and justice, human dignity, abolition of slavery in the Western world, universities, modern science, hospitals, musical innovations, and the importance of the written word—just to name a few.[1] While the evil actions of certain Christians get far more press (especially as of late), it is simply a matter of historical record that Christianity has been a redemptive force for good in our world from the beginning.*

---

* Again, *religion* is not dangerous, *people* are. We have already acknowledged that Christianity has done its fair share of harm, which needs to be openly recognized so that we can prevent such evils in the future. But this harm has oc-

To read the New Atheists, you would think that Christianity has been a blot on civilization rather than playing a pivotal role in both shaping and providing a rational and moral context in which humanity could flourish.*

We recognize that Christianity has its stains and responsibility needs to be taken where appropriate. As we have seen, history reveals that the darkness of the human heart can find expression in *any* worldview. But in the interest of telling the rest of the story, we want to highlight two of the significant ways in which Christianity, far from poisoning everything, has literally changed the world.[2] Christianity introduced charity to the world, as well as an elevated status for women.

THE BIRTH OF CHARITY

We take the existence of *charity* for granted, but compassion has not always been practiced. In fact, in stark contrast with the Romans, the early Christians practiced *caritas*, which was "giving to relieve the recipient's economic or physical distress without expecting anything in return."[3] The Romans practiced *liberalitas*, or "giving to please the recipient, who later would bestow a favor on the giver."[4] There is a big difference in giving to get something in return and selflessly giving to another in love.

Jesus taught this selfless ethic, which was recorded in the New Testament (e.g., the parable of the Good Samaritan in Luke

---

curred due to the misapplication of and disobedience to Jesus' life, example, and teachings. Christianity properly understood and applied leads to life characterized by kindness, love, generosity, and relationship as God originally intended.

* "Dawkins writes nothing about the great religious communities founded for the express purpose of building schools for the free education of the poor. Nothing about the thousands of monastic lives dedicated to the delicate and exhausting labor of copying by hand the great manuscripts of the past ... during which there were no printing presses. Nothing about the founding of the Vatican Library and its importance for the genesis of nearly a dozen modern sciences. Nothing of the faithful who have made so many crucial discoveries in science, medicine, and technology. Yet on these matters a word or two of praise from Dawkins might have made his tiresome lists of accusations seem less unfair." Michael Novak, *No One Sees God: The Dark Night of Atheists and Believers* (New York: Doubleday, 2008), 39.

10:30–37) and practiced in the early church. This ethic formed the basis for compassion and charity in the Western world:*

- "For I was hungry and you gave me something to eat, I was thirsty and you gave me something to drink, I was a stranger and you invited me in, I needed clothes and you clothed me, I was sick and you looked after me, I was in prison and you came to visit me.... I tell you the truth, whatever you did for one of the least of these brothers of mine, you did for me." (Matt. 25:35–40)

- "Religion that God our Father accepts as pure and faultless is this: to look after orphans and widows in their distress and to keep oneself from being polluted by the world." (James 1:27)

- "This is love: not that we loved God, but that he loved us and sent his Son as an atoning sacrifice for our sins.... Since God so loved us, we also ought to love one another." (1 John 4:10–11)

- "In humility consider others better than yourselves. Each of you should look not only to your own interests, but also to the interests of others. Your attitude should be the same as that of Christ Jesus." (Phil. 2:3–5)

The Bible contains many more passages like these and they set quite a standard. What is clear from history is that the early Christians took these commands very seriously. Social historian Rodney Stark observes, "Pagan and Christian writers are unanimous not only that Christian Scripture stressed love and charity as the central duties of faith, but that they were sustained in everyday behavior."[5]

Though poor by Roman standards, the early Christians sacrificially gave to the poor—regardless of religious orientation—as they had need. This compassion was so contagious and was hav-

---

* This ethic was also present in the Old Testament. For example, Jeremiah 22:16–17 reveals that defending the cause of the poor and needy is part of what it means to know God.

ing such an impact that it caused the pagan emperor Julian in 362 to write letters to his high priests saying, "The impious Galileans [his word for Christians] support not only their own poor, but ours as well, everyone can see that our people lack aid from us."[6]

The early Christians also took care of the sick. They actually viewed the great epidemic of 260 as an opportunity to love people. The logical response would have been to run away, but these Christians acted unnaturally by staying and caring for the sick— even at the risk of their own lives. Read the powerful words of Bishop Dionysus of Alexandria in his Easter letter that year:

> Most of our brother Christians showed unbounded love and loyalty, never sparing themselves and thinking only of one another. Heedless of danger, they took charge of the sick, attending to their every need and ministering to them in Christ, and with them departed this life serenely happy; for they were infected by others with disease, drawing on themselves the sickness of their neighbors and cheerfully accepting their pains. Many, in nursing and curing others, transferred their death to themselves and died in their stead.... The best of our brothers lost their life in this manner, a number of presbyters, deacons, and laymen winning high commendation so that death in this form, the result of great piety and strong faith, seems in every way the equal of martyrdom.[7]

Now note how the pagan responded:

> The heathen behaved in the very opposite way. At the first onset of the disease, they pushed the sufferers away and fled from their dearest, throwing them into the roads before they were dead and treated unburied corpses as dirt, hoping thereby to avert the spread and contagion of the fatal disease; but do what they might, they found it difficult to escape.[8]

Lest one accuse Dionysus of fabricating the pagan response to make Christians look good, the Greek historian Thucydides describes similar responses of desertion by those in his day when a plague struck Athens in 431 B.C.[9] Additionally, Plato thought that the poor who became sick should be left to die.[10] While everyone was running the other way in self-preservation, followers of Jesus, motivated by his words, moved toward the afflicted and diseased with compassion.

Infants and children benefited from the Christian belief that all human life was sacred. Christians were instrumental in outlawing infanticide in the middle of the fourth century. This heinous practice existed in virtually every ancient civilization, as well as in the more advanced Greco-Roman world. It was even recommended as legitimate state policy by both Plato and Aristotle.[11] (Poverty and population control were the two largest motivating factors.) Along with infanticide, Christians have also condemned abortion as murder from the earliest days of Christianity. Furthermore, Christians took care of abandoned children. The unwanted children not killed immediately following birth (usually girls) were often abandoned and left to die. Christians would literally pick them up off the streets and adopt them. Moreover, the short life expectancy in the ancient world (about thirty years) left many children orphaned. Based on the admonition in James 1:27, early Christians cared for orphans when no one else would—in family homes before Christianity was legalized in 313 and in official orphanages after that.[12]

After Christianity was legalized, Christians founded hospitals. (St. Basil of Caesarea in Cappadocia built the first hospital around 369.) Christians' high view of life also led them to oppose the gruesome gladiatorial games that killed hundreds of thousands for entertainment. We could go on, but we simply don't have room to describe the many other ways Christians applied Jesus' ethic throughout the centuries. Christ-followers cared for the elderly, the blind, the mentally handicapped, and countless others when no one else did. Their compassion led them to care for people that society largely had forgotten or that were culturally invisible.

JESUS IS GOOD NEWS FOR WOMEN

There is an unfortunate perception today that Christianity is antifemale. This is simply false. Throughout history, some Christians have abused or diminished women, as have people of various faiths and those who profess no faith at all. All abuse is shameful and a departure from God's design. Unfortunately the brokenness of the human heart can lead to a corruption of religion or ideology that is then used to oppress women. However, Christianity, properly understood and applied, does not lead to this oppression.

Christianity is unique in its elevation of women compared to other religions and Greek and Roman civilizations.* To say that being a woman in the ancient world was extremely challenging would be an understatement. Rodney Stark writes that in Athens,

> Women were in relative short supply owing to female infanticide, practiced by all classes, and to the additional deaths caused by abortion. The status of women was very low. Girls received little or no education … were married at puberty and often before. Under Athenian law a woman was classified as a child, regardless of age, and therefore was the legal property of some man at all stages of her life. Males could divorce by simply ordering a wife out of the household.[13]

Women did not fair much better in Rome, as indicated by the following laws. The Roman law of *manus* "placed her under the

---

* For example, Dale and Jonalyn Fincher observe that "Though Muhammad did act to protect females, such as prohibiting the practice of infanticide upon baby girls, his own words about women are not always consistent. He writes about wayward wives, 'those whose disobedience you suspect, admonish them and send them to separate beds and beat them' (Qu'ran 4:34); [and] sexual conduct, 'Wives are fields to seed as you please' (Qu'ran 2:223)." "The Treatment of Women: Jesus Outshines Muhammad," available at http://www.soulation.org/articles/Fledge-v3i13.html (accessed December 20, 2009). Also, see the information regarding other religions in Jonalyn Grace Fincher, "Defending Femininity: Why Jesus Is Good News for Women," in *Apologetics for a New Generation: A Biblical and Culturally Relevant Approach to Talking About God*, ed. Sean McDowell (Eugene, OR: Harvest House, 2009), 222–26.

absolute control of her husband, who had ownership of her and all her possessions."[14] In addition, *patria potestas* and *paterfamilias* gave the husband and father "supreme, absolute power over his children and grandchildren, even when they were grown. He alone had the power to divorce his wife, and he also possessed the power to execute his children. He could even execute his married daughter if she committed adultery in his or her husband's house."[15] Incidentally, you can see how radical the apostle Paul's teaching to fathers in Ephesians 6:4 would have been: "Fathers, do not exasperate your children; instead, bring them up in the training and instruction of the Lord."

With the Greco-Roman backdrop in mind, we are prepared to see just how radical Jesus' view of women really was. He healed several women of diseases, interacted with women of different races, and extended forgiveness to women who had committed sexual sin.[16] Jewish rabbinical tradition of the day (i.e., not the Bible) taught, "Let the words of law [Torah] be burned rather than committed to a woman,"[17] but Jesus had many female followers and disciples and he taught them.[18] Women supported his ministry financially, and he used women as positive examples in his teaching.[19] Jesus' female followers were the last to leave at his crucifixion and the first at his empty tomb. New Testament scholar D. M. Scholer concludes, "Jesus' respect for and inclusion of women as disciples and proclaimers provided the foundation for the positive place of women in the earliest churches and their ministry."[20]

Paul, who often gets a bad rap for his *perceived* low view of women, considered at least twelve women coworkers in his ministry.* Paul clearly had a high view of women: "There is neither Jew nor Greek, slave nor free, male nor female, for you are all one

---

* For passages where Paul mentions women as coworkers, see Acts 16:14–15, 40; Romans 16:1–16; 1 Corinthians 1:11; Philippians 4:2–3; Colossians 4:15. It is important to admit that power plays, male chauvinism, and bad theology have been used to subjugate and diminish women throughout church history. But again, these actions and attitudes are not consistent with New Testament theology or, more importantly, the example and teachings of the founder of Christianity, Jesus of Nazareth.

in Christ Jesus."[21] The earliest Christians recited these remarkable, countercultural words as a baptismal confession. Widows, far from being abandoned, were cared for, and older women were given a place of honor.[22] In light of all of this, is it any wonder "the ancient sources and modern historians agree that primary conversion to Christianity was far more prevalent among females than males"?[23]

In recent history, Christians were responsible for the banning of three despicable practices inflicted upon women around the world. Christian missionaries pressured the Chinese government to abolish foot binding in 1912. This practice was done for the sole reason of pleasing men—"it made a woman with her feet bound in an arch walk tiptoe and sway seductively."[24] In 1829 the English outlawed the Indian practice of *suttee*, in which widows were burned alive on the funeral pyres of their husbands, because of Christianity's teaching regarding widows and women. Finally, Western countries influenced by a Christian view of women and sexuality have condemned clitoridectomy (female genital mutilation), a gruesome practice that is still common in Muslim countries in Africa and the Middle East.

Today the entertainment industry views women as commodities—sex objects—to help sell anything and everything. This doesn't even consider the dehumanization that occurs in the multi-billion-dollar porn industry. Christian theology elevates women to a place of value because they are created in the image of God, not because they look or behave a certain way. Christopher Hitchens writes, "The Old Testament, as Christians condescendingly call it, has woman cloned from man for his use and comfort."[25] But this is not at all accurate. Contrary to Hitchens's claim, woman and man are *both* created in the image of God.[26] Further, when God said, "It is not good for the man to be alone. I will make a helper suitable for him,"[27] he did not mean a servant to bring men their beer. The Hebrew word "helper" is also used of members of the Trinity.[28] So if *helper* were a diminutive term, it would be news to God.

Criticism of the Bible's portrayal of women needs to be viewed through the lens of what is *accurately described* versus *actually endorsed* in Scripture, specifically for the Old Testament. As we have seen in the chapter on slavery, the realities of poverty and war added to the complexity of living in the ancient Near East. In a similar fashion, gender and family relationships as they play out in the narratives of the Old Testament are also broken and corrupted by sin and complicated by other sociological pressures. The New Atheists must look at the larger context. Hitchens conveniently left out of his analysis Bible passages that call Christian husbands to "show her honor as a fellow heir of the grace of life" and love their wives "just as Christ loved the church and gave himself up for her."* And if you will recall, Jesus loved so selflessly he ended up carrying the cross he was crucified on for the benefit of others.

Whatever one makes of Jesus' other claims, what is undeniable is that he has definitely been good news for women. Social historian Alvin Schmidt observes, "Neither Christ nor the early Christians ever preached outright revolution. Rather, it was his example that his followers reflected in their relationships with women, raising their dignity, freedom, and rights to a level previously unknown in any culture."[29] The elevated status of women continued throughout history after Christianity came on the scene and serves as the basis for women's rights today in Western countries.

THE GOOD NEWS CONTINUES

In this chapter, we have intentionally focused on the past because it is so easy for us to forget what kind of world it would be without the influence of Christianity. But you need to know that Christianity is still a force for good in this world. We could

---

* 1 Peter 3:7 NASB; Ephesians 5:25 NIV. Regarding the perversion of biblically informed submission, it needs to be stated emphatically that a man's domination, humiliation, manipulation, and abuse of his wife is an abomination to God and is contrary to God's design of marriage and oneness. The example of Christ is selfless love.

share plenty of statistics and facts, but instead we want to tell you about Jimmy Wambua of Kenya.

When Jimmy was four years old, his mother became ill and was bedridden. Jimmy, who did not know his father, was faced with starvation and scavenged on the streets for food. At age seven, he watched his ten-month-old sister die of starvation in his mother's lap. In April 1990 when Jimmy was eight, his mother found out about a place that helped children, so she sent him to a town twelve hours away. A young Christian named Mark decided he was going to sponsor Jimmy for thirty-eight dollars a month. This decision saved Jimmy's life.

Today Jimmy is studying the Bible in graduate school so he can go back to Kenya to *share* and *be* the good news of Jesus Christ for other children without hope. Jimmy is just one of the more than one million children cared for by Compassion International. He would definitely say that Christianity was good news for him.[30]

This story could be multiplied again and again by the outstanding work being done by Christ-followers through ministries like International Justice Mission, the Mocha Club, and Living Water International.[31] When the New Atheists make claims that religion poisons everything, they are flat wrong.[32] A more accurate conclusion is that "Christian ideals have permeated society until non-Christians, who claim to live a 'decent life' without religion, have forgotten the origin of the very content and context of their 'decency.'"[33] Stark summarizes, "Perhaps above all else, Christianity brought a new conception of humanity to a world saturated with capricious cruelty and the vicarious love of death."[34]

Historians have filled books discussing the compassion and charity of Christians. Christianity has been a force for good in the past, continues to be so today, and will be tomorrow as long as Christians pay close attention to the teaching and example of Jesus.

FOR FURTHER ENGAGEMENT

Haugen, Gary A. *Good News About Injustice: A Witness of Courage in a Hurting World.* 10th anniversary ed. Downers Grove, IL: InterVarsity Press, 2009.

Schmidt, Alvin J. *How Christianity Changed the World.* Grand Rapids: Zondervan, 2004.

[why it matters]

EMBRACING ALL OF LIFE

When I first came to faith as a junior high school student, my concept of Christianity was very limited. The main point was salvation, followed by living a life of clear morality that would make me distinct and different from the people around me. (Looking back, the spiritual pride involved in that is obvious, but somehow I missed it then.) Serious Christians became missionaries; those a bit less serious became pastors. Everything else was pretty unimportant from a spiritual perspective, though I knew that whatever we did, we should do it "for the Lord," whatever that meant.

In college, I encountered a different vision of Christianity, one that did not deny the importance of salvation and right living, but that also saw every area of life as sacred and all legitimate activities as a means of loving and serving God and my neighbor. In other words, whatever my job might be, it should not simply be a career but a *vocation*, a calling by God for my life. I am called to bring the kingdom of God to bear in every area of life, working under Christ for the redemption and restoration of all things to their proper place in God's purpose for the world. This idea, known as the cultural mandate, freed me to pursue my passion for scholarship and university teaching. Among other things, I wanted to be an encouragement to Christian students in hostile campus environments, and to provide an example of good scholarship from a Christian perspective to my secular colleagues.

The broader vision provided by the cultural mandate led me to study history and helped shape how I approach the field. Rather than pursuing a standard program in the history of Christianity, my studies have focused on social, intellectual, and economic history, with theology thrown in as well. Since all of these areas are important to God, I thought they should be important to me as well. And since human society is an integrated whole, I was particularly interested in how these different subdisciplines interact with each other, an interest which has allowed me to draw connections that are often missed and that highlight the influence of Christianity in shaping Western culture.

Studying these disciplines has left me in awe of the incredible scope of the biblical worldview and its power to shape history. Is the record perfect? Of course not, a fact explained by the Christian worldview itself, which recognizes the sinfulness of humanity. But the faults often laid at the feet of Christians (usually limited to the Crusades, the Inquisition and related areas, and the Galileo affair) are more than outweighed by the positive contributions of the biblical worldview, including the development of modern science, technology, economics, limited government, concepts of universal human rights (including property rights, women's rights, and the abolition of slavery), and belief in the dignity of work.

Seeing the impact of faithful but flawed Christians in all of these areas has given me a much bigger vision of the gospel and a greater confidence that what I do *matters*. Knowing God's sovereignty over history and recognizing the incredible things accomplished by his people over the centuries gives me a greater sense of peace, security, and hope in our chaotic and uncertain world.

—Glenn S. Sunshine

Glenn S. Sunshine is a professor of history at Central Connecticut State University, a research fellow of the Acton Institute, and a faculty member of the Centurions Program, a worldview teaching program. His latest book is *Why You Think the Way You Do: The Story of Western Worldviews from Rome to Home.*

CHAPTER 18

Why Jesus Instead of the Flying Spaghetti Monster?

There is no good historical evidence that he [Jesus] ever thought he was divine. The fact that something is written down is persuasive to people not used to asking questions like: "Who wrote it, and when?" "How did they know what to write?" "Did they, in their time, really mean what we, in our time, understand them to be saying?" "Were they unbiased observers, or did they have an agenda that coloured their writings?" Ever since the nineteenth century, scholarly theologians have made an overwhelming case that the gospels are not reliable accounts of what happened in the history of the real world. All were written long after the death of Jesus, and also after the epistles of Paul, which mention almost none of the alleged facts of Jesus' life.

—Richard Dawkins

Christianity is not a fairy tale; it is rooted in the events of history. The same cannot be said of the Tooth Fairy, the Easter Bunny, or even the beloved Santa Claus. Adults are not converting to belief in Santa Claus on their deathbeds or after a life of investigating the evidence for good old Saint Nicholas (though after investigating the evidence, you'll discover that Saint Nick definitely believed in Jesus[1]). Nor is Zeus a viable option. And while the flying spaghetti monster's popularity of late has been growing on the Internet thanks to Richard Dawkins, it does not boast 2 billion followers and counting.* So Jesus of Nazareth was either who he claimed to be or he wasn't. It really is that simple.

Christianity does not hide behind assertions of blind faith; it can be investigated with eyes wide open:

> Christianity is not a code for living or a philosophy of religion; rather it is rooted in real events of history. To some this is scandalous, because it means that the truth of Christianity is bound up with the truth of certain historical facts, such that if those facts should be disproved, so would Christianity. But at the same time, this makes Christianity unique because, unlike most other world religions, we now have a means of verifying its truth by historical evidence.[2]

By this point in the book, you may admit that it is possible (maybe even probable) that God exists. But with the exception of our brief discussion of Jesus' resurrection in chapter 3, we haven't said much about why someone ought to take the claims of Jesus, as recorded in the New Testament documents, seriously. The New Atheists are clearly skeptics when approaching Jesus— in fact Dawkins actually entertains the possibility that he may never have existed at all.† Is this kind of historical skepticism warranted? Can we know who the historical Jesus really was?

---

* The flying spaghetti monster is a parody of an invisible being you can't prove, similar to Bertrand Russell's Teapot. It was originally conceived by Bobby Henderson to be a spoof of intelligent design in 2005. More popularly, it has become a symbol that represents the supposed ridiculousness of belief in God. There is now even a church and gospel of the flying spaghetti monster and its followers are called pastafarians. While we disagree with the ultimate point of this satirical creation, we do applaud the creativity and humor!

† What becomes clear from their bibliographies is that none of them seriously engage with contemporary New Testament studies to see if their skepticism is warranted. To doubt the existence of Jesus is pretty remarkable because Jesus' death by crucifixion at the hands of the Romans is one of the most well-established facts in all of ancient history.

ARE THE NEW TESTAMENT GOSPELS RELIABLE HISTORY?

New Testament historian Ben Witherington observes, "The most the historian can establish about events in the past is a good probability one way or another that this or that event did or did not happen. There is no such thing as absolute certainty on such matters."[3] Now this doesn't mean that we should become historical skeptics, only that we should have realistic expectations. Let's look at the unique challenges that emerge when we apply the normal rules of historical investigation to the Gospels.

One objection to the Gospels is that appealing to them is an example of circular reasoning. The objection goes like this, "You can't use one book of the Bible to support what another book of the Bible says because you're just arguing in a circle or assuming what you are trying to prove." This is a common but faulty argument. First, we are not treating the Bible as a divinely inspired book that must be received as if it descended from heaven in calfskin leather.[4] Rather, we are approaching the New Testament documents as works of ancient literature just like the writings of Herodotus, Livy, or Aristotle.[5] Also, because anyone can buy a Bible at the local bookstore (booking a single volume), many people think that it was originally composed *as one book*. In reality, the New Testament is a collection of twenty-seven separate texts, written in Greek by nine different authors who wrote in distinctive styles and for different purposes over a period of sixty years. These writers didn't sit down in a room somewhere and decide that they needed to get their story straight and write the Bible. They were either eyewitnesses to the events themselves or they interviewed the eyewitnesses. Moreover, it is significant when multiple authors, writing independently of one another, agree on the same historical facts. So the Christian is not guilty of special pleading here or using the Bible to prove the Bible.

Another objection is that the Gospel writers were biased. Wouldn't Jesus' followers have had a theological axe to grind? If by this someone means that the disciples had convictions about the identity and teachings of Jesus, then yes, they were biased. But so is every other writer of history because *everyone* has a worldview. The important question is whether being an advocate for a certain point of view necessarily renders that person incapable of recording reliable and accurate history. Gospels scholar Mark Strauss is helpful on this point: "If an American wrote a history of the United States, would that history necessarily be unreliable or distorted? Or more pointedly, some of the most important accounts of the Nazi Holocaust have been composed by Jews. Does this fact render them inaccurate? On the contrary, those passionately interested in the events are often the most meticulous in recording them. To claim that the Gospels cannot be historical because they were written by believers is fallacious."[6]

Did the Gospel writers intend to write accurate history? Luke is a good case study for this question. Read how he begins his gospel in verses 1–4 (NASB):

> Inasmuch as many have undertaken to compile an account of the things accomplished among us, just as they were handed down to us by those who from the beginning were eyewitnesses and servants of the word, it seemed fitting for me as well, having investigated everything carefully from the beginning, to write it out for you in consecutive order, most excellent Theophilus; so that you may know the exact truth about the things you have been taught.

While he was doing more than just reporting the facts, Luke has also been shown to be a first-rate historian. His writings of Luke and Acts contain detailed and reliable information that only could have come from someone familiar with local geography, history, politics, and customs. For example, historian Colin Hemer has documented eighty-four facts in the last sixteen chapters of Acts that have been confirmed by historical and archaeological research.[7] Luke clearly took great care to get his historical facts straight, which indicates that he would have been careful to accurately record early teaching concerning Jesus of Nazareth.

The conclusion historians are willing to draw concerning the Gospels depends in large part on what presuppositions they bring to their investigation. British New Testament scholar R. T. France comments,

> At the level of their literary and historical character we have good reasons to treat the Gospels seriously as a source of information on the life and teaching of Jesus, and thus on the historical origins of Christianity.... Beyond that point, the decision as to how far a scholar is willing to accept the record they offer is likely to be influenced more by his openness to a "supernaturalist" world-view than by strictly historical considerations.[8]

In many cases, a rejection of this "supernaturalist" worldview or bias against the possibility of miracles is to blame for a person's skepticism of the Gospels. We have already seen in chapter 3 that it is not warranted to reject the possibility of miracles *a priori* (i.e., before examining the evidence).[9] A more reasonable approach would involve employing an "open" historical-critical method and making an inference to the best explanation.[10]

HOW DO WE KNOW WHAT THE *EARLIEST* CHRISTIANS BELIEVED ABOUT JESUS?

The ancient world was an oral culture. That is, societies were used to functioning without books. We, however, live in a post-Guttenberg world, so many of us have a hard time imagining how an oral culture could produce reliable history. Oral tradition is often caricatured as crude storytelling along the lines of the telephone game we all played as kids. This is an inaccurate picture to say the least.

Richard Bauckham, professor of New Testament studies at the University of St. Andrews, has done extensive research on oral tradition and eyewitness testimony in the first-century Jewish context. He writes, "Trusting testimony is not an irrational act of faith that leaves critical rationality aside; it is, on the contrary, the rationally appropriate way of responding to authentic testimony. Gospels understood as testimony are the entirely appropriate means of access to the historical Jesus."[11] He further notes that modern skeptics of testimony find themselves in an awkward position because "it is also a rather neglected fact that all history... relies on testimony."[12] In other words, you can dispense with testimony as a legitimate source of knowledge *only* if you are willing to dispense with the ability to discover *anything* about the past.

So what did the early church believe and proclaim from the very beginning? The New Testament documents were written between A.D. 49 and 95. If Jesus was crucified in A.D. 30 or 33, then how was what the earliest followers believed about Jesus reliably passed down until the texts were written and circulated? New Testament scholar Darrell Bock points to three lines of evidence that demonstrate what the earliest Christians believed (conveniently alliterated in three S's):[13]

- *Summaries*—Early Christians memorized and recited doctrinal summaries alongside the Hebrew Scriptures when they gathered for worship in house churches.[14] These oral texts were later *embedded* in written texts.[15] It is important to highlight that these summaries often included the technical language of "delivered" and "received," language that related to how Jewish rabbis passed on formal tradition to their disciples.[16] (Jesus is called "rabbi" fourteen times and "teacher" forty times in the Gospels.)
- *Singing*—When they gathered, early Christians sang their theology in hymns to show their devotion to the Lord Jesus Christ.[17] Did you sit down and memorize "Amazing Grace" or did you absorb it over time? The same was true for them.
- *Sacraments*—Baptism and the Lord's Supper were practiced on a regular basis and pictured the basic elements of the salvation story as core theology.[18]

These creeds, hymns, and practices *predated* the writing of the New Testament documents (remember that this was an oral culture and most people could not read). Think of these three S's as "oral texts" that the earliest Christian community recited and practiced *before* a completed Bible existed. These foundational beliefs (sometimes called the "rule of faith") set the boundaries for orthodoxy.*

DID EARLY CHRISTIANITY BORROW FROM PAGAN MYTHOLOGY?

A common Internet objection to Christianity is that it is not all that unique—that Christianity borrowed much of the language of dying and rising gods and baptismal rituals from mystery religions, where the language was already prevalent. Dawkins even says "all the essential features of the Jesus Legend ... are borrowed—every last one of them—from other religions already in existence in the Mediterranean and Near East region."[19] But this is not a new objection. This view originated with the "history of religions school" in the late nineteenth century.[20] Since then the theory has been soundly refuted and virtually no professional New Testament scholar argues for this anymore.

All of the sources cited by those who argue that Christianity was heavily dependent on mystery religions *postdate* the oral and written sources for Christianity. So if borrowing was going on, it was the mystery religions that borrowed from Christianity in order to gain new converts. As Ed Komoszewski, James Sawyer, and Daniel Wallace conclude, "Only after the rise of Christianity did mystery religions begin to look suspiciously like the Christian faith."[21]

Because this objection is so popular, we will allow N. T. Wright to put to rest any thoughts of substantive similarity between the historical, bodily resurrection of Jesus as recorded in the New Testament documents and the accounts of dying and rising gods in the mystery religions:

---

* Despite claims by some contemporary scholars (e.g., Bart Ehrman and Elaine Pagels) that there were lots of alternative Christianities and so it is hard to know which one is the "true" one, the fact remains that later Gnosticism was clearly inconsistent with the earliest teaching and beliefs of Christianity. See Darrell L. Bock, *The Missing Gospels: Unearthing the Truth Behind Alternative Christianities* (Nashville: Thomas Nelson, 2006).

At the heart of cults was the ritual re-enactment of the death and rebirth of the god, coupled with sundry fertility rites. The productivity of the soil, and of the tribe or nation, was at stake; by getting in touch with the mysterious forces that underlay the natural world, by sympathetic and symbolic re-enactment of them, one might hope to guarantee both crops and offspring. The myth which accompanied these rituals was indeed the story of resurrection, of new life the other side of death.... Did any worshiper in these cults, from Egypt to Norway, at any time in antiquity, think that actual human beings, having died, actually came back to life? Of course not. These multifarious and sophisticated cults enacted the god's death as a *metaphor*, whose concrete referent was the cycle of seed-time and harvest, of human reproduction and fertility. Sometimes, as in Egypt, the myths and rituals included funerary practices: the aspiration of the dead was to become united with Osiris. But the new life they might thereby experience was not a return to life in the present world. Nobody actually expected the actual mummies to get up, walk about and resume normal living; nobody in that world would have wanted such a thing, either.*

---

* N. T. Wright, *The Resurrection of the Son of God* (Minneapolis: Fortress Press, 2003), 80–81. Here is Ronald Nash's assessment of the Isis-Osiris myth:

The basic myth of the Isis cult concerned Osiris, her husband during the earlier Egyptian and nonmystery stage of the religion. According to the most common version of the myth, Osiris was murdered by his brother who then sank the coffin containing Osiris's body into the Nile River. Isis discovered the body and returned it to Egypt. But her brother-in-law once again gained access to the body, this time dismembering it into fourteen pieces which he scattered widely. Following a long search, Isis recovered each part of the body. It is at this point that the language used to describe what followed is crucial. Sometimes those telling the story are satisfied to say that Osiris came back to life, even though such language claims far more than the myth allows. Some writers go even further and refer to the alleged "resurrection" of Osiris. One liberal scholar illustrates how biased some writers are when they describe the pagan myth in Christian language: "The dead body of Osiris floated in the Nile and he returned to life, this being accomplished by a baptism in the waters of the Nile" (Joseph Klausner, *From Jesus to Paul* [New

DID JESUS CLAIM TO BE GOD?

Often it is asserted that claims to be God were read back onto the lips of Jesus by later generations of Christians. So, did early followers of Christ invent Jesus' deity as Dawkins asserts? Was he merely a peasant philosopher or good moral teacher until Constantine got hold of him for political reasons in the fourth century?

We first must recognize that devotion to Jesus Christ *as God* emerged in a Jewish monotheistic context. Larry Hurtado of the University of Edinburgh, who has exhaustively researched the origins of devotion to Jesus in earliest Christianity, observes:

> Certainly, various deities were reverenced in the Roman period, and it was in principle no problem to enfranchise another divine figure in the religious "cafeteria" of the time. But it was a major and unprecedented move for people influenced by the exclusivist monotheistic stance of Second-Temple Judaism to include another figure singularly alongside God as recipient of cultic devotion in their worship gatherings.[22]

In other words, this wasn't like adding another god to the pantheon. If the Jewish people had learned anything in the seven hundred years leading up to the time of Jesus, it was that idolatry (the practice of worshiping any other gods but Yahweh) was a really bad idea.* They had other theological shortcomings, but the belief

---

York: Macmillan, 1943], 104). This biased and sloppy use of language suggests three misleading analogies between Osiris and Christ: (1) a savior god dies and (2) experiences a resurrection accompanied by (3) water baptism. But the alleged similarities, as well as the language used to describe them, turn out to be fabrications of the modern scholar and are not part of the original myth.

From "Was the New Testament Influenced by Pagan Religions?" available at the Christian Research Institute's Web site, http://www.equip.org/articles/was-the-new-testament-influenced-by-pagan-religions- (accessed October 20, 2009). Nash's book-length treatment is *The Gospel and the Greeks* (1992).

* Archaeological evidence confirms this point. Ephraim Stern of the Hebrew University of Jerusalem says, "Before the destruction of the First Temple, wherever we dig, in whatever part of the Judean country, we find sanctuaries, and, more

in *one* God was not one of them. They weren't open to or interested in adding another deity. Something pretty remarkable would have had to occur to account for this radical change. Perhaps being raised from the dead would qualify?

The historical evidence reveals that the earliest Christians believed and worshiped Jesus as God. But did Jesus ever claim this of himself? We will briefly point out two occasions that clearly answer yes to that question. Both are found in Mark, which most scholars agree was the first gospel written.

In Mark 2:1–12, Jesus is teaching to a packed house at Capernaum. There is a paralytic man there and his friends are trying to get him to Jesus, but they can't because of the crowds. So they boldly lower him down through the roof to see if Jesus will heal him. How does Jesus respond? He says, "Your sins are forgiven." This surprised both the religious leaders in the crowd and the paralytic. The paralytic was probably thinking, "Hey, I asked to be healed, not forgiven!" And the religious leaders responded, "Why does this fellow talk like that? He's blaspheming! Who can forgive sins but God alone?" But Jesus wanted to make a point, so he said, "Which is easier: to say to the paralytic, 'Your sins are forgiven,' or to say, 'Get up, take your mat and walk'? But that you may know that the Son of Man has authority on earth to forgive sins," he said to the paralytic, "I tell you, get up, take your mat and go home." So the paralytic was healed *and* forgiven. The point was this: anyone could have said that the paralytic's sins were forgiven, but how would anyone have known that it really happened? Jesus gave a visible demonstration of his authority, proving by the miracle that he could also forgive sins. According to the Old Testament, only God could forgive sins,[23] so this miracle was a clear audiovisual illustration of Jesus claiming to be God.

---

often, we find hundreds and thousands of figurines [idols], even in Jerusalem itself.... We are speaking about thousands before [Jerusalem's destruction] and nothing—completely nothing at all—after." "The Bible's Buried Secrets," *Nova*, first broadcast November 18, 2008, by PBS. Transcript available at http://www .pbs.org/wgbh/nova/transcripts/3516_bible.html.

Mark 14:60–64 describes Jesus' trial before the Jewish leadership. They asked him point-blank, "Are you the Christ [Messiah], the Son of the Blessed One?" Jesus' response is powerful: "I am," said Jesus. "And you will see the Son of Man sitting at the right hand of the Mighty One and coming on the clouds of heaven." Now there is a lot here. But the most important point is this: Jesus refers to himself as the "Son of Man" who is described in Daniel 7:13–14:

> In my vision at night I looked, and there before me was one like a son of man, coming with the clouds of heaven. He approached the Ancient of Days and was led into his presence. He was given authority, glory and sovereign power; all peoples, nations and men of every language worshiped him. His dominion is an everlasting dominion that will not pass away, and his kingdom is one that will never be destroyed.

The Son of Man is in the presence of the Ancient of Days (God himself) and is given authority by him.[24] The Jewish leadership—who knew their Scriptures well—got the message loud and clear. Hearing Jesus' claim, they were indignant, declaring it blasphemy. In verses 63–64, they began scheming to condemn Jesus to death for claiming to be God.

Given the context of Jewish monotheism, Jesus would have had to come at claiming his deity sideways rather than head-on. He needed to bring them along step by step. But make no mistake; these were radical claims to his audience and they clearly got the point he was making on both occasions.[25] In addition to these texts in Mark, many other passages in the New Testament teach directly (and indirectly) that Jesus claimed to be God and was affirmed as God.[26]

SOME THOUGHTS ON THE EXCLUSIVITY OF JESUS

Almost everybody respects and admires the life of Jesus. What people struggle with is how he could be the *only* way to

God. We want to briefly address important issues regarding the exclusivity of Jesus.[27]

It has become popular in our culture to claim that "All roads lead to God." New Atheist Sam Harris doesn't think so and we commend him for that. He speaks plainly, "We agree, for instance, that if one of us is right, the other is wrong.... Either Jesus offers humanity the one true path to salvation (John 14:6), or he does not."[28] Truth is exclusive *by definition*. And every belief system—even atheism—makes truth claims. Ravi Zacharias artfully points out:

> The truth is that all religions are not the same. All religions do not point to God. All religions do not say that all religions are the same. In fact, some religions do not even believe in God. At the heart of every religion is an uncompromising commitment to a particular way of defining who God is or is not. Buddhism, for example, was based on Buddha's rejection of two of Hinduism's fundamental doctrines. Islam rejects both Buddhism and Hinduism. So it does no good to put a halo on the notion of tolerance and act as if everything is equally true. In fact, even all-inclusive religions such as Bahaism end up being exclusivistic by excluding the exclusivists![29]

Christianity may be exclusive in its belief about Jesus being the only way, but it doesn't exclude anyone who desires to come. *All* are welcome regardless of gender, race, socioeconomic status, or geographic location.[30] This illustrates the radical inclusivity of the gospel. Jesus offers the free gift of forgiveness to all who will accept it; he doesn't force anyone to receive his grace. As Paul makes clear in Acts 17:24–27, anyone who seeks after God will find him.*

---

* It is at this point that the objection of "What about those who have never heard of Jesus?" is raised. This is a legitimate question—one that we have wrestled with. But there are various plausible answers that Christians have put forth. See Paul Copan, *True for You, but Not for Me*, 183–215. The clear teaching of Acts

A common objection used to silence Christians is that they are arrogant and immoral for believing that there is only one way to God. In response to this charge, philosopher Alvin Plantinga asks:

> Suppose I think the matter over, consider the objections as carefully as I can, realize that I am finite and furthermore a sinner, certainly no better than those with whom I disagree, and indeed inferior both morally and intellectually to many who do not believe what I do; but suppose it still seems clear to me that the proposition in question is true [e.g., that Jesus Christ is the only way to God]: can I really be behaving immorally in continuing to believe it?[31]

It seems not. Moreover, the charge of arrogance and immorality cuts both ways because implicit in the objectors' view is the claim that everyone else *but them* has it wrong. That is, all of the devout adherents of the world's major religions—billions of people—have it wrong. Now unfortunately Christians are arrogant sometimes, but their shortcomings or misunderstandings do not count against the truthfulness of the life, message, and teachings of Jesus.

WHO DO YOU SAY THAT I AM?

Where does this all leave us? Contrary to the buffet of Dawkins's unsupported assertions in this chapter's epigraph, the New Testament documents provide solid historical data about Jesus that can be reasonably assessed. Laypeople and scholars have investigated and found the person of Jesus compelling for two thousand years now. Objections much more sophisticated than the ones Dawkins marshals have been raised and responded to through the years. But the question still remains—*Who do you say that I am?*[32] While you can guess how Dawkins would

---

17:24–27 is that God desires to be found and that if people seek him, they will find him, for God's Spirit is at work in the world (see also John 16:8–11).

respond, everyone who encounters the carpenter from Nazareth must give an answer.

FOR FURTHER ENGAGEMENT

Komoszewski, J. Ed, M. James Sawyer, and Daniel B. Wallace. *Reinventing Jesus: How Contemporary Skeptics Miss the Real Jesus and Mislead Popular Culture.* Grand Rapids: Kregel, 2006.

Strauss, Mark L. *Four Portraits, One Jesus: An Introduction to Jesus and the Gospels.* Grand Rapids: Zondervan, 2007.

[why it matters]

FINDING REAL LIFE

Little did I know when I started college that I would be doing what I do now. I was headed toward a career in radio, TV, and film, hoping to be a sports broadcaster or work in a sports department. I was an officially declared agnostic. I grew up in a church where belief in the resurrection of Jesus was optional. I thought Jesus was a great cultural figure who served our culture as a prophet in challenging us to live well before God. I knew that much, but was not sure how much of it I believed, including what one could believe about the Bible—a valuable book perhaps, but not the Word of God (after all, how could one know when God had spoken!).

Over a five-year period stretching back to high school, believers had urged me to believe in Jesus for the sake of my soul, but I was not interested. I thought they were a bunch of fanatics. But they were good friends so I tolerated their forays into the well-being of my soul. During my freshman year at Southern Methodist University, my roommate and fellow Mustangs challenged me to take a hard look at Jesus' claims and the Bible. I began a journey during that year that has kept me in the Bible ever since.

I came to see that the manuscript base for the content of the New Testament was unparalleled among ancient documents. I began to recognize that no group would make up a religion like Christianity to make itself feel better, because Christianity is so forthright about the sin of all of us and how we cannot fix the problem on our own. I came to appreciate the Gospels presenting a Jesus who did more than make ethical claims. I came to see that he was the issue in these books. One either embraced his message and embraced him at the same time, or one had to reject his message, since he was in the middle of that message.

I began to sense that the Jesus my culture had sold me was not the Jesus I was reading about in the only sources we have that reach back to and give us a glimpse of him. I had no doubt that God existed and acted when I had prayed not to have a Bible-carrying Southern Baptist roommate at college so I could enjoy my time in college, and my roommate ended up being a Bible-carrying Southern Baptist whose life matched his profession of faith. That prayer had begun the night before I left for college with the affirmation, "God, I do not know if you exist, but if you do, then . . ." God was keeping an eye out for me by answering my prayer with a heartfelt *no*.

So now I write about Jesus and the Bible. I have given my life to studying it. It is not only worth the study; it is a book that points us to the one person who can help us make things right with God. I do not broadcast sporting events today. I write about finding real life.

—Darrell L. Bock

Darrell L. Bock is research professor of New Testament studies at Dallas Theological Seminary. He has written several books, including *Dethroning Jesus, The Missing Gospels,* and the *New York Times* best-seller *Breaking the Da Vinci Code.* He is professor for spiritual development and culture for the *Center for Christian Leadership* and the editor-at-large for *Christianity Today.*

A Tale of Two Ordinary Believers

I believe in Christianity as I believe that the sun has risen: not only because I see it, but because by it I see everything else.

—C. S. Lewis

We aren't Oxford-trained, PhD-holding guys, and odds are that most people who read this book aren't either. So what does the journey of faith look like for two ordinary believers?

JONATHAN MORROW'S STORY

All journeys have beginnings. For me, I guess you could say that it all began in Ms. Lacy's class in sophomore English. But we'll get to that.

My life began in Las Vegas, Nevada. Unfortunately the early part of my story was marked by more pain than happiness.[1] I grew up in the home of an alcoholic father and a mother who struggled with mental illness—a combination that proved too much for their marriage. They divorced when I was eight.

When I was seven, my family moved to a town in rural east Tennessee because my dad was in search of a fresh start. My childhood revolved around my older brothers and the latest Nintendo games (the original Zelda, Final Fantasy, and Super Mario

253

Brothers). There are happy memories from those days, but also wounds I feel to this day.

During my sophomore year in high school, I was living with my dad, stepmom, and new little sister in Knoxville, Tennessee. Throughout middle and high school I had been searching for something to fill the emptiness I felt inside and to distract me from the loss I had already experienced in life. This took the form of everything from video games, drinking, and playing football to chasing girls (but thankfully, all the girls ran in the other direction).

Most days, English class was filled with grammar, required reading, and quizzes to make sure we were actually reading. One day, however, was different; we watched the movie *Dead Poets Society*. I watched as Mr. Keating (Robin Williams) gathered the young men of his English literature class around him and talked to them about life. Through a Walt Whitman poem, he made this striking point: "'What good amid these, O me, O life?' Answer: That you are here. That life exists, and identity; that the powerful play goes on and you may contribute a verse. *That the powerful play goes on and you may contribute a verse. What will your verse be?*"[2] These last words resonated deep within me. What *would* my verse be?

I left class not knowing what I wanted to do or who I wanted to become; I had realized for the first time that I did not want to come to the end of my life only to find out that I'd never really lived. I wanted my life to count. This thought stayed in the back of my mind while I started to search for what "living" would be.

Fast-forward to September of my junior year. It was homecoming and I had no date for the dance. My classmate Mike didn't either (though at least his girlfriend was grounded rather than nonexistent). The two of us ended up grabbing some chicken wings for dinner. We didn't know each other very well, but he took a huge risk by sharing the gospel with me that night. For the first time, I actually understood that the point of Jesus' life and death was to forgive me of my sins, restore my broken relationship with God, and offer me new life—eternal life.[3] That night, with the little I understood, I put my trust in Jesus and asked God to come into my life and change me. That choice has changed everything.

My college years were some of the most formative of my life. Early on, I got involved with Campus Crusade for Christ at Middle Tennessee State University and ended up spending three summers with them, living and working in Clearwater Beach, Florida. These were foundational times for me when I intensely studied the Bible and lived in community with other students who were actually following Jesus (as opposed to just "playing church"). During these summers I experienced a life-transforming closeness with God.

My experience in the college classroom shaped me as well. I encountered several professors who were openly hostile to Christianity, and they raised some objections to my faith that I had never heard before. I had no answers myself and began looking for them because I had no interest in believing in fairy tales, even if they made me feel better. But as I investigated my faith in God, I found it stood up to the test of scrutiny and doubt. I discovered good reasons to be a Christian. (I share part of my college journey in my book *Welcome to College*.)

Moving forward, I found the love of my life and was married the same day I graduated from college. It would take another book to begin to describe how healing Mandi's unconditional love has been for me these past nine years, or how much fun it is to face the adventure of life with your best friend. I have learned so much from watching her walk with God through the years.

After college I became increasingly driven by the thought that if people were created to know and love God, then that's what I wanted to be about. This was the genesis of my Web site, www.thinkchristianly.org, and led to my graduate studies in Bible, philosophy of religion and ethics, and theology—first in Dallas and then Los Angeles. Today, I am an equipping pastor, and, as opportunities arise, I speak and write to help people engage the most important questions of life. That is my passion.

I have encountered doubts and depression along the way. I

have faced tough questions (mostly my own). There have been times when God seemed right next to me and others when he seemed universes away. I have made mistakes and done things well. I have experienced the loss of my oldest brother to suicide and the death of my father—both far too young. I have also experienced the joys of becoming a father, twice. I have friends that know and love me and mentors who have marked my life.

I have literally walked where Jesus walked. I stumble more often than I would like to admit. Like most stories, mine has its share of comedy and tragedy. But most importantly, Jesus has been with me every step of the way, changing my life.

SEAN MCDOWELL'S STORY

My story is very different from Jonathan's. Even though I grew up in a Christian home, I hit a point in my life when certain questions came crashing down on me like never before:

- How do I really know Christianity is true?
- What if I had been raised in a different family?
- Is Jesus really the only way to God?
- What is going to bring real happiness and meaning in life?
- What about other religions?

Before this period in my life, my faith was simply something I took for granted. I have fond memories of attending Christian conferences, going on mission trips, and listening to my father as he taught the Bible. My parents raised me in the Christian faith. In fact, as a child growing up, I can never remember *not* believing the Christian story about the world.

Yet as a college student, the answers I had based my faith on were no longer enough. Nagging doubts about my faith simply wouldn't go away. Rather than basing my faith on the opinions of others, I wanted a faith based on fact. I had to know with confidence that what I believed was really true. At times, these questions led me to feel the despair that existentialist writers such as Albert Camus and Jean Paul Sartre said follows from the nonexistence of God. I remember staying up late at night reading the psalms of David as he wondered why God seemed so absent in his time of need.

As I began to wrestle with the big questions of life, I realized there was one person I needed to be honest with—my father. To understand how difficult this was for me, it's necessary to understand my dad's story as well.

If you haven't figured it out by now, my father is the well-known apologist Josh McDowell. He's the author of more than a hundred books and is probably best known for his book *Evidence That Demands a Verdict*, in which he documents the historical evidence that persuaded him to seriously consider the claims of Christ. He grew up in a small Michigan town in a deeply dysfunctional family. In fact, my father can never remember his father (my grandfather) being sober until he was in his twenties. His older brother sued his father for everything, just out of spite; and one of his older sisters committed suicide. In the recently updated version of *More Than a Carpenter*, my dad shared an even more devastating reality about his childhood—he was sexually abused for about eight years.

As you can imagine, my father was desperate for a life of happiness and meaning. As a student, he excelled—he made a lot of money and was elected to student government—yet nothing seemed to fill the void in his heart. After meeting some Christian students whose lives were genuinely different, he decided to write a book disproving the Christian faith. While he records his story in more depth in *More Than a Carpenter*, the bottom line is that he became convinced that Christianity was in fact true. He has since committed his entire life to defending and sharing his faith with the world.

This is why my conversation with my father was so tough. How would he react to his own son questioning the faith he so deeply cherished? As we sat at a small café in the mountains of Breckenridge, Colorado, I told my dad about my doubts. His response completely took me by surprise. "I think it's great that you want to find truth," he said. "It's wise not simply to accept things just because you were told them. You need to find out if Christianity is true. You know that your mom and I love you regardless of what you conclude. Seek after truth and take to heart the things your mom and I have taught you. And let me know if I can help along the way."

That is exactly what I did. I started reading books by Christian apologists such as J. P. Moreland and William Lane Craig. I also read skeptics such as Michael Martin (*The Case Against Christianity*) and Dan Barker (*Losing Faith*). I had to read as much of both sides as possible. After much thought, deliberation, and soul-searching, I came to the conclusion that my faith was well grounded. Here's (very) briefly what persuaded me.

While there is much compelling evidence for Christianity (as we have attempted to lay out in this book), I just couldn't explain away Jesus of Nazareth. His public ministry was only three years. He never wrote a book. He had no political or military power. And he had little money. Yet he turned the world upside down through his teachings.

The claims Jesus made struck me as utterly profound. He didn't just claim to know how to get to God—he claimed to *be* God. He didn't claim simply to know truth—he claimed to *be* the truth.[4] Jesus asked his disciples, "Who do you say I am?"[5] I realized that how I answered this question determined my eternal destiny. The evidence convinced me that Jesus really was who he claimed to be.

Yet it wasn't solely the historical evidence that I found persuasive. It was also Jesus' profound insight into the human condition that humbled me. In Mark 7:21–23 Jesus said, "For from within, out of people's hearts, come evil thoughts, sexual immoralities, thefts, murders, adulteries, greed, evil actions, deceit, lewdness, stinginess, blasphemy, pride, and foolishness. All these evil things come from within and defile a person" (HCSB). The core problem with the world, according to Jesus, is not economic inequality (à la Marxism) or our forgetfulness that we are divine (New Age), but the wickedness of the human heart. As Frank Sinatra observed, we want to do it our way. Although I was a pretty good kid growing up (i.e., I didn't do any of the "big" sins), I began to realize the depths of my own pride and rebellion against God. I, too, needed a savior.

Even though I had been in a Christian family my entire life, the message of Christ reached my heart like never before. I still have questions. And I still make mistakes (just ask my wife!). But following Jesus has been the best decision of my life.

OUR TALE OF TWO OXFORD ATHEISTS RESUMED

Before we wrap up this book, we need to finish our Tale of Two Oxford Atheists. As we pointed out in the introduction, both Richard Dawkins and Alister McGrath are intelligent, Oxford-trained, tenured professors. So what are we to make of why one detests God and the other embraces him?

There is a revealing interchange involving Richard Dawkins that Barbara Hagerty, National Public Radio religion correspondent, recounts in her thought-provoking work *Fingerprints of God*:

> John Barrow, a brilliant Cambridge mathematician, was speed walking us through the hypothesis of a "fine-tuned" universe that is exquisitely and astonishingly calibrated to allow for life. He explained the concept of "multiverses," which posits that we live in one of 10,500 universes. Then he said, almost as an aside, "I'm quite happy with a traditional theistic view of the universe."
>
> He might as well have dropped an anvil on Richard Dawkins's foot. Dawkins is a renowned evolutionary biologist at Oxford University and possibly the world's most famous atheist, certainly one of the most militant. Two days earlier, Dawkins had delivered a talk that he believed would prove the impossibility of God, and which later would be published as a book called *The God Delusion*. He had remained in Cambridge to hear the lectures of other researchers, particularly world-class John Barrow. When Barrow, who turned out to be an Anglican, mentioned his

belief in God, Dawkins began roiling with frustration like a teakettle about to blow.

"Why on earth do you believe in God?" Dawkins blurted. All heads turned to Barrow.

"If you want to look for divine action, physicists look at the rationality of the universe and the mathematical structure of the world."

"Yes, but *why do you want to look for divine action?*" Dawkins demanded.

"For the same reason that someone might *not* want to," Barrow responded with a little smile, as all of us erupted in laughter—except for Dawkins.[6]

This exchange is fascinating because both men are experts in their field and highly conversant in the language of science. And yet, we see them at opposite ends of the spectrum. Dawkins struggles to comprehend why anyone would want to look for evidence of a divine hand in the universe and Barrow, on the basis of the available data and not in spite of it, is completely content to see the fine-tuning of the universe as evidence of a divine hand.

Dawkins doesn't want there to be a God. And he is not alone. One of the leading philosophical atheists of our day, Thomas Nagel, candidly admits,

> I want atheism to be true and am made uneasy by the fact that some of the most intelligent and well-informed people I know are religious believers. It just isn't that I don't believe in God and, naturally, hope that I am right in my belief. It's that I hope there is no God! I don't want the universe to be like that.[7]

Statements like Dawkins's and Nagel's remind us of what we have known all along—*belief is a complex and mysterious process.* The choice to believe or not believe is never just a rational decision.* Tim Keller observes that our beliefs are comprised of three kinds of reasons.[8] First, there are rational reasons that have to do with weighing the evidence and arguments for and against a particular belief (much of this book deals with rational reasons for or against God). Reason is very important and is consistent with faith, but reason *alone* does not tell the whole story. Next, there are personal reasons that involve our experiences, disappointments, achievements, and desires. While much harder to quantify, personal reasons are shaped—*but not determined*—by what we have experienced and how we have interpreted those experiences. So personal reasons must be factored into the equation of belief. Finally, there are social reasons that consist of the relationships we either have or want to have. For example, maybe the group of people that accepts me (or that I want to accept me) strongly disbelieves in God. This doesn't make God exist or not exist because people and communities don't determine truth. Relationships, however, do influence how plausible I may find the belief in God to be.

At the end of the day, our beliefs are formed in the context of rational, personal, and social reasons. What we are open to believing is often influenced by personal and social experiences; but while these experiences may influence what we are open to believing, they do not determine reality. That is why rational investigation is so important to this process. In a way, it keeps our internal and relational worlds honest.

A CHALLENGING QUESTION

We believe that the rational evidence for God's existence and the truth of Christianity is persuasive. We have not found the New Atheists' arguments against Christianity compelling (in fact, many of their objections appeal to emotion rather than to reason). And we think that you are well within your intellectual rights to believe in God *if you want to.*

---

* In fact, the Bible reveals that it is possible for people to suppress the truth and that God gives people the freedom to do so (Rom. 1:18ff).

You have hung with us to the end. Perhaps you are already a believer and this book has encouraged your faith. Or perhaps you are still not sure what to think about the whole God thing. We challenge you to ask yourself a courageous question: "Would I at least want it to be the case that Jesus was who he claimed to be?" In other words, "Would I want it to be the case that forgiveness, restoration, and purpose are actually possible in this life and the next?"[9] This will tell you where you are on your faith journey. Notice we are not asking if you think there is good evidence for Jesus or not—we are only asking if you think it would be a good thing if Jesus was who he claimed to be. How you answer this question may provide some insight on how your personal and social reasons are affecting your openness to the question of God.

When it comes to God, one of the temptations is to withhold judgment until all the information is in and every possible issue has been investigated. To be honest, that's a pretty tall order. You will never know everything about everything. We sure don't. If you wait until then, well, you will be waiting a long time! And this question is too important. Just as an employer can't know if an employee will be reliable until she is hired, and a person can't know everything about their would-be spouse before they say "I do," so too you can't experience God—really get to know him—until you have entered into a personal relationship.[10] Pastor John Ortberg offers some really good advice: "There is no way to God that bypasses the call to let go [i.e., to choose to trust him]. You may have many intellectual doubts, and it is really important to be honest about those, to talk about them and study. However, thinking and studying alone never remove the need to choose. The question of faith is never just an intellectual decision."[11]

We have made our choice; we're all in. In light of the solid historical, scientific, philosophical, and personal evidence, we have chosen to follow Jesus. We have invited him to be our leader, savior, and teacher, and we are trying to learn from him how to live each day.

So what about you? Everyone follows someone and there is

always a choice. We hope that you will seriously consider Jesus' offer for a different kind of life: "Come to me, all of you who are weary and carry heavy burdens, and I will give you rest. Take my yoke upon you. Let me teach you, because I am humble and gentle at heart, and you will find rest for your souls."[12]

FOR FURTHER ENGAGEMENT

McDowell, Josh, and Sean McDowell. *More Than a Carpenter: His Story Might Change Yours.* Carol Stream, IL: Tyndale, 2009.

Moreland, J. P. *The God Question: An Invitation to a Life of Meaning.* Eugene, OR: Harvest House, 2009.

Resources for Engaging the New Atheism and Thinking About God

BOOKS

Berlinski, David. *The Devil's Delusion: Atheism and Its Scientific Pretensions.* New York: Basic Books, 2009.

Craig, William Lane, and Chad Meister. *God Is Great, God Is Good: Why Believing in God is Reasonable and Responsible.* Downers Grove, IL: Intervarsity Press, 2009.

D'Souza, Dinesh. *What's So Great About Christianity?* Washington, DC: Regnery, 2007.

Ganssle, Gregory E. *A Reasonable God: Engaging the New Face of Atheism.* Waco, TX: Baylor University Press, 2009.

Hart, David Bentley. *Atheist Delusions: The Christian Revolution and Its Fashionable Enemies.* New Haven, CT: Yale University Press, 2009.

Keller, Timothy. *The Reason for God: Belief in an Age of Skepticism.* New York: Dutton, 2008.

Lennox, John C. *God's Undertaker: Has Science Buried God?* Updated ed. Oxford: Lion, 2009.

Strobel, Lee. *The Case for the Real Jesus: A Journalist Investigates Current Attacks on the Identity of Christ.* Grand Rapids: Zondervan, 2007.

DVDS

The Case for a Creator. Directed by Wayne P. Allen. La Habra, CA: Illustra Media, 2006.

The Case for Christ. Directed by Michael and Timothy Eaton. Orange County, CA: Carmel Entertainment Group, 2007.

The Case for Faith. Directed by Lad Allen. La Habra, CA: La Mirada Films, 2008.

Darwin's Dilemma. Directed by Lad Allen. La Habra, CA: Illustra Media, 2009.

Expelled: No Intelligence Allowed. Directed by Nathan Frankowski. Premise Media, 2008.

Is Faith Delusional? An Evening with John Lennox and Ravi Zacharias. Norcross, GA: Ravi Zacharias International Ministries, 2009.

The Privileged Planet. Directed by Lad Allen. La Habra, CA: Illustra Media, 2004.

Unlocking the Mystery of Life. Directed by Lad Allen. La Habra, CA: Illustra Media, 2002.

WEB SITES

- Jonathan Morrow (www.thinkchristianly.org)
- Sean McDowell, Worldview Ministries (www.sean mcdowell.org)
- Stand to Reason (www.str.org)
- Ravi Zacharias International Ministries (www.rzim.org)
- William Lane Craig, Reasonable Faith (www.reasonable faith.org)
- Lee Strobel, Investigating Faith (www.leestrobel.com)
- John Lennox, Science and Ethics (www.johnlennox.org)
- The Veritas Forum (www.veritas.org)
- Confident Christianity (www.confidentchristianity.com)
- Be Thinking (www.bethinking.org)
- Reclaiming the Mind Ministries—Making Theology Accessible (www.reclaimingthemind.org)
- Biblical Training (www.biblicaltraining.org)
- Dinesh D'Souza's debates, YGod Institute (www.greatgod debates.org)

Dealing with Doubt on the Journey of Faith

Questions... *everybody has them.* But what do we do with them? And what happens when questions about God, the Bible, or Christianity turn into doubts? Real Christians aren't supposed to doubt, are they? Tim Keller offers a helpful and important observation:

> A faith without some doubts is like a human body without any antibodies in it. People who blithely go through life too busy or indifferent to ask hard questions about why they believe as they do will find themselves defenseless against either the experience of tragedy or the probing questions of a smart skeptic. A person's faith can collapse almost overnight if she has failed over the years to listen patiently to her own doubts, which should only be discarded after long reflection.[1]

Doubt is a natural part of being human because part of what it means to be human is to have limitations. Every one of us, including our New Atheist friends, have limitations in energy, time, and even knowledge. We all experience doubts at one time or another simply because we *cannot* know everything about everything. So be encouraged, you are not alone. But in order to live with our doubts in a spiritually healthy and faith-building way, we need to be clear about what doubt is and isn't.

COMING TO TERMS WITH FAITH, DOUBT, AND UNBELIEF

We have already seen that a biblical understanding of faith is not blind or opposed to evidence, but it doesn't require *complete* information either. Rather, faith is simply trusting in what you have good reason to believe is true. It is also important to remember that faith is only as good as the object in which it is placed. Sincerity is important, but trying really hard to believe something doesn't make it true or false. A great way to find out if you really believe something is whether you are ready to act as if (fill in the blank) were true or real in everyday life. For example, do you really believe being pure in your thought life and relationships is the best way to live? Do your viewing habits and moral boundaries match this belief?

To doubt means to be between two minds or opinions. It is the middle ground between faith and unbelief. Unbelief, as Os Guinness notes, "is a state of mind that is closed against God, an attitude of the heart that disobeys God as much as it disbelieves the truth. Unbelief is the result of a settled choice."[2] There is a big difference between *struggling to believe* in God and *setting oneself against* him. Richard Dawkins and Christopher Hitchens are exhibits A and B of "unbelief."

THE DASHBOARD OF YOUR SOUL

A helpful way to understand faith and doubt is to think about the dashboard in your car. When no warning lights are on, things are working pretty well. But when the check engine light comes on, you know there's a problem. However, this light indicates there could be *several different* problems, but you won't know which problem it is until you go to a mechanic to have your car hooked up to a diagnostic reader.

Doubt is like the warning lights on your dashboard. Just as you wouldn't address all the warning lights in the same way (e.g., changing the oil every time the gas light comes on), you also need to recognize that each kind of doubt will require a unique approach. The most common forms of doubt originate from *intellectual* issues, *emotional* issues, and *lack of spiritual growth*. Here are some suggestions about how to deal with these. Also, we refer you to Os Guinness's excellent book on understanding and overcoming doubt, *God in the Dark*.

Intellectual Doubts

Regarding intellectual doubts, the most important thing you can do is to become very clear and specific concerning what your question or doubt actually is. The longer it remains foggy, the harder it is to address. It's often helpful to dig through your thoughts with others to get at the root intellectual issue or question. During times of doubt, the temptation will be to isolate yourself and not share with friends what you are struggling with because you may be ashamed to admit it. Bad idea—you need community most during times of doubt. Remember, doubt can be an opportunity for your faith to grow.

Of all the varieties of doubt, intellectual doubt is the one that is best helped by reading and study. You must be persistent. If something is really bothering you, work at finding a *reasonable* answer. We promise that you are not the only one who has ever asked the question you're struggling with, and you should have confidence that others have provided good answers to consider (see appendix A). As you process your thoughts, it is important to try to make sure your intellectual doubt isn't an emotional doubt in disguise.

Emotional Doubts

Sometimes emotional doubts look like intellectual ones, but the root cause turns out to be something other than unanswered questions. Guinness offers a vivid picture of how this sometimes looks:

> The problem is not that reason attacks faith but that emotions overwhelm reason as well as faith, and it is impos-

sible for reason to dissuade them.... [This kind of] doubt comes just at the point where the believer's emotions (vivid imagination, changing moods, erratic feelings, intense reactions) rise up and overpower the understanding of faith. Out-voted, out-gunned, faith is pressed back and hemmed in by the unruly mob of raging emotions that only a while earlier were quiet, orderly citizens of the personality. Reason is cut down, obedience is thrown out, and for a while the rule of emotions is as sovereign as it is violent. The coup d'état is complete.[3]

We've all been there. Sources of emotional doubts can be experiencing disappointment, failure, pain, or loss; having unresolved conflict or wounds from the past that need to be addressed; letting unruly emotions carry us away for no good reason; being spiritually dry and relationally distant; and fearing to truly commit to someone (whether that "someone" be God or another person).

Emotions are good and normal but they aren't always right. In other words, they are an accurate barometer of what is going on inside our hearts, but they don't tell us whether we should or shouldn't be feeling the way we are. Emotions need to be examined. So you may be emotionally drained after a long week or a conflict at work, but that shouldn't impact your confidence that the New Testament is reliable or God exists. What happens is that our emotions get projected onto an intellectual question, and it becomes really easy to confuse the two. This is another reason community is so important. Others can usually help us discern what is going on if we are in emotional white water. Don't be afraid to invite other mature believers into your faith journey.

Doubts from Lack of Growth

If you are a follower of Jesus, then it is always good to ask yourself if you are growing spiritually. Are you reading your Bible on a regular basis, praying, sharing your faith, and living in community with others? (Not in a legalistic, "God will love me more if…" sort of way, but because these are necessary ingredients for spiritual growth.) "Just as a plant grows or withers, so a worldview must be developed and practiced and produce results or it will be discarded as impractical."[4]

Also, when we sin and are disobedient to God, our sin creates relational distance from him. God doesn't love us any less and we aren't at risk of losing our salvation, but we may need to ask him to show us if we need to confess anything so that our fellowship with him can be restored. A great prayer to meditate on is Psalm 139:23–24: "Search me, O God, and know my heart; test me and know my anxious thoughts. See if there is any offensive way in me, and lead me in the way everlasting."

If you find yourself with doubts, you're in good company.[5] But having the courage to doubt your doubts and investigate the root of these issues over time will lead to greater confidence as a follower of Jesus. This is what the journey of faith is all about.[6]

FOR FURTHER ENGAGEMENT

Guinness, Os. *God in the Dark: The Assurance of Faith Beyond a Shadow of Doubt.* Wheaton, IL: Crossway, 1996.

Moreland, J. P., and Klaus Issler. *In Search of a Confident Faith: Overcoming Barriers to Trusting in God.* Downers Grove, IL: InterVarsity Press, 2008.

Is the New Testament Filled with Contradictions and Corrupted Texts?

Richard Dawkins and Christopher Hitchens, who have no formal training in biblical studies, often appeal to New Testament scholar Bart Ehrman to do their heavy lifting.[1] Briefly, Ehrman is the darling of the New Atheists because he was once one of the deluded fundamentalists that the New Atheists rail against in their writings—Ehrman was an insider who studied at evangelical institutions like Moody and Wheaton. But when he did his doctorate at Princeton, he lost his faith in the Bible and eventually abandoned Christianity. Unfortunately it appears that Ehrman's rejection of the Bible had more to do with a misunderstanding of the doctrine of biblical inerrancy than it did with the actual issue that triggered his crisis of faith.[2]

While technically not one of the New Atheists (he describes himself as a "happy agnostic"), Ehrman gets honorable mention status in this book because of his recent attacks on historic Christianity. In *Misquoting Jesus: The Story Behind Who Changed the Bible and Why* and *Jesus, Interrupted: Revealing the Hidden Contradictions in the Bible (And Why We Don't Know About Them)*, he claims the Bible has been corrupted by scribes throughout the centuries and is riddled with errors and contradictions.* And to heighten the air of conspiracy, he informs the reader that all of this has been covered up by the church and kept from them.[3] (Ehrman has also written *God's Problem* on the problem of evil and suffering in the world and admits that this is his fundamental barrier to belief in God.[4])

So what are we to make of Bart Ehrman? I (Jonathan) recently interacted with a college student who was being persuaded by the writings of the New Atheists and who was also reading Ehrman's *Misquoting Jesus*. As we talked, it became clear that this was the only book on the origin and reliability of the Bible he was reading or planning to read, which is unfortunate because Ehrman offers an alarmist portrait of New Testament studies. He is also a capable writer who—like the New Atheists—employs powerful rhetoric. His modus operandi is to popularize discussions that have been known in scholarship for decades, serve them up for a generally skeptical and biblically illiterate culture, and then presto, discredit historic or traditional Christianity. New Testament scholar Ben Witherington, who also studied at Princeton but did not reject his faith, observes that Ehrman's writings read like one who is "exorcising the demons of his fundamentalist past."[5]

We don't point all of this out to dismiss Ehrman's conclusions without an argument, but we do want you to be aware that you are not getting an unbiased, dispassionate analysis of the facts if you *only* read Ehrman. So if you are investigating the origin and reliability of the New Testament documents for the first time, then you owe it to yourself to hear both sides of the story. Ehrman is an accomplished scholar and textual critic, but so is someone like Dan Wallace, coauthor of *Dethroning Jesus: Expos-*

---

* "Apparent contradictions in the Gospels often disappear when it is recognized that the Evangelists were not producing verbatim accounts but had the freedom to paraphrase, interpret, abbreviate, and reorder events and sayings to fit their theological purposes. They were not just reporters but inspired interpreters of the Jesus event." Mark L. Strauss, *Four Portraits, One Jesus: An Introduction to Jesus and the Gospels* (Grand Rapids: Zondervan, 2007), 396.

ing Popular Culture's Quest to Unseat the Biblical Christ. Wallace has the same credentials and level of expertise in textual criticism and has arrived at very different conclusions than Ehrman after examining the same evidence (in fact, they publically debated these differences in 2008).

TEXTUAL CRITICISM 101

To begin with, you need to know that none of the original manuscripts of either the Old or New Testaments are still in existence—all that remain are imperfect copies. But this is exactly the same situation of every other ancient work of literature. No one has the originals. While this may come as a surprise, this fact should not turn us into skeptics regarding ancient texts. Scholars use the copies we have to reconstruct the original Old and New Testaments. Generally speaking, the more copies we have to examine and the closer they are to when they were written, the better. This practice of reconstruction is known as textual criticism.

It's simply not possible to cover all the ins and outs of textual criticism in an appendix, but we do want to answer two critical questions.[6] First, do scholars have enough copies of the New Testament to work with in order to reconstruct? And second, have the New Testament texts been corrupted beyond recovery? Regarding the number of copies:

> The wealth of material that is available for determining the wording of the original New Testament is staggering: more than fifty-seven hundred Greek New Testament manuscripts, as many as twenty thousand versions, and more than one million quotations by patristic writers. In comparison with the average ancient Greek author, the New Testament copies are well over a thousand times more plentiful. If the average-sized manuscript were two and one-half inches thick, all the copies of the works of an average Greek author would stack up four feet high, while the

copies of the New Testament would stack up to over a mile high! This is indeed an embarrassment of riches.[7]

You can consider the first question sufficiently answered.

Regarding corruption beyond recovery, Ehrman claims, "There are more variations among our manuscripts than there are words in the New Testament."[8] He uses the number of 400,000 textual variants (the entire Greek New Testament contains only 138,162 words). While his account of textual variants is technically accurate, the statistic is very misleading to those not familiar with how textual criticism works. Wallace breaks down the kinds of variants into four categories:[9]

- *Spelling differences.* The great majority of variants (70–80 percent, or 320,000) are spelling errors and easily correctable upon manuscript comparison.
- *Minor differences that involve synonyms or do not affect translation.* These differences include whether or not definite articles are used with proper names (e.g., "The Joseph or The Mary" in Luke 2:16) or words are transposed (word order is very important in English, but in an inflected language like Greek, word order is not nearly as important). Another cause of differences is the flexibility of the language, evident in the fact that you can say something like "Jesus loves John" in at least sixteen different ways in the Greek language.
- *Meaningful* but not *viable differences.* Sometimes a single manuscript will differ from the rest of the manuscripts that contain the same alternate reading (e.g., 1 Thess. 2:9 either reads "gospel of God" or "gospel of Christ").
- *Meaningful* and *viable differences.* These meaningful and viable differences are not things like "Jesus was a liar" or "Jesus was not compassionate." One of the most famous differences is Romans 5:1, which either reads "let us have peace with God" or "we have peace with God." The manuscripts are pretty evenly divided.

Wallace summarizes, "less than 1 percent of all textual variants are both meaningful and viable, and by 'meaningful' we don't mean to imply earth-shattering significance but rather, almost always, minor alterations to the meaning of the text."[10] That comes out to less than 4,000 of the original 400,000 variants *having any real significance at all for the meaning of a verse.* And regarding the verses where questions remain, "significant textual variants that alter core doctrines of the New Testament have not been produced."[11]

FAITH WELL PLACED

While at Princeton, Ehrman studied under arguably the leading textual critic of the late twentieth century, Bruce Metzger. If the New Testament text had skeletons in the closet and dirty little secrets, he knew all about them. Here is the conclusion of an interview that Lee Strobel had with Metzger:

All the decades of scholarship, of study, of writing textbooks, of delving into the minutiae of the New Testament text—what has all that done to your personal faith? "It has increased the basis of my personal faith to see the firmness with which these materials have come down to us, with a multiplicity of copies, some of which are very, very ancient," Metzger responded. So, scholarship has not diluted your faith—. He jumped in before I could finish my sentence. "On the contrary, it has built it. I've asked questions all my life, I've dug into the text, I've studied this thoroughly, and today I know with confidence that my trust in Jesus has been well placed ... *very* well placed."[12]

FOR FURTHER ENGAGEMENT

Blomberg, Craig. *The Historical Reliability of the Gospels.* 2nd ed. Downers Grove, IL: InterVarsity Press, 2007.

Bock, Darrell L., and Daniel B. Wallace. *Dethroning Jesus: Exposing Popular Culture's Quest to Unseat the Biblical Christ.* Nashville: Thomas Nelson, 2007.

Notes

INTRODUCTION A TALE OF TWO OXFORD ATHEISTS

Epigraph. Antony Flew and Roy Abraham Varghese, *There Is a God: How the World's Most Notorious Atheist Changed His Mind* (New York: HarperOne, 2007), 88.

1. Simon Hattenstone, "Darwin's Child," The Guardian, February 10, 2003,http://www.guardian.co.uk/world/2003/feb/10/religion.science andnature; and the "God Delusion" debate between Dawkins and Lennox, http://www.fixed-point.org/index.php/video/35-full-length/164-the-dawkins-lennox-debate (accessed December 7, 2009).

2. AlisterMcGrath,"Biography,"http://users.ox.ac.uk/~mcgrath/biography .html (accessed April 17, 2009).

3. Alister McGrath, *Dawkins' God: Genes, Memes, and the Meaning of Life* (Malden, MA: Blackwell, 2005), 2.

4. Ibid.

5. Ibid.

6. "A Brief History of the University," University of Oxford, http://www .ox.ac.uk/about_the_university/introducing_oxford/a_brief_history _of_the_university/index.html (accessed March 30, 2009).

7. See http://www.atheistbus.org.uk.

8. Richard Dawkins, *The God Delusion* (New York: Houghton Mifflin, 2008), 5.

9. See the blog post by Darrel Ray ("American Atheist Conference," April 12, 2009) on Atheist Nexus: A Community of Nontheists, http://www.atheistnexus.org/profiles/blogs/american-atheist-conference.

10. Christopher Hitchens, *God Is Not Great: How Religion Poisons Everything* (New York: Twelve, 2007), 282.

11. Dawkins, *The God Delusion*, 5.

12. Ibid., 31.

13. Sam Harris, *Letter to a Christian Nation* (New York: Knopf, 2007), 87–88.

14. From the cover of Alister McGrath and Joanna Collicut McGrath, *The Dawkins Delusion? Atheist Fundamentalism and the Denial of the Divine* (Downers Grove, IL: InterVarsity Press, 2007).

15. John Meacham, "The End of Christian America," *Newsweek*, April 4, 2009, http://www.newsweek.com/id/192583 (accessed April 16, 2009). See Darrell Bock, "Making Sense of the *Newsweek* Article on the Decline and Fall of American Christianity," April 10, 2009, http://blog.bible.org/bock/node/459 (accessed April 17, 2009).

16. Timothy Keller, *The Reason for God: Belief in an Age of Skepticism* (New York: Dutton, 2008), xv.

17. Alister McGrath, *The Twilight of Atheism: The Rise and Fall of Disbelief in the Modern World*, 1st ed. (New York: Doubleday, 2004).

18. An exceptional work detailing this research is David Kinnaman and Gabe Lyons, *UnChristian: What a New Generation Really Thinks About Christianity—and Why It Matters* (Grand Rapids: Baker, 2007).

19. Michael Novak, *No One Sees God: The Dark Night of Atheists and Believers* (New York: Doubleday, 2008), xxiii.

20. For more on changing the tone of the cultural conversation, see Sean McDowell, ed. *Apologetics for a New Generation* (Eugene, OR: Harvest House, 2009).

CHAPTER 1 IS FAITH IRRATIONAL?

Epigraph. Victor J. Stenger, *The New Atheism: Taking a Stand for Science and Reason* (Amherst, NY: Prometheus, 2009), 15.

1. Richard Dawkins, "The Faith Trap" panelists blog "On Faith: A Conversation on Religion and Politics with Jon Meacham and Sally Quinn," posted March 20, 2010, *The Washington Post*, http://newsweek.washingtonpost.com/onfaith/panelists/richard_dawkins/2010/03/the_faith_trap.html.

2. Ibid.

3. Richard Dawkins, *The God Delusion* (New York: Houghton Mifflin, 2008), 28.

4. Daniel C. Dennett, *Breaking the Spell: Religion as a Natural Phenomenon* (New York: Penguin, 2006), 230–31.

5. Sam Harris, *Letter to a Christian Nation* (New York: Vintage Books, 2008), 110.

6. Sam Harris, *The End of Faith: Religion, Terror, and the Future of Reason* (New York: W. W. Norton, 2004), 15.

7. John 20:29.

8. Richard Dawkins, *The Selfish Gene* (Oxford: Oxford University Press, 1976), 198.

9. Matthew 12:39–40; 16:4; Mark 8:31; 9:31; 10:33–34; Luke 11:29.

10. John 20:31 HCSB.

11. See J. P. Moreland, *Love Your God with All Your Mind: The Role of Reason in the Life of the Soul* (Colorado Springs, CO: Navpress, 1997).
12. Mark 12:30.
13. Isaiah 1:18.
14. See Exodus 7–14.
15. Mark 2:10–11.
16. David K. Clark, *Dialogical Apologetics: A Person-Centered Approach to Christian Defense* (Grand Rapids: Baker, 1993), 20.
17. David Marshall, "Faith and Reason," http://christthetao.homestead.com/articles/FaithandReason.pdf (accessed July 25, 2009).
18. Alister McGrath and Joanna Collicutt McGrath, *The Dawkins Delusion? Atheist Fundamentalism and the Denial of the Divine* (Downers Grove, IL: InterVarsity Press, 2007), 17.
19. Christopher Hitchens, *God Is Not Great* (New York: Twelve, 2007), 5.
20. Norman L. Geisler and Frank Turek, *I Don't Have Enough Faith to Be an Atheist* (Wheaton, IL: Crossway, 2004).
21. Dawkins, *The God Delusion*, 165.
22. Ibid., 188–89.
23. See Daniel C. Dennett, *Consciousness Explained* (Boston: Back Bay, 1992).
24. Ibid., 35.
25. William Lane Craig, "God Is Not Dead Yet," *Christianity Today*, July 2008, 22–27.
26. Ibid., 22.
27. Quentin Smith, "The Metaphilosophy of Naturalism," *Philo* 4, no. 2 (2001): 4.
28. Ibid.
29. "Modernizing the Case for God," *Time*, April 7, 1980, available at http://www.time.com/time/magazine/article/0,9171,921990,00.html.
30. David Berlinski, *The Devil's Delusion: Atheism and Its Scientific Pretensions* (New York: Basic Books, 2009), 136.
31. 1 Thessalonians 2:8.

CHAPTER 2 ARE SCIENCE AND CHRISTIANITY AT ODDS?

Epigraph. Sam Harris, *Letter to a Christian Nation* (New York: Knopf, 2007), 63.
1. David Van Biema, "God vs. Science" *Time*, November 5, 2006; Christopher Hitchens, *God Is Not Great: How Religion Poisons Everything* (New York: Twelve, 2007), 64–65; Richard Dawkins, *The God Delusion* (New York: Houghton Mifflin, 2008), 321.
2. Alister McGrath and Joanna Collicutt McGrath, *The Dawkins Delusion? Atheist Fundamentalism and the Denial of the Divine* (Downers Grove, IL: InterVarsity Press, 2007), 46.
3. Johannes Kepler, quoted in John C. Lennox, *God's Undertaker: Has Science Buried God?* (Oxford: Lion Hudson, 2007), 20.
4. Isaac Newton, *The General Scholium*, quoted in Nancy Pearcey and

Charles Thaxton, *The Soul of Science* (Wheaton, IL: Crossway, 1994), 91. Newton also believed the ear and eye indicated intelligent design.

5. "The Jewish God, the Christian God, or No God?" debate between Christopher Hitchens, Dennis Prager, and Dinesh D'Souza, May 1, 2008, at Temple Baht Yam in Newport Beach, CA.

6. "Religion poisons everything" is found in the subtitle of Hitchens's book *God Is Not Great*.

7. Dawkins, *The God Delusion*, 125.

8. McGrath and McGrath make this point in *The Dawkins Delusion?* 42.

9. See, e.g., Pearcey and Thaxton, *Soul of Science*; and Ian Barbour, *When Science Meets Religion: Enemies, Strangers, or Partners* (New York: HarperOne, 2000).

10. Sam Harris, *The End of Faith: Religion, Terror, and the Future of Reason* (New York: W. W. Norton, 2005), 105.

11. Guillermo Gonzalez and Jay W. Richards, *The Privileged Planet* (Washington, DC: Regnery, 2004), 222–28.

12. Ibid.

13. There are two official online sources for the trial of Galileo that substantiate this discussion. The Scripture references that were in the Galileo trial are at http://www.law.umkc.edu/faculty/projects/ftrials/ galileo/scripture.html. The prosecutors accused him of misusing Scripture. Second, the papal condemnation, which includes their renunciation of his use of Scripture is at http://www.law.umkc.edu/ faculty/projects/ftrials/galileo/condemnation.html. These Web sites are from the University of Missouri-Kansas City School of Law.

14. Dinesh D'Souza, *What's So Great About Christianity* (Washington, DC: Regnery, 2007), 110.

15. Dawkins, *The God Delusion*, 35 (emphasis in original).

16. Romans 1:4.

17. Lennox, *God's Undertaker*, 19.

18. Dawkins, *The God Delusion*, 411–17.

19. Patricia Churchland, "Epistemology in the Age of Neuroscience," *Journal of Philosophy*, October 1987, 548.

20. C. S. Lewis, *Miracles: A Preliminary Study*, Macmillan Paperbacks Edition (New York: Macmillan, 1978), 12–24.

21. From a letter to W. Graham (July 3, 1881), quoted in the *Autobiography of Charles Darwin and Selected Letters* (1892; reprint, New York: Dover, 1958).

22. Lewis, *Miracles*, 21.

23. Paul Davies, "What Happened Before the Big Bang?" in *God for the 21st Century*, ed. Russell Stannard (Philadelphia: Templeton Foundation Press, 2000), 12.

24. Alvin Plantinga, "The Dawkins Confusion," review of *The God Delusion*, by Richard Dawkins, *Books and Culture*, March/April 2007, http://www.booksandculture.com/articles/2007/marapr/1.21.html (accessed April 17, 2009).

CHAPTER 3 ARE MIRACLES POSSIBLE?

Epigraph. Richard Dawkins, *The God Delusion* (New York: Houghton Mifflin, 2008), 187.

1. "Mount Kenya Region—Past and Present," http://www.visitkenya .com/guide/4_0_64_1_Mount-Kenya-Region-.:-VisitKenya.com.html (accessed November 18, 2009).

2. Dawkins, *The God Delusion*, 35 (emphasis in original); Christopher Hitchens, *God Is Not Great* (New York: Twelve, 2007), 141.

3. Gerd Ludemann, *The Resurrection of Christ: A Historical Inquiry* (Amherst, NY: Prometheus, 2004).

4. See Sara Goudarzi, "Did Jesus Walk on Water? Or Ice?" MSNBC, April 4, 2006, http://www.msnbc.msn.com/id/12152740/ (accessed August 6, 2009), which discusses findings published by Doran Nof, Ian McKeague, and Nathan Paldor, "Is There a Paleolimnological Explanation for 'Walking on Water' in the Sea of Galilee?" *Journal of Paleolimnology* 35 (2006): 417–39.

5. 1 Corinthians 15:17 HCSB. See also verse 14.

6. Dawkins, *The God Delusion*, 419.

7. Michael Goulder, "The Explanatory Value of Conversion-Visions," in *Jesus' Resurrection: Fact or Fiction? A Debate Between William Lane Craig and Gerd Ludemann*, edited by Paul Copan and Ronald Tacelli (Downers Grove, IL: InterVarsity Press, 2000), 102.

8. Hitchens, *God Is Not Great*, 141.

9. See John Earman, *Hume's Abject Failure: The Argument Against Miracles* (Oxford: Oxford University Press, 2000).

10. C. S. Lewis, *Miracles* (New York: Macmillan, 1947), 105.

11. Paul Rhodes Eddy and Gregory A. Boyd, *The Jesus Legend: A Case for the Historical Reliability of the Synoptic Jesus Tradition* (Grand Rapids: Baker, 2007).

12. J. P. Meier, *A Marginal Jew: Rethinking the Historical Jesus*, vol. 1 (New York: Doubleday, 1991), 275.

13. Eddy and Boyd, *The Jesus Legend*, 246.

14. 2 Timothy 2:15.

15. See Graham H. Twelftree, *Jesus the Miracle Worker: A Historical and Theological Study* (Downers Grove, IL: InterVarsity Press, 1999).

16. Gary L. Habermas and Michael R. Licona, *The Case for the Resurrection of Jesus* (Grand Rapids: Kregel, 2004), 143.

17. Hitchens, *God Is Not Great*, 143.

18. Habermas and Licona, *Case for the Resurrection*, 43–77.

19. Matthew 27:35–50; Mark 15:27–37; Luke 23:33–46; John 19:23–30.

20. Will Durant, *Caesar and Christ* (New York: Simon and Schuster, 1944), 572.

21. John 19:34. See William D. Edwards, Wesley J. Gabel, and Floyd E. Hosmer, "On the Physical Death of Jesus Christ," *Journal of the American Medical Association* 255 (March 21, 1986): 1462–63; C. Truman

Davis, "The Crucifixion of Jesus," *Arizona Medicine*, March 1965, 185–86; Stuart Bergsma, "Did Jesus Die of a Broken Heart?" *The Calvin Forum*, March 1948, 165.

22. John Dominic Crossan, *Jesus: A Revolutionary Biography* (San Francisco: HarperCollins, 1991), 145.
23. Stephen T. Davis, *Risen Indeed: Making Sense of the Resurrection* (Grand Rapids: Eerdmans, 1993), 79–80.
24. See Josh McDowell and Sean McDowell, "Attempts to 'Explain Away' the Resurrection," chap. 17 in *Evidence for the Resurrection* (Ventura, CA: Gospel Light, 2009), 199–214.

CHAPTER 4 IS DARWINIAN EVOLUTION THE ONLY GAME IN TOWN?

Epigraph. Richard Dawkins, *The Greatest Show on Earth* (New York: Free Press, 2009), 8.

1. Sam Harris, *Letter to a Christian Nation* (New York: Knopf, 2007), 70; Christopher Hitchens, *God Is Not Great* (New York: Twelve, 2007), 85; Dawkins, *Greatest Show on Earth*, 9.
2. See "A Scientific Dissent from Darwinism," Discovery Institute, www.dissentfromdarwin.org (accessed October 28, 2009).
3. Dawkins, *Greatest Show on Earth*, 35.
4. Jerry Coyne, *Why Evolution Is True* (New York: Viking, 2009), 1.
5. Richard Dawkins, *The Blind Watchmaker: Why the Evidence Reveals a Universe Without Design* (New York: Norton, 1987), 1.
6. Dawkins, *Greatest Show on Earth*, 216.
7. Harris, *Letter to a Christian Nation*, 76; Dawkins, *Greatest Show on Earth*, 116.
8. Michael Behe, *The Edge of Evolution* (New York: Free Press, 2006), 15 (emphasis in original).
9. Dawkins, *Greatest Show on Earth*, 295.
10. Ibid., 283.
11. Stephen C. Meyer, Scott Minnich, Jonathan Moneymaker, Paul A. Nelson, and Ralph Seelke, *Explore Evolution* (Melbourne: Hill House, 2007), 77.
12. Harris, *Letter to a Christian Nation*, x (emphasis in original).
13. Hitchens, *God Is Not Great*, 82; Dawkins, *Greatest Show on Earth*, 356.
14. Dawkins, *Greatest Show on Earth*, 70.
15. Ibid., 353.
16. William A. Dembski and Sean McDowell, *Understanding Intelligent Design* (Eugene, OR: Harvest House, 2008), 54–55.
17. Dawkins, *Greatest Show on Earth*, 332.
18. Fazale Rana and Hugh Ross, *Who Was Adam?* (Colorado Springs, CO: NavPress, 2005), 237–38.
19. Benjamin Wiker, *The Darwin Myth: The Life and Lies of Charles Darwin* (Washington, DC: Regnery, 2009), 77.

20. Dawkins, *Greatest Show on Earth*, 402.
21. Richard Dawkins, *Blind Watchmaker*, 6.
22. Victor J. Stenger, *The New Atheism: Taking a Stand for Science and Reason* (Amherst, NY: Prometheus, 2009), 76.
23. Stephen C. Meyer, "Jefferson's Support for Intelligent Design" *Boston Globe*, July 15, 2009, available at www.boston.com/bostonglobe/editorial_opinion/oped/articles/2009/07/15/jeffersons_support_for_intelligent_design/.
24. Ibid.
25. Ibid.

CHAPTER 5 HOW DID THE UNIVERSE BEGIN?

Epigraph. Sam Harris, *Letter to a Christian Nation* (New York: Vintage Books, 2006), 73.
1. Michael Turner, "The Origin of the Universe" *Scientific American*, September 2009, 36–43.
2. Simon Singh, *Big Bang: The Origin of the Universe* (New York: Harper-Collins, 2004), 144–61, 249–61.
3. P. C. W. Davies, "Spacetime Singularities in Cosmology" in *The Study of Time III*, ed. J. T. Fraser (Berlin: Springer Verlag, 1978), 78–79.
4. Antony Flew and Roy Abraham Varghese, *There Is a God: How the World's Most Notorious Atheist Changed His Mind* (New York: Harper-One, 2007), 136.
5. William Lane Craig, *Reasonable Faith: Christian Truth and Apologetics*, 3rd ed. (Wheaton, IL: Crossway, 2008), 111.
6. J. Y. T. Greig, ed., *The Letters of David Hume*, vol. 1 (Oxford: Clarendon Press, 1932), 187.
7. J. P. Moreland, *The God Question: An Invitation to a Life of Meaning* (Eugene, OR: Harvest House, 2009), 58–60.
8. Alexander Vilenkin, *Many Worlds in One: The Search for Other Universes* (New York: Hill and Wang, 2006), 176.
9. Daniel C. Dennett, *Breaking the Spell: Religion as a Natural Phenomenon* (New York: Viking, 2006), 244.
10. Craig, *Reasonable Faith*, 111.
11. Richard Dawkins, *The God Delusion* (New York: Houghton Mifflin, 2008), 174.
12. Stephen Hawking, *A Brief History of Time* (New York: Bantam, 1988), 136–39.
13. Dawkins, *The God Delusion*, 136.
14. Genesis 1:1 (emphasis added).
15. Sam Harris, "The Language of Ignorance," Truthdig, posted on August 15, 2006, http://www.truthdig.com/report/item/20060815_sam_harris_language_ignorance/.
16. Craig, *Reasonable Faith*, 154.

17. Paul Draper, "A Critique of the Kalam Cosmological Argument" in *Philosophy of Religion: An Anthology*, ed. Louis P. Pojman, 3rd ed. (Belmont, CA: Wadsworth, 1997), 45–46.

18. Robert Jastrow, *God and the Astronomers*, 2nd ed. (Toronto: Reader's Library, 2000), 107.

CHAPTER 6 HOW DID LIFE BEGIN?

Epigraph. Richard Dawkins, *The God Delusion* (New York: Houghton Mifflin, 2008), 162, 168.

1. *Dumb and Dumber*, directed by Peter Farrelly (New York: New Line Cinema, 1994).

2. Sam Harris, *Letter to a Christian Nation* (New York: Vintage Books, 2008), 71.

3. Origins of Life Initiative, Harvard University, http://origins.harvard.edu.

4. Andy Knoll, "Origins: How Life Began," *Nova*, first broadcast September 28, 2004, by PBS. Transcript available at http://www.pbs.org/wgbh/nova/transcripts/3112_origins.html.

5. Stuart Kauffman, *At Home in the Universe: The Search for Laws of Self-Organization and Complexity* (New York: Oxford University Press, 1995), 31.

6. Charles Darwin, in a letter written in 1871 to Joseph Hooker, in F. Darwin, ed., *The Life and Letters of Charles Darwin*, vol. 3 (London: John Murray, 1888), 18.

7. John C. Lennox, *God's Undertaker: Has Science Buried God?* (Oxford: Lion Hudson, 2007), 117.

8. Michael Denton, *Evolution: A Theory in Crisis* (Chevy Chase, MD: Adler and Adler, 1986), 250.

9. Richard Dawkins, *River Out of Eden: A Darwinian View of Life* (New York: Basic Books, 1996), 17. 10. Mark Whorton and Hill Roberts, *Holman QuickSource Guide to Understanding Creation* (Nashville: B & H Publishing, 2008), 323.

11. Bill Gates, *The Road Ahead* (Boulder, CO: Blue Penguin, 1996), 228.

12. As quoted in Antony Flew and Roy Abraham Varghese, *There Is a God: How the World's Most Notorious Atheist Changed His Mind* (New York: HarperOne, 2007), 128.

13. Stephen C. Meyer, *Signature in the Cell: DNA and the Evidence for Intelligent Design* (New York: HarperCollins, 2009), 206–7.

14. Ibid., 212.

15. Ibid.

16. Dean H. Kenyon and Gary Steinman, *Biochemical Predestination* (New York: McGraw-Hill, 1969).

17. Dean Kenyon, *Unlocking the Mystery of Life*, DVD, directed by Wayne P. Allen and Timothy Eaton (La Habra, CA: Illustra Media, 2002).

18. Kenyon recounts his journey in the DVD *Unlocking the Mystery of Life*.
19. Ibid.
20. Dawkins, *The God Delusion*, 164.
21. Meyer, *Signature in the Cell*, 314.
22. Quoted in Robert Irion, "RNA Can't Take the Heat," *Science* 279 (1998): 1303.
23. See William A. Dembski and Jonathan Wells, *How to Be an Intellectually Fulfilled Atheist (Or Not)* (Wilmington, DE: Intercollegiate Studies Institute, 2008).
24. Flew and Varghese, *There Is a God*, 132.
25. Nancy Pearcey, *Total Truth: Liberating Christianity from Its Cultural Captivity* (Wheaton, IL: Crossway, 2004), 201.

CHAPTER 7 WHY IS THE UNIVERSE JUST RIGHT FOR LIFE?

Epigraph. Richard Dawkins, *The God Delusion* (New York: Houghton Mifflin, 2008), 78.
1. Tim Folger, "Science's Alternative to an Intelligent Creator: The Multiverse Theory," *Discover* (December 2008), published online November 10, 2008, available at http://discovermagazine.com/2008/dec/10-sciences-alternative-to-an-intelligent-creator.
2. Quoted in Paul Davies, *The Accidental Universe* (Cambridge: Cambridge University Press, 1982), 118.
3. Mark Whorton and Hill Roberts, *Holman QuickSource Guide to Understanding Creation* (Nashville: B & H Publishing, 2008), 308.
4. Hugh Ross, *The Creator and the Cosmos* (Colorado Springs, CO: NavPress, 1995), 117.
5. This section first appeared in Sean McDowell, "Is There Any Evidence for God? Physics and Astronomy," *The Apologetics Study Bible for Students*, gen. ed. Sean McDowell (Nashville: B & H Publishing, 2010).
6. Roger Penrose, *The Emperor's New Mind* (New York: Oxford, 1989), 344.
7. Paul Davies, *Cosmic Jackpot* (New York: Houghton Mifflin, 2007), 149.
8. Ibid., 2–3.
9. John Leslie, *Universes* (New York: Routledge, 1989), 108.
10. Dawkins, *The God Delusion*, 188.
11. Victor Stenger, *The New Atheism: Taking a Stand for Science and Reason* (Amherst, NY: Prometheus, 2009), 193.
12. Reasonablefaith.org, Q&A Archive question #1, "What do you think of Richard Dawkins' argument for atheism in *The God Delusion*?" (last accessed on March 20, 2010).
13. Folger, "Science's Alternative to an Intelligent Creator," http://discovermagazine.com/2008/dec/10-sciences-alternative-to-an-intelligent-creator.

14. Dawkins, *The God Delusion*, 173–74.
15. Bradley Monton, *Seeking God in Science: An Atheist Defends Intelligent Design* (Peterborough, Ontario: Broadview, 2009), 85.
16. Robin Collins, "The Teleological Argument," *The Blackwell Companion to Natural Theology*, ed. J. P. Moreland and William Lane Craig (Malden, MA: Wiley-Blackwell, 2009), 263.
17. John C. Lennox, *God's Undertaker: Has Science Buried God?* (Oxford: Lion Hudson, 2007), 73.
18. William Lane Craig, *Reasonable Faith: Christian Truth and Apologetics*, 3rd ed. (Wheaton, IL: Crossway, 2008), 159.
19. Guillermo Gonzalez and Jay W. Richards, *The Privileged Planet: How Our Place in the Cosmos Is Designed for Discovery* (Washington, DC: Regnery, 2004), 32–33.
20. Ibid., 35.
21. Stenger, *The New Atheism*, 77.
22. Alister McGrath, *A Fine-Tuned Universe: The Quest for God in Science and Theology* (Louisville, KY: Westminster John Knox Press, 2009), 180–81.
23. Ibid., 156.
24. Ibid., 164.
25. Carl Sagan, *Pale Blue Dot: A Vision of the Human Future in Space* (New York: Random House, 1994).
26. Douglas Adams, *The Hitchhiker's Guide to the Galaxy*, 25th anniversary ed. (1979; London: Harmony, 2004). Monty Python also did a song on this same theme, adding the following commentary at the end: "It sort of makes you feel insignificant, doesn't it?"
27. Folger, "Science's Alternative to an Intelligent Creator," http://discover magazine.com/2008/dec/10-sciences-alternative-to-an-intelligent -creator.

CHAPTER 8 HAS SCIENCE SHOWN THERE IS NO SOUL?

Epigraph. Victor Stenger, *The New Atheism: Taking a Stand for Science and Reason* (Amherst, NY: Prometheus, 2009), 16.
1. Daniel C. Dennett, *Breaking the Spell: Religion as a Natural Phenomenon* (New York: Viking Press, 2006), 107 (emphasis in original).
2. Matthew 10:28 NASB.
3. Ecclesiastes 3:11.
4. Richard Dawkins, *The God Delusion* (New York: Houghton Mifflin, 2008), 210.
5. Sam Harris, *Letter to a Christian Nation* (New York: Vintage Books, 2008), 51.
6. Barbara Bradley Hagerty, "The God Choice," *USA Today*, June 22, 2009, 9A.

7. Barbara Bradley Hagerty, *Fingerprints of God* (New York: Riverhead, 2008), 205.
8. Gary Habermas and J. P. Moreland, *Beyond Death* (Wheaton, IL: Crossway, 1998), 157–58.
9. Ibid., 159.
10. Mario Beauregard and Denyse O'Leary, *The Spiritual Brain: A Neuroscientist's Case for the Existence of the Soul* (New York: HarperCollins, 2007), 163.
11. See also Dinesh D'Souza, *Life After Death: The Evidence* (Washington, DC: Regnery, 2009).
12. Tom Wolfe, "Sorry, But Your Soul Just Died," originally published in *Forbes ASAP* (1996). Reprinted with permission at http://orthodoxy today.org/articles/Wolfe-Sorry-But-Your-Soul-Just-Died.php.
13. John Searle, *Freedom and Neurobiology* (New York: Columbia University Press, 2007), 43.
14. Interestingly, Sam Harris seems to deny the existence of free will in *The End of Faith: Religion, Terror, and the Future of Reason* (New York: W. W. Norton, 2005), 262–63.
15. William Lane Craig and J. P. Moreland, *Philosophical Foundations for a Christian Worldview* (Downers Grove, IL: InterVarsity Press, 2003), 233–38.
16. Dennett, *Breaking the Spell,* 107.
17. Dawkins, *The God Delusion,* 168.
18. J. P. Moreland, *Consciousness and the Existence of God: A Theistic Argument,* Routledge Studies in the Philosophy of Religion (New York: Routledge, 2008).
19. Beauregard and O'Leary, *The Spiritual Brain,* 104.

CHAPTER 9 IS GOD JUST A HUMAN INVENTION?

Epigraph. Christopher Hitchens, *God Is Not Great: How Religion Poisons Everything* (New York: Twelve, 2007), 103.
1. Gerald R. McDermott, *The Baker Pocket Guide to World Religions: What Every Christian Needs to Know* (Grands Rapids: Baker, 2008).
2. Yann Martel, *Life of Pi* (San Diego: Harvest, 2003), 28.
3. Sigmund Freud, *The Future of an Illusion,* trans. James Strachey (New York: Norton, 1989), 38.
4. See, for example, William Lane Craig and J. P. Moreland, *The Blackwell Companion to Natural Theology* (Malden, MA: Wiley-Blackwell, 2009).
5. Paul Copan and Paul K. Moser, *The Rationality of Theism* (London: Routledge, 2003), 5.
6. Interestingly, there is some evidence of this. See Paul C. Vitz, *Faith of the Fatherless: The Psychology of Atheism* (Dallas: Spence, 1999), 17–57.
7. C. S. Lewis, *Mere Christianity* (New York: Simon and Schuster, 1996), 119–22.

8. However, we certainly need to move forward responsibly and humanely. See the excellent work by C. Ben Mitchell et al., *Biotechnology and the Human Good* (Washington, DC: Georgetown University Press, 2007).

9. Quoted in Barbara Bradley Hagerty, *Fingerprints of God: The Search for the Science of Spirituality* (New York: Riverhead, 2009), 93.

10. Ibid., 94–95.

11. Francis S. Collins, *The Language of God: A Scientist Presents Evidence for Belief* (New York: Free Press, 2006), 263.

12. Keith Ward, *Is Religion Dangerous?* (Grand Rapids: Eerdmans, 2007), 176.

13. Richard Dawkins, *The God Delusion* (New York: Houghton Mifflin, 2008), 193.

14. Ibid., 222.

15. Richard Dawkins, *A Devil's Chaplain: Reflections on Hope, Lies, Science, and Love* (New York: Houghton Mifflin, 2003), 117.

16. Ibid.

17. These points are summarized from Alister McGrath, *Dawkins' God: Genes, Memes, and the Meaning of Life* (Malden, MA: Blackwell, 2005), 119–38.

18. Dawkins, *Devil's Chaplain*, 124.

19. McGrath, *Dawkins' God*, 134.

20. Ibid., 135.

21. Ibid., 130.

22. Ibid., 137.

23. Dawkins, *The God Delusion*, 208–9.

24. See the arguments for and against in Michael J. Murray and Jeffrey Schloss, *The Believing Primate: Scientific, Philosophical, and Theological Reflections on the Origin of Religion* (Oxford: Oxford University Press, 2009).

25. Michael J. Murray, "Belief in God: A Trick of Our Brain?" in *Contending with Christianity's Critics: Answering New Atheists and Other Objectors*, ed. Paul Copan and William Lane Craig (Nashville: B & H Publishing, 2009), 47.

26. Murray, "Belief in God," 52.

27. Justin L. Barrett, *Why Would Anyone Believe in God?* Cognitive Science of Religion Series (Lanham, MD: AltaMira, 2004), 124. For a philosophical/theological argument for this same conclusion, see Alvin Plantinga, *Warranted Christian Belief* (Oxford: Oxford University Press, 2000).

28. Ecclesiastes 3:11.

CHAPTER 10 IS RELIGION DANGEROUS?

Epigraph. Christopher Hitchens, *God Is Not Great: How Religion Poisons Everything* (New York: Twelve, 2007), 56.

NOTES

1. Sam Harris, *Letter to a Christian Nation* (New York: Knopf, 2007), 87.
2. Hitchens, *God Is Not Great*, 283.
3. Richard Dawkins, *The God Delusion* (New York: Houghton Mifflin, 2008), 36.
4. Ibid., 58.
5. Keith Ward, *Is Religion Dangerous?* (Grand Rapids: Eerdmans, 2007), 27.
6. Alister McGrath, "Challenges from Atheism," in *Beyond Opinion: Living the Faith We Defend*, ed. Ravi Zacharias (Nashville: Thomas Nelson, 2007), 31.
7. Ward, *Is Religion Dangerous?* 27.
8. For more on the sociological and historical factors surrounding the Crusades, see Rodney Stark, *God's Battalions: The Case for the Crusades* (New York: HarperOne, 2009).
9. John Ortberg, *Faith and Doubt* (Grand Rapids: Zondervan, 2008), 111–12.
10. Ward, *Is Religion Dangerous*, 73.
11. Dinesh D'Souza, *What's So Great About Christianity* (Washington, DC: Regnery, 2007), 215.
12. Ibid., 216.
13. For a more thorough reckoning of what has been called "the most murderous idea ever invented," see Stéphane Courtois and Mark Kramer, *The Black Book of Communism: Crimes, Terror, Repression* (Cambridge, MA: Harvard University Press, 1999); and Zbigniew Brzezinski, *Out of Control: Global Turmoil on the Eve of the Twenty-first Century* (New York: Collier, 1994).
14. Dawkins, *The God Delusion*, 316.
15. D'Souza, *What's So Great About Christianity*, 215.
16. Hitchens, *God Is Not Great*, 5.
17. Victor J. Stenger, *The New Atheism: Taking a Stand for Science and Reason* (Amherst, NY: Prometheus, 2009), 21.
18. Ronald H. Nash, *Faith and Reason: Searching for a Rational Faith* (Grand Rapids: Zondervan, 1988), 24.
19. Kenneth R. Samples, *A World of Difference: Putting Christian Truth-Claims to the Worldview Test* (Grand Rapids: Baker, 2007), 21.
20. Victor J. Stenger, *God: The Failed Hypothesis* (Amherst, NY: Prometheus, 2007), 257.
21. David Berlinski, *The Devil's Delusion: Atheism and Its Scientific Pretensions* (New York: Basic Books, 2009), 26–27.
22. Ibid.
23. Richard Dawkins, *River Out of Eden: A Darwinian View of Life* (New York: Basic Books, 1995), 133.
24. Dallas Willard, *Renovation of the Heart: Putting on the Character of Christ* (Colorado Springs, CO: NavPress, 2002), 46.
25. Ibid.
26. Willard, *Renovation of the Heart*, 14.

27. In addition to *Renovation of the Heart*, see Willard, *The Divine Conspiracy: Rediscovering Our Hidden Life in God* (San Francisco: HarperSanFrancisco, 1997).
28. Ezekiel 36:26.
29. For more on how this plays out in society, see Hunter Baker, *The End of Secularism* (Wheaton, IL: Crossway, 2009).
30. Ravi K. Zacharias, *The End of Reason: A Response to the New Atheists* (Grand Rapids: Zondervan, 2008), 52.
31. Os Guinness, *The Case for Civility: And Why Our Future Depends on It* (New York: HarperOne, 2008).
32. Ibid., 135–37. For more on this topic, see Brendan Sweetman, *Why Politics Needs Religion: The Place of Religious Arguments in the Public Square* (Downers Grove, IL: InterVarsity Press, 2006).

CHAPTER 11 DOES GOD INTEND FOR US TO KEEP SLAVES?

Epigraph. Sam Harris, *Letter to a Christian Nation* (New York: Knopf, 2007), 14.

1. Ephesians 6:5.
2. Terry Eagleton, "Lunging, Flailing, Mispunching," *London Review of Books*, October 19, 2006, http://www.lrb.co.uk/v28/n20/eagl01_.html (accessed August 21, 2009). Eagleton is an agnostic and Marxist who has written a book-length critique of Richard Dawkins and Christopher Hitchens (who he refers to as "Ditchkins") in *Reason, Faith, and Revolution: Reflections on the God Debate*, The Terry Lecture Series (New Haven: Yale University Press, 2009).
3. Dinesh D'Souza, *What's So Great About Christianity* (Washington, DC: Regnery, 2007), 70.
4. Orlando Patterson, *Slavery and Social Death: A Comparative Study* (Cambridge, MA: Harvard University Press, 1982).
5. Christopher J. H. Wright, *Old Testament Ethics for the People of God* (Downers Grove, IL: InterVarsity Press, 2004), 333.
6. Ibid.
7. Ibid., 334.
8. Exodus 12:44; 20:10; 21:26–27; Deuteronomy 15:12; and 23:15–16, respectively.
9. Job 31:13–14.
10. Genesis 1:27.
11. Gerald F. Hawthorne, Ralph P. Martin, and Daniel G. Reid, *Dictionary of Paul and His Letters* (Downers Grove, IL: InterVarsity Press, 1993), 881.
12. Galatians 3:28 NLT.
13. Philemon 16–17.
14. Paul Copan, *That's Just Your Interpretation: Responding to Skeptics Who Challenge Your Faith* (Grand Rapids: Baker, 2001), 178.

15. For a summary of this throughout history, see Alvin J. Schmidt, *How Christianity Changed the World* (Grand Rapids: Zondervan, 2004).

16. Harris, *Letter to a Christian Nation*, 16.

17. Luke 4:18 ESV (quoting Isaiah 61:1–2).

18. I (Jonathan) first heard this vivid way of putting the idea of the kingdom of God in a sermon from John Ortberg, "The Offer That Changes Everything," available at http://mppc.org/learn/sermons?page=26 (accessed December 16, 2009). This way of thinking reflects the tension we feel in God's Kingdom being already here but not yet what it will one day be. A foretaste and preview has begun, but the fullness of God's reign will occur in the future at his second coming.

19. Ravi K. Zacharias, *The End of Reason: A Response to the New Atheists* (Grand Rapids: Zondervan, 2008), 100.

20. As quoted in Zacharias, *End of Reason*, 98.

CHAPTER 12 IS HELL A DIVINE TORTURE CHAMBER?

Epigraph. Sam Harris, *Letter to a Christian Nation* (New York: Knopf, 2007), 13.

1. Albert L. Winseman, "Eternal Destinations: Americans Believe in Heaven, Hell," Gallup, http://www.gallup.com/poll/11770/Eternal-Destinations-Americans-Believe-Heaven-Hell.aspx (accessed July 27, 2009).

2. Christopher Hitchens, *God Is Not Great: How Religion Poisons Everything* (New York: Twelve, 2007), 175–76, 219.

3. Ibid., 58.

4. Richard Dawkins, *The God Delusion* (New York: Houghton Mifflin, 2008), 361.

5. Matthew 25:41, 46.

6. Matthew 25:30.

7. Matthew 10:28.

8. Luke 14:26.

9. George Eldon Ladd, *A Theology of the New Testament*, rev. ed., ed. Donald Alfred Hagner (Grand Rapids: Eerdmans, 1993), 196.

10. Tim Keller, "The Importance of Hell," http://www.redeemer.com/news_and_events/articles/the_importance_of_hell.html (accessed August 4, 2009).

11. Lee Strobel, *The Case for Faith: A Journalist Investigates the Toughest Objections to Christianity* (Grand Rapids: Zondervan, 2000), 174.

12. 2 Thessalonians 1:9 NASB (emphasis added).

13. Timothy Keller, *The Reason for God: Belief in an Age of Skepticism* (New York: Dutton, 2008), 76.

14. C. S. Lewis, *The Abolition of Man* (New York: Simon and Schuster, 1996), 46.

15. Keller, *Reason for God*, 76–77.

16. I (Jonathan) first heard the phrase "echoes of Eden" in a lecture Stuart

McAllister gave on setting forth the case for Christianity. "Setting Forth the Case for Christianity" available for purchase from Ravi Zacharias International Ministries, http://store.rzim.org/product/tabid/61/p-312-setting-forth-the-case-for-christianity.aspx (accessed October 15, 2009).

17. Lewis, *Abolition of Man*, 69.
18. Strobel, *Case for Faith*, 175. Strobel is recounting an interview with J. P. Moreland.
19. Hitchens, *God Is Not Great*, 55.
20. Ezekiel 18:23, 32.
21. C. S. Lewis, *The Problem of Pain* (New York: HarperSanFrancisco, 2001), 130.
22. See Matthew 11:20–24 (cf. Luke 12:47–48).
23. Romans 6:23.
24. Mark 10:14–16 NIV; Matthew 18:14 NASB.
25. See Deuteronomy 1:39. For those wanting to explore the theological reasons behind this and the nature and extent of Christ's atonement, see Millard Erickson, *Christian Theology*, 2nd ed. (Grand Rapids: Baker, 2001), 654–56.
26. Genesis 18:25.
27. Lewis, *Problem of Pain*, 124.
28. J. I. Packer, *Knowing God*, 20th anniversary ed. (Downers Grove, IL: InterVarsity Press, 1993), 143.
29. Becky Pippert, as quoted in Will Metzger, *Tell the Truth: The Whole Gospel to the Whole Person by Whole People* (Downers Grove, IL: InterVarsity Press, 2002), 49.
30. Matthew 27:46.
31. Lewis, *Problem of Pain*, 120.
32. John 5:24.

CHAPTER 13 IS GOD A GENOCIDAL BULLY?

Epigraph. Richard Dawkins, *The God Delusion* (New York: Houghton Mifflin, 2008), 281–82.

1. Deuteronomy 20:16–18.
2. Two helpful treatments on the debated ethics of war for Christians are J. Daryl Charles, *Between Pacifism and Jihad: Just War and Christian Tradition* (Downers Grove, IL: InterVarsity Press, 2005); and Scott B. Rae, *Moral Choices: An Introduction to Ethics*, 3rd ed. (Grand Rapids: Zondervan, 2009), 302–28.
3. We refer you to those who have labored to deal faithfully and honestly with these texts: Paul Copan, "Is Yahweh a Moral Monster? The New Atheists and Old Testament Ethics," *Philosophia Christi* 10, no. 1 (2008); and Richard S. Hess, "War in the Hebrew Bible: An Overview," in *War in the Bible and Terrorism in the Twenty-First Century*,

eds. Richard S. Hess and Elmer A. Martens (Winona Lake, IN: Eisenbrauns, 2008).

4. We would like to acknowledge our gratitude for the honest and thoughtful insights of Old Testament scholar and ethicist Christopher J. H. Wright. We highly recommend his book *The God I Don't Understand* (Grand Rapids: Zondervan, 2008) for further investigation. We relied heavily on his expertise in this area along with Paul Copan, whose synthesis and analysis have been invaluable. Finally, we want to thank Clay Jones for his thoughtful feedback on this chapter.

5. Cornelius Plantinga, *Not the Way It's Supposed to Be: A Breviary of Sin* (Grand Rapids: Eerdmans, 1995), 13 (emphasis in original).

6. Ibid., 14.

7. See John 18:36.

8. Wright, *The God I Don't Understand*, 90 (emphasis in original).

9. See the excellent treatment of these issues in Paul Copan, *When God Goes to Starbucks: A Guide to Everyday Apologetics* (Grand Rapids: Baker, 2008), 136–61.

10. E.g., Dawkins, *The God Delusion*, 279. There is much confusion about what prompted the Crusades. For a helpful treatment of the sociological and historical factors involved, see Rodney Stark, *God's Battalions: The Case for the Crusades* (New York: HarperOne, 2009).

11. Christopher Hitchens, *God Is Not Great: How Religion Poisons Everything* (New York: Twelve, 2007), 101.

12. God warned the Israelites not to fall into Canaanite depravity. See Leviticus 18:24–25; 20:22–24; Deuteronomy 9:5; 12:29–31.

13. Clay Jones, "We Don't Hate Sin So We Don't Understand What Happened to the Canaanites," *Philosophia Christi* 11, no. 1 (2009): 61.

14. Wright, *The God I Don't Understand*, 92 (emphasis in original).

15. Ibid.

16. See Leviticus 18:28; Deuteronomy 28:25–68.

17. Wright, *The God I Don't Understand*, 101.

18. Hebrews 11:31; James 2:25; Matthew 1:5.

19. Dawkins, *The God Delusion*, 280 (emphasis in original).

20. John 10:9.

21. See, for example, Robert H. Stein, *Playing by the Rules: A Basic Guide to Interpreting the Bible* (Grand Rapids: Baker, 1994).

22. Wright, *The God I Don't Understand*, 88.

23. Ibid.

24. Deuteronomy 7:2–5 (emphasis added). Scholars have also interpreted this passage to mean that the prohibitions against intermarriage was a way of saying, "Don't even think about ways around this."

25. Joshua 2:9–11.

26. Joshua 10:40–42 (NASB; emphasis added). Cf. Joshua 11:16–20.

27. Wright, *The God I Don't Understand*, 88.

28. This observation is from Copan, *When God Goes to Starbucks*, 141.

29. Deuteronomy 28:61.
30. See Deuteronomy 7:5. Gordon J. Wenham, *Exploring the Old Testament: A Guide to the Pentateuch* (Downers Grove, IL: InterVarsity Press, 2003), 137.
31. See Genesis 12:1–3.
32. Galatians 3:8.
33. See Genesis 3–11.
34. Deuteronomy 7:6–7.
35. See the excellent development in Christopher J. H. Wright, *The Mission of God: Unlocking the Bible's Grand Narrative* (Downers Grove, IL: InterVarsity Press, 2006).
36. Wright, *The God I Don't Understand*, 102. See also Zechariah 9:7. This passage could also be understood as God's mercy later being extended to a people that Israel should have destroyed, but did not. The ban should have included the Jebusites, but God worked redemptively even in Israel's disobedience. Our thanks to Clay Jones for pointing this out.
37. See Psalm 103; Jeremiah 22:16; 1 John 4:8–9; Revelation 19:11–16.
38. See Romans 8:18–25.

CHAPTER 14 IS CHRISTIANITY THE CAUSE OF DANGEROUS SEXUAL REPRESSION?

Epigraph. Christopher Hitchens, *God Is Not Great: How Religion Poisons Everything* (New York: Twelve, 2007), 215.
1. Ibid., 4.
2. Richard Dawkins, *The God Delusion* (New York: Houghton Mifflin, 2008), 263.
3. Sam Harris, *Letter to a Christian Nation* (New York: Knopf, 2007), 25–26.
4. Jennifer Roback Morse, *Smart Sex: Finding Life-Long Love in a Hook-Up World* (Dallas: Spence, 2005), 104–8.
5. Ibid., 106.
6. Proverbs 5:18–19 HCSB.
7. See Tommy Nelson, *The Book of Romance: What Solomon Says About Love, Sex, and Intimacy* (Nashville: Thomas Nelson, 1998).
8. Josh McDowell, "Is the Bible Sexually Oppressive?" *The Apologetics Study Bible*, gen. ed. Ted Cabal (Nashville: Holman, 2007), 987.
9. See Genesis 2:24.
10. "Oxytocin: Don't Sniff It If You Want to Hang On to Your Money," *The Medical News*, June 2005, http://www.news-medical.net/news/2005/06/01/10597.aspx (accessed January 15, 2010).
11. Joe S. McIlhaney and Freda McKissic Bush, *Hooked: New Science on How Casual Sex Is Affecting Our Children* (Chicago: Northfield, 2008), 35–41.

12. Ibid., 105.
13. Ibid., 101.
14. Phil Brennan, "Doctor: Teen Sex Is Killing Our Children," February 3, 2003, http://archive.newsmax.com/archives/articles/2003/2/3/173601.shtml (accessed January 15, 2010).
15. See John 10:10.
16. William R. Mattox Jr., "Aha! Call It the Revenge of the Church Ladies," *USA Today*, February 11, 1999, 15A. Maggie Gallagher makes a similar case for the benefits of married sex in *The Case for Marriage: Why Married People Are Happier, Healthier, and Better Off Financially* (New York: Broadway, 2001). A more recent study that comes to the same conclusion is McIlhaney and Bush, *Hooked.*
17. Mattox, "Revenge of the Church Ladies."
18. McIlhaney and Bush, *Hooked*, 136.
19. Mattox, "Revenge of the Church Ladies."
20. Ibid.
21. Morse, *Smart Sex*, 151–52.
22. Ephesians 4:15.
23. McIlhaney and Bush, *Hooked*, 138–39.

CHAPTER 15 CAN PEOPLE BE GOOD WITHOUT GOD?

Epigraph. Richard Dawkins, *The God Delusion* (New York: Houghton Mifflin, 2008), 241.
1. Romans 2:14–15 NLT. Note that "Gentiles" in this passage contextually refers to people who do not believe in God or who were not given the Torah like the Israelites were.
2. William Lane Craig, *Reasonable Faith: Christian Truth and Apologetics*, 3rd ed. (Wheaton, IL: Crossway, 2008), 173.
3. Richard Dawkins, *A Devil's Chaplain: Reflections on Hope, Lies, Science, and Love* (New York: Houghton Mifflin, 2003), 34.
4. Sam Harris, *The End of Faith: Religion, Terror, and the Future of Reason* (New York: W. W. Norton, 2005), 178.
5. Ibid., 170.
6. Dawkins, *The God Delusion*, 247.
7. Ibid., 251.
8. Harris, *The End of Faith*, 185.
9. Richard Dawkins, *The Selfish Gene* (New York: Oxford University Press, 1989), 2–3 (emphasis in original).
10. Dinesh D'Souza, *Life After Death: The Evidence* (Washington, DC: Regnery, 2009), 221.
11. Craig, *Reasonable Faith*, 174.
12. See Victor Reppert, *C. S. Lewis's Dangerous Idea: A Philosophical Defense of Lewis's Argument from Reason* (Downers Grove, IL: InterVarsity Press, 2003).

13. Richard Dawkins, *River Out of Eden: A Darwinian View of Life* (New York: Basic Books, 1995), 95–96.
14. Michael Ruse, "Evolutionary Theory and Christian Ethics," in *The Darwinian Paradigm* (London: Routledge, 1989), 262–69.
15. From Dr. Provine's interview in the documentary film *Expelled: No Intelligence Allowed*, directed by Nathan Frankowski (Premise Media, 2008).
16. As quoted in Louis P. Pojman, *Ethics: Discovering Right and Wrong*, 3rd ed. (Belmont, CA: Wadsworth, 1999), 31–32.
17. Dawkins, *The God Delusion*, 266. Note that *absolute* means "a value or principle that is regarded as universally valid or that may be viewed without relation to other things."
18. This version of the moral argument is developed and defended in William Lane Craig, *Reasonable Faith: Christian Truth and Apologetics*, 3rd ed. (Wheaton, IL: Crossway, 2008), 172–82. We are indebted to his work in this area.
19. Dawkins, *The God Delusion*, 265.
20. "God Debate: Sam Harris vs. Rick Warren," *Newsweek*, April 9, 2007, available online at http://www.msnbc.msn.com/id/17889148/site/newsweek/print/1/displaymode/1098/ (accessed October 5, 2009).
21. Richard Weikart, *From Darwin to Hitler: Evolutionary Ethics, Eugenics, and Racism in Germany* (New York: Palgrave Macmillan, 2004).
22. Francis J. Beckwith and Gregory Koukl, *Relativism: Feet Firmly Planted in Mid-Air* (Grand Rapids: Baker, 1998), 69. Further, relativism is ultimately self-refuting. Consider the famous slogan "that's true for you but not for me." Is this statement true for *both* of us? For more, see Beckwith and Koukl's excellent book.
23. Dawkins, *The God Delusion*, 245–46.
24. While this conclusion doesn't take us all the way to the Christian God, it fits well with the picture of God as described in the Bible.
25. "The Universal Declaration of Human Rights," United Nations, December 10, 1948, http://www.un.org/en/documents/udhr/ (accessed October 5, 2009).
26. This observation came to me (Jonathan) while reading Paul Copan, "God, Naturalism, and the Foundations of Morality" in *The Future of Atheism: Alister McGrath and Daniel Dennett in Dialogue*, ed. Robert B. Stewart (Minneapolis: Fortress Press, 2008).

CHAPTER 16 IS EVIL ONLY A PROBLEM FOR CHRISTIANS?

Epigraph. Sam Harris, *Letter to a Christian Nation* (New York: Knopf, 2007), 55–56.
1. Sam Harris, *The End of Faith: Religion, Terror, and the Future of Reason* (New York: W. W. Norton, 2005), 172.
2. Alvin Plantinga, *God, Freedom, and Evil* (Grand Rapids: Eerdmans, 1977), 30.

3. Dr. Norman Geisler gave this helpful illustration in a lecture at Saddleback Church, September 6, 2009, titled "If God Exists, Why Is There Evil?" available at http://saddleback.com/mediacenter/services/currentseries.aspx?site=yDi0V4EwP58=&s=OsqcpA0SUkE= (accessed October 30, 2009).

4. William Lane Craig, Hard Questions, Real Answers (Wheaton, IL: Crossway, 2003), 90–91.

5. N. T. Wright, "The Bible Does Answer the Problem—Here's How," Beliefnet, April 25, 2008, http://blog.beliefnet.com/blogalogue/2008/04/thanks-bart-for-a-further.html#more (accessed September 28, 2009).

6. Timothy J. Keller, The Reason for God: Belief in an Age of Skepticism (New York: Dutton, 2008), 25.

7. 2 Corinthians 5:21; Matthew 27:46.

8. I (Jonathan) heard Ravi say this in a lecture many years ago. Unfortunately, I don't remember any more than this.

9. Alister McGrath, The Mystery of the Cross (Grand Rapids: Zondervan, 1988), 159.

10. N. T. Wright, Evil and the Justice of God (Downers Grove, IL: InterVarsity Press, 2006).

11. Genesis 50:20 NASB. See also Romans 8:28.

12. As cited in Randy C. Alcorn, If God Is Good: Faith in the Midst of Suffering and Evil (Colorado Springs, CO: Multnomah, 2009), 406. This book is a very helpful treatment of evil from a biblical, theological, and pastoral perspective.

13. Romans 8:28.

14. 1 Peter 1:6–7; 2 Corinthians 4:16–18.

15. Psalm 56:8; Isaiah 25:8.

16. 2 Peter 3:8–10 NET.

17. John W. Loftus, Why I Became an Atheist (Amherst, NY: Prometheus, 2008), 243.

18. C. S. Lewis, The Problem of Pain (New York: HarperSanFrancisco, 2001), 91.

19. Craig, Hard Questions, Real Answers, 112.

CHAPTER 17 **WHAT GOOD IS CHRISTIANITY?**

Epigraph. Christopher Hitchens, God Is Not Great: How Religion Poisons Everything (New York: Twelve, 2007), 13.

1. See the endnotes in this chapter along with Jonathan Hill, What Has Christianity Ever Done for Us? How It Shaped the Modern World (Downers Grove, IL: InterVarsity Press, 2005); Rodney Stark, For the Glory of God: How Monotheism Led to Reformations, Science, Witch-Hunts, and the End of Slavery (Princeton, NJ: Princeton University Press, 2003); Rodney Stark; and Vincent Carroll and Dave Shiflett,

Christianity on Trial: Arguments Against Anti-Religious Bigotry (San Francisco: Encounter Books, 2002).

2. If you are looking for only one book to read on this, then see the excellent study of social historian Alvin J. Schmidt, *How Christianity Changed the World* (Grand Rapids: Zondervan, 2004).
3. Schmidt, *How Christianity Changed the World*, 126.
4. Ibid.
5. Rodney Stark, *The Rise of Christianity: A Sociologist Reconsiders History* (Princeton, NJ: Princeton University Press, 1996), 86.
6. As quoted in ibid., 84.
7. Ibid., 82.
8. Ibid., 83.
9. Ibid., 84–85.
10. Schmidt, *How Christianity Changed the World*, 128.
11. Stark, *The Rise of Christianity*, 118.
12. Schmidt, *How Christianity Changed the World*, 132.
13. Stark, *The Rise of Christianity*, 102.
14. Schmidt, *How Christianity Changed the World*, 100.
15. Laws found in Table 4 of the Twelve Tables of Roman Law, quoted in ibid.
16. Matthew 9:18–26; John 4:9; and Luke 7:36–50, respectively.
17. *Sotah* 3.4, quoted in Schmidt, *How Christianity Changed the World*, 102.
18. Mark 15:41; Luke 10:39.
19. Luke 8:1–3; 18:1–8.
20. D. M. Scholer, "Women," in *Dictionary of Jesus and the Gospels*, ed. Joel B. Green, Scot McKnight, and I. Howard Marshall (Downers Grove, IL: InterVarsity Press, 1992), 886.
21. Galatians 3:28.
22. 1 Timothy 5:1–16.
23. Stark, *The Rise of Christianity*, 100.
24. Schmidt, *How Christianity Changed the World*, 118.
25. Hitchens, *God Is Not Great*, 54.
26. Genesis 1:27.
27. Genesis 2:18.
28. Psalms 30:10; 54:4.
29. Schmidt, *How Christianity Changed the World*, 122.
30. To watch a video of the powerful moment when Jimmy Wambua meets Mark, his Compassion sponsor of nineteen years, see http://www.catalystspace.com/catablog/full/2009_catalyst_compassion_moment/ (accessed October 25, 2009).
31. See, for example, the movement to end modern slavery (including the sex slave trade) spearheaded by Christians at www.attheendofslavery.com.
32. Actually, major studies have shown that being religious is actually good for your health. See Harold G. Koenig, *Medicine, Religion,*

and Health: Where Science and Spirituality Meet, Templeton Science and Religion Series (West Conshohocken, PA: Templeton Foundation Press, 2008). Also, it has been empirically shown that religious people, specifically church-attending, evangelical Christians, are the most generous Americans with their money. See sociologist Arthur C. Brooks, Who Really Cares: The Surprising Truth About Compassionate Conservatism (New York: Basic Books, 2006).

33. Josiah Smith as quoted in Schmidt, How Christianity Changed the World, 131.

34. Stark, The Rise of Christianity, 214.

CHAPTER 18 WHY JESUS INSTEAD OF THE FLYING SPAGHETTI MONSTER?

Epigraph. Richard Dawkins, The God Delusion (New York: Houghton Mifflin, 2008), 117–18.

1. We came across this observation in Alister McGrath, Dawkins' God: Genes, Memes, and the Meaning of Life (Malden, MA: Blackwell, 2005), 87.

2. William Lane Craig, Reasonable Faith: Christian Truth and Apologetics, 3rd ed. (Wheaton, IL: Crossway, 2008), 207.

3. Ben Witherington, New Testament History: A Narrative Account (Grand Rapids: Baker, 2001), 17.

4. First and foremost, these are historical documents and should be considered as such. One can approach them in this way whether or not one thinks they are the inspired Word of God (that is a further commitment that goes beyond historicity).

5. See Robert H. Stein, "Criteria for the Gospels' Authenticity," in Contending with Christianity's Critics: Answering New Atheists and Other Objectors, ed. Paul Copan and William Lane Craig (Nashville: B & H Publishing, 2009).

6. Mark L. Strauss, Four Portraits, One Jesus: An Introduction to Jesus and the Gospels (Grand Rapids: Zondervan, 2007), 385. For more on the historical reliability of the Gospels, see the detailed study of Craig Blomberg, The Historical Reliability of the Gospels, 2nd ed. (Downers Grove, IL: InterVarsity Press, 2007). Also, for an understanding of the kind of literature the Gospel writers composed and what that means for how the texts are to be understood, see Richard A. Burridge, What Are the Gospels? A Comparison with Graeco-Roman Biography, 2nd ed. (Grand Rapids: Eerdmans, 2004).

7. Norman L. Geisler and Frank Turek, I Don't Have Enough Faith to Be an Atheist (Wheaton, IL: Crossway, 2004), 256–59. See Colin J. Hemer and Conrad H. Gempf, The Book of Acts in the Setting of Hellenistic History (Tübingen: Mohr, 1989).

8. As quoted in Craig, Reasonable Faith, 238.

9. See the excellent study by Graham H. Twelftree, Jesus the Miracle

Worker: A Historical and Theological Study (Downers Grove, IL: Inter-Varsity Press, 1999).

10. For a compelling argument for this approach, see Paul R. Eddy and Gregory A. Boyd, *The Jesus Legend: A Case for the Historical Reliability of the Synoptic Jesus Tradition* (Grand Rapids: Baker, 2007), 39–90.

11. Richard Bauckham, *Jesus and the Eyewitnesses: The Gospels as Eyewitness Testimony* (Grand Rapids: Eerdmans, 2006), 5.

12. Ibid.

13. Darrell L. Bock and Daniel B. Wallace, *Dethroning Jesus: Exposing Popular Culture's Quest to Unseat the Biblical Christ* (Nashville: Thomas Nelson, 2007), 221.

14. See, for example, Romans 1:2–4; 1 Corinthians 8:4–6; 11:23–24; 15:1–5.

15. Greek scholars know this is from oral tradition because it leaves the telltale signs of rhythm and meter, has a balanced structure in the Greek, and is a crisp summary that would be easy to memorize.

16. Bauckham explains, "By 'formal' here, I mean that there were specific practices employed to ensure that tradition was faithfully handed on from a qualified traditioner to others." See Bauckham, *Jesus and the Eyewitnesses*, 264–71.

17. See Philippians 2:5–11 and Colossians 1:15–20 for instances of early hymns.

18. See Matthew 28:19–20; 1 Corinthians 11:23–26; Ephesians 4:4–6.

19. Dawkins, *The God Delusion*, 119–20.

20. For case-by-case refutations of charges that Christianity borrowed from pagan mystery religions, see the excellent work of J. Ed Komoszewski, M. James Sawyer, and Daniel B. Wallace, *Reinventing Jesus: How Contemporary Skeptics Miss the Real Jesus and Mislead Popular Culture* (Grand Rapids: Kregel, 2006), 220–58. See also Lee Strobel, *The Case for the Real Jesus: A Journalist Investigates Current Attacks on the Identity of Christ* (Grand Rapids: Zondervan, 2007), 157–87. For a fuller treatment, see Ronald H. Nash, *The Gospel and the Greeks: Did the New Testament Borrow from Pagan Thought?* 2nd ed. (Phillipsburg, NJ: P & R, 2003).

21. Komoszewski, Sawyer, and Wallace, *Reinventing Jesus*, 234.

22. Larry W. Hurtado, *How on Earth Did Jesus Become a God? Historical Questions About Earliest Devotion to Jesus* (Cambridge, U.K.: Eerdmans, 2005), 25. Hurtado's most thorough treatment is in *Lord Jesus Christ: Devotion to Jesus in Earliest Christianity* (Cambridge, U.K.: Eerdmans, 2003).

23. See, e.g., Isaiah 43:25; cf. Mark 2:7.

24. See Psalm 110.

25. I first encountered these arguments for the deity of Jesus from the lectures of Darrell Bock. For an excellent and accessible treatment of the biblical data that shows that what was attributed to Yahweh (honors, attributes, names, deeds, and seat) is also attributed to

Jesus, see Robert M. Bowman and J. Ed Komoszewski, *Putting Jesus in His Place: The Case for the Deity of Christ* (Grand Rapids: Kregel, 2007).

26. See Matthew 14:33; 28:19; John 10:30–33; Hebrews 1:3; Titus 2:13; etc.

27. There is obviously much more to this topic than can be addressed in the space we have here, so be sure to check out Paul Copan, *True for You, but Not for Me: Countering the Slogans That Leave Christians Speechless*, rev. ed. (Minneapolis: Bethany, 2009); and Harold A. Netland, *Encountering Religious Pluralism: The Challenge to Christian Faith and Mission* (Downers Grove, IL: InterVarsity Press, 2001).

28. Sam Harris, *Letter to a Christian Nation* (New York: Knopf, 2007), 3.

29. Ravi Zacharias, "Why I Believe Jesus Christ Is the Ultimate Source for Meaning," in *Why I Am a Christian: Leading Thinkers Explain Why They Believe*, ed. Norman L. Geisler and Paul K. Hoffman (Grand Rapids: Baker, 2001), 268.

30. Galatians 3:28.

31. Alvin Plantinga, "Pluralism," in *The Philosophical Challenge of Religious Diversity*, ed. Phillip L. Quinn and Kevin Meeker (New York: Oxford University Press, 2000), 179.

32. See Mark 8:27–29.

CONCLUSION A TALE OF TWO ORDINARY BELIEVERS

Epigraph. C. S. Lewis, *The Weight of Glory* (San Francisco: HarperSanFrancisco, 2001), 140.

1. In such a short space it is hard to share all of the qualifications and nuances of life. One thing that I want to make clear is that I love my family and want to honor them. There have been some significant redemptive moments amidst the brokenness and dysfunction that I didn't share.

2. *Dead Poets Society*, directed by Peter Weir (Burbank, CA: Touchstone Pictures, 1989).

3. John 17:3.

4. John 14:6.

5. Matthew 16:15; Mark 8:29; Luke 9:20.

6. Barbara Bradley Hagerty, *Fingerprints of God: The Search for the Science of Spirituality* (New York: Riverhead, 2009), 269–70.

7. Thomas Nagel, *The Last Word* (New York: Oxford University Press, 1997), 130.

8. Keller eloquently makes this point in a lecture at Northwestern University for the Veritas Forum. See "The Reason for God" at http://veritas.org/media/talks/611 (accessed November 1, 2009). For more on the impact of immorality and stubbornness on our willingness to believe, see James S. Spiegel, *The Making of an Atheist: How Immorality Leads to Unbelief* (Chicago: Moody, 2010).

9. I (Jonathan) first heard this insightful question in a lecture several years ago by Dallas Willard. He often uses it to gently expose what a person really desires. See "Tough Questions with Dallas Willard," posted on December 12, 2009, at http://mppc.org/series/can-smart -people-believe-god/smart-people-tough-questions-dallas-willard (accessed December 30, 2009).
10. From Tim Keller's "The Reason for God."
11. John Ortberg, *Faith and Doubt* (Grand Rapids: Zondervan, 2008), 175–76.
12. Matthew 11:28–29 (NLT).

APPENDIX B DEALING WITH DOUBT ON THE JOURNEY OF FAITH

1. Timothy J. Keller, *The Reason for God: Belief in an Age of Skepticism* (New York: Dutton, 2008), xvi–xvii.
2. Os Guinness, *God in the Dark: The Assurance of Faith Beyond a Shadow of Doubt* (Wheaton, IL: Crossway, 1996), 26.
3. Ibid., 125–26.
4. Ibid., 115.
5. See Mark 9:24, and also John the Baptist in Luke 7:19-20.
6. 2 Thessalonians 1:3.

APPENDIX C IS THE NEW TESTAMENT FILLED WITH CONTRADICTIONS AND CORRUPTED TEXTS?

1. Richard Dawkins, *The God Delusion* (New York: Houghton Mifflin, 2008), 120–21; Christopher Hitchens, *God Is Not Great: How Religion Poisons Everything* (New York: Twelve, 2007), 120–22.
2. See Craig A. Evans, *Fabricating Jesus: How Modern Scholars Distort the Gospels* (Downers Grove, IL: InterVarsity Press, 2006), chapter 1. Dan Wallace offers some clarity on the doctrine of inerrancy: "So if we were to build a pyramid of bibliology, the broader foundation would be: 'I believe that God has done great acts in history and the Bible has recorded some of those.' On top of that would be: 'The Bible is telling me the truth when it comes to matters of faith and practice.' And on top would be: 'The Bible is true in what it touches.' Unfortunately, some have inverted the pyramid and tried to make it stand on its head. Then if you take someone like Ehrman, when a professor tries to kick the legs out from under inerrancy, it's like the whole pyramid falls over. Ehrman ends up throwing out everything. The problem was that he was putting his priorities in the wrong place." From Lee Strobel, *The Case for the Real Jesus: A Journalist Investigates Current Attacks on the Identity of Christ* (Grand Rapids: Zondervan, 2007), 75. For an excellent article on how to make sense of differences in wording among the Gospel writers, see Darrell L.

Bock, "The Words of Jesus in the Gospels: Live, Jive, or Memorex?" in *Jesus Under Fire: Modern Scholarship Reinvents the Historical Jesus*, ed. Michael J. Wilkins and J. P. Moreland (Grand Rapids: Zondervan, 1995).

3. Ehrman also raises issues regarding missing gospels and alternative Christianities. This has been responded to as well; see Darrell L. Bock, *The Missing Gospels: Unearthing the Truth Behind Alternative Christianities* (Nashville: Thomas Nelson, 2006).

4. In Ehrman's words, "Eventually, though, I felt compelled to leave Christianity altogether. I did not go easily. On the contrary, I left kicking and screaming, wanting desperately to hold on to the faith I had known since childhood and had come to know intimately from my teenaged years onward. But I came to a point where I could no longer believe. It's a very long story, but the short version is this: I realized that I could no longer reconcile the claims of faith with the facts of life. In particular, I could no longer explain how there can be a good and all-powerful God actively involved with this world, given the state of things. For many people who inhabit this planet, life is a cesspool of misery and suffering. I came to a point where I simply could not believe that there is a good and kindly disposed Ruler who is in charge of it." "Bart Ehrman: Questioning Religion on Why We Suffer," NPR, February 19, 2008, http://www.npr.org/templates/story/story.php?storyId=19096131 (accessed December 23, 2009).

5. Ben Witherington, interview by Stand to Reason, June 14, 2008, available at http://www.str.org/site/PageServer?pagename=Radio_Archives (accessed October 22, 2009).

6. Wallace provides an excellent and accessible introduction to this in J. Ed Komoszewski, M. James Sawyer, and Daniel B. Wallace, *Reinventing Jesus: How Contemporary Skeptics Miss the Real Jesus and Mislead Popular Culture* (Grand Rapids: Kregel, 2006), 53–117.

7. Ibid., 82.

8. Bart D. Ehrman, *Misquoting Jesus: The Story Behind Who Changed the Bible and Why* (New York: HarperSanFrancisco, 2005), 90.

9. Darrell L. Bock and Daniel B. Wallace, *Dethroning Jesus: Exposing Popular Culture's Quest to Unseat the Biblical Christ* (Nashville: Thomas Nelson, 2007), 55–58.

10. Ibid., 60.

11. Ibid., 70.

12. Lee Strobel, *The Case for Christ: A Journalist's Personal Investigation of the Evidence for Jesus* (Grand Rapids: Zondervan, 1998), 71.

About the Authors

Sean McDowell is head of the Bible Department at Capistrano Valley Christian Schools, where he teaches courses on philosophy, theology, and apologetics. He graduated from Talbot Theological Seminary with a double Master's degree in theology and philosophy. He is pursuing a PhD in apologetics and worldview studies from Southern Baptist Theological Seminary.

A contributor to books and magazines and regular blogger at www.seanmcdowell.org, Sean is the general editor for *Apologetics for a New Generation* and *The Apologetics Study Bible for Students.* He is the coauthor of *Understanding Intelligent Design* with William A. Dembski, and *Evidence for the Resurrection* and *More Than a Carpenter* with Josh McDowell.

Sean is the national spokesman for Wheatstone Academy, an organization committed to training young people with a biblical worldview, and is listed among the top one hundred apologists on Apologetics315.com.

Sean married his high school sweetheart, Stephanie. They have two children and live in San Juan Capistrano, California.

Jonathan Morrow is the founder of www.thinkChristianly.org and the author of *Welcome to College: A Christ-Follower's Guide for the Journey.* Jonathan holds an MDiv and a Master's in philosophy from Talbot School of Theology, where he is pursuing a DMin in engaging mind and culture.

Jonathan contributed several articles to *The Apologetics Study Bible for Students* and a chapter to *Foundations of Spiritual Formation: A Community Approach to Becoming Like Christ*. His book *Welcome to College* has been featured on *Family Life Today, Stand to Reason, Point of View*, Crosswalk.com, and Apologetics.com.

Presently Jonathan is the equipping pastor at Fellowship Bible Church in Murfreesboro, Tennessee. He and his wife, Mandi, have two children.